The whole Southwest was a House Made of Dawn. It was made of pollen and of rain. The land was old and everlasting. There were many colors on the hills and on the plain, and there was a dark wilderness on the mountains beyond. The land was tilled and strong and it was beautiful all around.

From a Southwest Indian song

Navajo woman and child at village of Walpi, First Mesa, Hopi Reservation. Photograph by Emry Kopta, Courtesy Museum of Northern Arizona Photo Archives.

CHILDREN OF SACRED GROUND

AMERICA'S LAST INDIAN WAR

by Catherine Feher-Elston
Foreword by Dr. Joann Kealiinohomoku

 Northland Publishing

To the Navajo, Hopi, and Paiute people,
and to the memory of my grandmother,
Dorothy Frances MacPherin, who taught
me compassion.

Cover design by David Jenney
Book design by Lisa Dunning
Typeset in Phoenix by ProType

CONTENTS

FOREWORD

The emotional charge of the Navajo-Hopi land dispute has intensified since the passage of Public Law 93-531 during the mid-1970s. At that time the public became aware of its own vested interest in the problem. The conflict of land stewardship versus land residency, acute under any circumstances, has become exacerbated. Well-meaning outsiders have assumed the roles of movers and shakers vis-a-vis PL 93-531—some to express approval of the legislation, some to urge its modification, and some to demand its repeal. Often, indeed usually, responders have had a narrow perspective on the issue, either because of insufficient information, or because of a willingness to take a fervent, biased position no matter how ill-informed. This has sharpened the polarity of an already divisive situation.

When I first met Catherine Feher-Elston in 1981, she was a graduate student in anthropology at Northern Arizona University in Flagstaff. Already concerned about the relocation issue, she was investigating how relocation threatened the health and well-being of relocatees. Not content with researching the end results alone, Feher-Elston wanted to learn why this problem had arisen. She wanted to comprehend those divergent world views that made two neighboring native American tribes hold such contrastive opinions about the land, and how these, in turn, varied from the attitudes of outsiders. Because of this, I soon perceived that Feher-Elston was practically unique in her determination to be objective as well as empathic.

From our first meeting to the present, I have watched Feher-Elston's development as a first-rate researcher and writer. Combining the techniques of the ethnographer with those of the investigative reporter, she has achieved an understanding of the Navajo and Hopi land and relocation issue that is rare, possibly unparalleled. To do this, Feher-Elston interviewed numerous Navajo and Hopi persons, including those who are traditional leaders, elected leaders, and relocatees. In addition, she has researched documents and talked with government officials. In order to guarantee accurate and responsible reportage, she has continually monitored her data and perceptions of the complicated cultural, historical, and legal factors that have influenced the nature and evolution of the problem. Toward this end, she has traveled thousands of miles and devoted countless hours.

To my knowledge, this book is the first truly comprehensive analysis of the Navajo and Hopi land use and relocation issue to appear in print, candidly objective with no hidden agenda. It provides expository materials that reveal the ethos of both the Navajo and Hopi tribes as they bear on the land issue. Feher-Elston has woven these into the chronologies and political maneuvers that have been the results of and the responses to varying internal factions and external pressures. She introduces other pertinent facets of the land dispute that have not been discussed openly before, as, for example, the dilemma of individuals who have loyalties to both tribes because of mixed ancestry or intermarriage. She describes the demographies that have caused generational gaps of knowledge concerning tribal histories. She examines the postures of outsiders, and they include native Americans from tribes other than the principles in this issue, as well as non-Indians whose pro-active stance reflects, more about themselves than about the facts of the situation. Finally, she explains the position of the United States government, trapped with no apparent comfortable resolution, and vulnerable to attacks by proponents of every persuasion.

The fact that the deadline for relocation has passed recently, the most significant event in the history of the dispute, makes the publication of this book particularly timely. The book will provide the necessary background for readers to make intelligent appraisals of other developments as they continue to unfold. Of immediate value to pertinent decision makers, especially legislators as well as involved parties from the public sector, the book will be useful for both the Navajo and Hopi tribes, also. Beyond its immediacy, the book will become an important historical document for future evaluative retrospectives of the Navajo-Hopi land dispute that began hundreds of years ago, and shows no sign of abatement as the twentieth century comes to a close.

JOANN W. KEALIINOHOMOKU, PH.D
Department of Anthropology
Center for Colorado Plateau Studies
Northern Arizona University
Flagstaff, Arizona

PREFACE

This book has been written in an attempt to explain the Navajo and Hopi land issue in a simple and direct way. Much has been written about the struggle for land between the two tribes, but because the problem is so complicated and painful to those affected by the dispute, many writers have allowed emotion to obstruct objectivity. As a result, much that has been written has been done from an advocacy perspective.

In a discussion between a God and a prince in one of the books of the Hindu epic *Mahabarta*, known to the West as the *Bhagavad Gita*, Krishna says to Arjuna, "All is clouded by desire, as a fire by smoke, as a mirror by dust." These words can aptly be applied to documents and discussions about the land dispute. Land is the key to indigenous cultural survival. The tribes love the land, they desire to retain the key to their survival, and perspectives are shaped by this desire. As the tribes teach non-Indians about the issue, what they hope to retain sometimes takes precedence over understanding and objectivity in explaining how the problem developed. In many cases, tribesmen themselves have forgotten the roots of the problem in the struggle to keep what they feel is their birthright.

Americans, like others of European origins, like to see the world in terms of good and evil, black and white. The Navajo-Hopi land dispute, similar to many other tense situations in the world, is not something that can be reduced to a matter of right and wrong. It is a complicated struggle, one which has taken centuries to evolve, and one that affects cultures constantly in conflict and in flux. The problems accelerated with the coming of the Americans to the region. Ultimately, in the search for a clear and simple solution, American courts and Congress imposed a type of judgment so simple it seems obvious only from a great distance. It is possible that the American desire for easy justice coupled with ignorance of tribal histories clouded the mirror of the land dispute. Americans imposed a solution that neither tribe enjoyed, and American taxpayers continue to pay for this "simple" solution today.

Indeed, when one considers the staggering problems that the relocation of ten thousand people entails, it is difficult not to let emotionalism take over and objectivity disappear. But out of fairness to the people involved, I felt it necessary to study as many aspects of the histories and cultures involved as I could. I studied the situation for six years before preparing this manuscript.

In other attempts to understand the land issue, problems with bias sometimes arise not merely because a writer becomes emotionally involved with the issue, but also because most of the documents involved in the Navajo and Hopi conflict have been written by outsiders, concerned about the well-being of one tribe or another, or by tribal propagandists interested in pursuing their own ends.

The first chroniclers of the Southwest were the Spanish, who saw witchcraft, Satan, and resources to exploit everywhere they went. Certainly, their perspectives were not comprehensive and unbiased. Mexicans and Americans followed, each with their own agendas. Later, Navajo and Hopi Indian agents presented reports and memoranda to Washington, D.C. Some of them actually profited from their work with the tribes, and all of them had their own motives for involvement, not necessarily correlating with the well-being of the Indians whose interests they were assigned to protect.

When I came to the Southwest in January 1981, I had been trained in history, anthropology, and ethnohistory through years of undergraduate and graduate study at Washington State University. In addition to anthropological training, I had lived abroad in Libya from 1964–67, had travelled extensively throughout the Mediterranean and Europe, and had worked with the Smithsonian on the Gaza Strip during the summer of 1977. I had some experience in cross-cultural communication, and that was much-needed preparation for the challenges I was about to face.

It was while studying reservation hunger that I started to learn about the land dispute. One day, while returning to Window Rock from a trip to Tuba City with my boss Katherine Arviso, Katherine stopped the car and told me to get out and look at the local landmarks. She had stopped at the turn-off to Dinebito Trading Post on Highway 264, on the western edge of the Hopi mesas.

"Look at these land formations and marks and remember them," Katherine ordered. "That road goes to Big Mountain. You should go there, you will learn something."

Within a few weeks, I had made my first trip to Big Mountain and had met Sally Tsosie and Annie Homes, who knew Katherine Arviso. Through them, I met Katherine Smith. I learned my first perspectives on the land dispute from these women.

In time, I completed my work with the hunger project and took a grantsmanship job with DNA Legal Services in Window Rock. At that time, Peterson Zah was the executive director of DNA. I learned a little bit about the world of Navajo politics while working there. But the most important person I met while working at DNA was a community relations specialist named Miller Nez. Nez was a great-great grandson of Nataani Hosteen Nez, a famous medicineman from White Cone, on the edge of the disputed area. Miller is a medicineman, too. After some time, Miller decided to teach me a little bit about Navajo religion, language, and culture. I learned the Creation story from Miller, and attended various ceremonies with him.

For my first year in the Southwest, most of what I learned about the land dispute was from the Navajo perspective. But I moved to Flagstaff and gradually came to learn more and more about the dispute from Dr. Joann Kealiinohomoku and Hopi Museum Curator Terrance Talaswaima (Honvantewa). I began to learn that there were at least two sides to the issue.

While working with former Navajo and Hopi Indian Relocation Commission Director Leon Berger at the Navajo-Hopi Task Force, which was headquartered in Flagstaff in 1982, I prepared an ethnohistoric survey paper for Dr. Bill Griffin of the Anthropology Department at Northern Arizona University. My subject was the land issue, and the paper I prepared was titled, "Perceptions of Land Ownership in the Navajo-Hopi Land Dispute: An Ethnohistoric Study." That same year, I prepared a preliminary study of mortality and natality among Joint Use Area Navajos along with anthropologist Bill Wilson.

It was while working with the task force that I became interested in journalism. I served as a consultant with CBS *60 Minutes* when their researcher, Patti Hassler, came out to prepare a piece for broadcast. We did the research in 1981, and the program aired in 1982. In 1982, I worked with Lucy Bruell, who produced a segment on the impacts of relocation on the people of Coal Mine Mesa Chapter for ABC-Newsweek Woman. It aired that same year.

While working with television and other journalists, I came to realize that a lot of news that came out of the Southwest needed the guidance of a historian or anthropologist in order to be accurate. So, in 1983, I embarked on a serious career in journalism. I became the news director for a small reservation newspaper, the *Navajo-Hopi Observer*. It was my work with the *Observer* that forced me to pursue some objectivity about the land issue, since Navajos and Hopis, as well as Anglos, Zunis, Utes, Paiutes, Hualapais, and Havasupais, read the paper. So do assorted members of Congress.

While working for the *Observer*, I worked out of an office based in the Hopi village of Moencopi, and lived there as well. I began to realize that the roots of the land dispute were hidden deep within the soil that is sacred to all tribes in the region. As the July 6, 1986, deadline drew nearer and nearer, press coverage of the situation became more and more emotional and more and more outrageous. Somehow, the whole truth and most of the facts just were not coming to the surface.

I tried to maintain objectivity in my own articles, and began steadily building a variety of correspondent and stringer relationships with a number of news services and regional and national publications. Among them were the *Arizona Republic*, the *Albuquerque Journal*, and the Associated Press.

In time, I began to realize that I was faced with the perfect opportunity to gather research for a book about migrations, past and present, to the House of Dawn. Through news-gathering, I came to meet past and present tribal chairmen like Hopi Abbott Sekaquaptewa, Hopi Ivan Sidney, Navajo Peter MacDonald, Navajo Peterson Zah, and their assorted vice-chairmen. I met Senators and Congressmen such as Senator Barry Goldwater of Arizona and Congressman Manuel Lujan of New Mexico. I learned about the people at the Navajo and Hopi Indian Relocation Commission, and the trials and tribulations that they go through with their unenviable job. I witnessed the founding of the Big Mountain Legal Defense/Offense Committee by attorney Lew Gurwitz. I got to know all types of tribal officials, Navajo medicinemen, Hopi priests and kikmongwis, as well as the parade of reporters and hangers-on who came to Arizona to find the land dispute.

Because of the many years I have spent researching the topic, I came to realize that I had a unique opportunity and an important obligation. I had the opportunity to write about the dispute from a humanist and anthropological perspective. I had the obligation to strive for objectivity, because Navajos, Hopis, and many, many other people had given me their time and told the feelings of their hearts to me. Because people have placed their trust in me, I have an obligation to tell their story.

I have tried to minimize analysis, and tell the story of these children of sacred ground in their own words, whenever possible. In some areas, it has been necessary to analyze, or interject my own perceptions, but by and large, I have wanted them to explain how things came to be the way they are in their own way.

I gathered material for this book through interviews with Indians, politicians, detectives, and anthropologists; research of historical documents; the review of news and magazine articles; reading other books written on the dispute; and the study of people who have been involved with the situation. My approach to the topic is ethnohistorical.

Compiling statistics and technical and demographic information for this project was a nightmare. For reasons of propaganda, and other reasons unclear to me, every tribe, federal agency, and advocacy group involved in the dispute disseminates different statistics. Each tribe has different statistics for how many people live in the disputed area. The advocacy groups sometimes seem to inflate their statistics, for obvious reasons; why the federal agencies do not agree on their figures is another mystery.

I have tried to keep the story simple and direct, so that Americans of all backgrounds can read and have some idea about what is really going on out here. There has been a lot of distortion about the struggle for land, and the impacts of relocation, and why relocation happened. The American people are footing the bill for relocation through their taxes. So, I am offering my years of experience in the Southwest and my perspectives on the problem. To the best of my ability, I have tried to present the perspectives of the people involved in the controversy and the feelings of Navajos and Hopis who are most critically affected by relocation.

ACKNOWLEDGMENTS

In any project of this scope and depth, the assistance of many knowledgeable people is essential. I want to express my gratitude to those people who have helped me, not only with research and information-gathering involved in this project, but also in helping me to understand the world and vision of tribal people in the Southwest. By understanding the perspectives of other people and cultures, I have come to a better understanding of myself, my ancestors, and how the world came to be as it is today. It is important that everyone who helped me receives my thanks, and if anyone is left unnamed in the listing, it may be because they requested anonymity or were inadvertently omitted.

First, I want to thank the many Hopi, Navajo, and Paiute people who gave me their time. Among these are the people of Big Mountain, Coal Mine Mesa, Teesto, and White Cone. Hopi people from all three mesas and Moencopi shared important experiences and feelings with me.

As far as religious leaders and medicinemen involved in my work, I want to especially thank Oraibi Kikmongwi Stanley Bahnimptewa and his spokesman, Caleb Johnson. I also thank Moencopi Kikmongwi Heber Dan and the people of Lower Village, for explaining many things to me about the history of Moencopi and the political strife between Upper and Lower Village and its possible ramifications in the 1934 case. I want to thank Ethel Mahle of Walpi for sharing history and her time with me. I also want to thank First Mesa Kikmongwi Ebin Leslie and Second Mesa leader Perry Honanie, and many other leaders who spoke with me in various news and research interviews. I owe a special debt to White Cone medicineman Miller Nez, who taught me Navajo origins and included me in many prayers and ceremonies. Nez taught me how Navajos view the world between the sacred mountains, and took me to numerous places held in respect by the tribes, including the San Francisco Peaks. I also want to thank Navajo herbalist, Sam Boone Sr., from Coppermine, and his wife Mary, who blessed my marriage. The blessing ceremony was held in the shadow of the holy mountain.

A special mention should be made to honor the memories of two people who heavily influenced my perspectives. One is Hopi, one is Navajo. The Hopi is Terrance Talaswaima (Honvantewa) of Shipalovi, who was first a friend of Dr. Joann Kealiinohomoku, and took an interest in my work after an introduction through her. Terrance has passed on, but he is often in my thoughts. He told me the story of Awatobi, and took me there. He explained the founding of Shungopovi, and how other villages came forth from the original Mother Village. He told me the origins of the Home Dance, and explained about Hopi weddings and gave me his book, *Hopi Bride at the Home Dance*. He explained the Water Serpent dance and the legend of Palotquopi and its ramifications and influence on Hopi culture and religion. Terrance was an exceptional man and a gifted artist. I miss him.

The Navajo is Alta Kahn of Pine Springs and Burnt Water. Alta and her children were the first people to take me in and begin teaching me about the Navajo Way. I attended my first sings at Alta's camp. She and her family were very kind to me, and I will never forget her.

A number of political and village leaders have helped me. I owe much to Navajo leader Katherine Dahozy Arviso and her family. Katherine chose me to come to Arizona to help her in a nutritional research program. Perhaps, if she had not invited me, I would never have come to the House of Dawn. Katherine introduced me to Sally Tsosie and told me to go to Big Mountain and learn about the conflict from Navajos upon whom it had an impact. I want to thank Navajo Tribal Chairman Peter MacDonald and his wife Wanda, who have always been helpful to me and explained things to the best of their abilities. I want to thank Hopi Tribal Chairman Ivan Sidney, whose political career I initially started covering in 1981, and who has since become more than a news story: a trusted source and an important tribal leader. I also want to thank Mrs. Evonne Sidney, the chairman's wife, who has often made time for me in her busy schedule, and gave me exclusive coverage of her trip to the United Nations Conference on Women in 1985. I want to thank former Hopi Tribal Chairman Abbott Sekaquaptewa and his brother, Eugene. The Sekaquaptewas have always been patient with me, willing to explain aspects of Hopi history and the struggles they have endured to protect their land and way of life. I want to express special thanks to former Navajo Tribal Chairman, former DNA Legal Services Director, and current Chairman of the

Navajo Scholarship and Education Fund Peterson Zah, for the years of useful information and cooperation he has given to me and all other members of the press. Zah's contributions to his people have been invaluable. He is a man of vision and a man of honor.

I also want to thank Upper Moencopi leaders LeRoy Shingoitewa, Roy Tuchawena, Leonard Dallas, and Sandra Honanie for all the time they have shared with me. These people always had time to explain things, whether it was how the Paiutes came to the area, or how the Rare Metals uranium mill was going to be cleaned up, or why a motel would help Moencopi. When I was the news director for the *Navajo-Hopi Observer*, my office was located in the Upper Village complex, and people were very kind and helpful to me.

A lot of people in Tuba City, across the road from Moencopi, have been kind to me, too, and helped with my work. Louise Yellowman, the Coconino County supervisor from Tuba City, has always been helpful and gracious in our interviews and visits. The Navajo Police Department at Tuba City has provided a lot of insight into the personal struggles of people in the region, as have the Hopi (BIA) police. Nancy Walters, the Tuba City librarian, and her family, mother and sisters, including Sally Tsosie, were always willing to help me with my work, and they have provided shelter for me on occasions over the years as well.

I want to thank former Tuba City DNA attorneys Irene and David Barrow for their valuable help. I also want to thank San Juan Paiute leader Evelyn James for the time she spent with me, helping me understand the Paiute past and their hopes for a new future.

Members of the Navajo and Hopi Indian Relocation Commission were also very helpful. Despite the stress of an unenviable job, former executive directors Leon Berger and Stephen Goodrich always took the time to answer questions, as has current director Chris Bavasi. The statistics analyst, Dave Shaw-Serdar, has always provided accurate and fair information, and I appreciate his time. Commission attorneys Sue Crystal and Paul Tessler have been valuable resources as well, as has Mike McAllister. Commissioners Hawley Atkinson, Sandra Massetto, and Ralph Watkins have always answered my questions, and have added valuable insights into the federal side of the dispute.

I also want to thank Dr. Joann Kealiinohomoku, professor emeritus of Northern Arizona University and the director of the Cross-Cultural Dance Resource Center in Flagstaff, Arizona. When I came to Flagstaff after almost a year of living on the Navajo Reservation, she forced me to look at many different perspectives on the land issue. With her expertise in contemporary Indian cultures, and her years of field experience, she has proven a valuable ally, and she encourages me to always think and perceive on a myriad of levels. This is important for objectivity and fairness, and it is essential in history and anthropology. Keeping an open mind can be a struggle, even for the most well-intentioned researcher.

I also want to thank Northern Arizona University anthropologist Dr. Charles Hoffman for the time he has taken over the years to share information about his research and work with the San Juan Paiutes. It was his interest in the band that made me realize that they existed as a separate people.

I especially want to thank Northern Arizona University historian Dr. Philip Reed Rulon for putting me in contact with my editor, Susan McDonald of Northland Publishing. Dr. Rulon had helped me with a number of news stories in past years, and when I discussed my manuscript ideas with him and asked who would be the most appropriate publisher, he highly recommended his former student, Susan McDonald.

I want to express my appreciation for the patience, time, and constructive criticism that Susan McDonald has put into my manuscript. Her suggestions and editorial comments greatly strengthened the work, and she deserves credit for her involvement.

I also want to thank a former editor of mine, Julia Betz, formerly of the *Lake Powell Chronicle* and the *Navajo-Hopi Observer*. Julia is now the director of the John Wesley Powell Museum in Page, Arizona. Julia was a good editor, and she has greatly influenced my work and my writing style. Through my work at the *Observer*, I was better able to understand the Navajos, Hopis, and Paiutes, and I had a forum to explain their lives and the events that shape their world to outsiders.

Finally, I would like to thank my parents, Mr. and Mrs. Ferenc X. Feher, for their support of my work. I also want to thank my husband, Kevin, for his editorial and emotional support through a difficult year of writing.

CATHERINE FEHER-ELSTON
May 1988

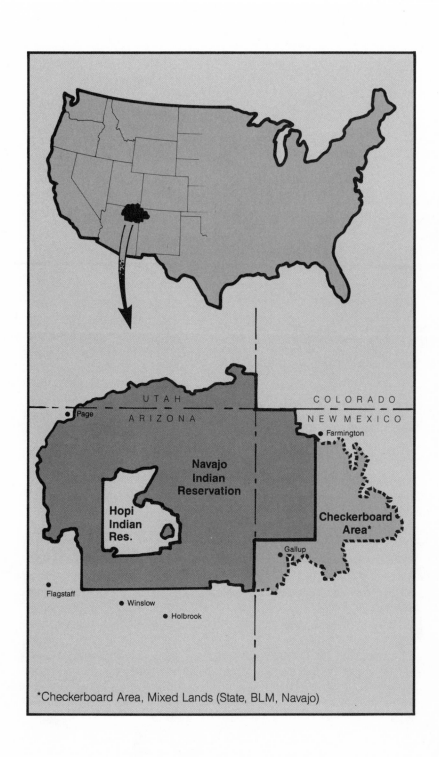

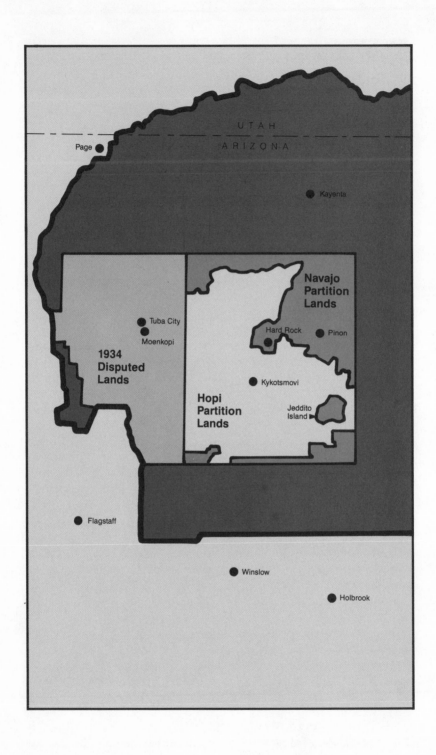

INTRODUCTION
Trouble in the House of Dawn

Land is life to the Indian people of the American Southwest. The native people of the Four Corners area believe that their homeland is the House Made of Dawn, and that they are the sworn caretakers of that house. But there is trouble in the House of Dawn; she can no longer contain her children, and as they try to divide their house, they are locked in a struggle for land and resources.

The House of Dawn can be found at the southern tip of the Rocky Mountains; it is a land of high plains, sacred mountains, canyons, and arroyos that floats serenely above the searing heat of the Sonoran desert. It is a land of broad grasslands, scattered springs and canyon oases, punctuated by dramatic mesas. Beautiful, but unforgiving, this is a fragile land that must be coaxed and cared for in order to provide life for its human creatures.

Mesquite bush, greasewood, cedar, and juniper grow here. Climate and lushness of vegetation are dictated by elevation in this country. At elevations of less than 5,000 feet, there is primarily dry desert. But much of the area lies above 5,000 feet and can be typified as high desert, alpine meadows, or forests. Here, the air is scented with creosote, sage, and pine. Humans share the land with a myriad of other life forms, including antelope, deer, coyotes, bobcats, wolves, badgers, porcupines, ravens, hummingbirds, lizards, and snakes.

In summer, it is a place of distant thunder and sudden afternoon rain. On the plains, mustard flowers bloom, vetch and lupine blossom. The earth is red and the sky is deepest blue. Sunlight is intense here, and as the sun illuminates the land, the land is bathed in a fierce golden glow; it shines with a clarity unmatched outside the Mediterranean world. Also in summer, dark clouds roll in like galleons from the distant ocean. Rolling thunder causes the earth to tremble before she is smitten by lightning flames and finally blessed by the gift of rain. In winter, bright, sunny mornings quickly give way to roaring blizzards of snow, sleet, and ice. Once the snows melt, oceans of mud trap the unwary traveller.

The history of the Great Southwest is itself a story of struggle for sustenance in an arid and unforgiving land. It is a story of migrations and conquest, cycles that continue even today. Southwestern Indian populations have exploded in the past century, straining the limits of their traditional world. Without a land base, a people have no future. More obviously and directly, without a land base, people have no place to live, religions are undermined, cultures die, and languages disappear. Today, the struggle for space in the Southwest has reached a breaking point. The Navajo are in conflict with the Hopi over what both perceive as their sacred homelands. The creation in 1882 of the Hopi reservation and the subsequent congressional partition of shared land (the Joint Use Area) have resulted in the government-supervised relocation of those who live on the wrong side of the boundary, i.e., Navajo on Hopi land, Hopi on Navajo land. The front pages of every major newspaper in North America have carried stories of the horror of relocation, and the struggle between the tribes continues as the July 6, 1986, deadline for completion of this controversial project has come and gone.

Struggles once resolved by natural processes like population control, starvation, and territorial warfare now are brought before the federal courts of the country that conquered the tribes. Up until the very recent past, warriors fought and died in defense of their sacred ground. Battles raged across the windswept land over the centuries, but with the advent of the twentieth century, after the annexation of the Southwest by the United States, the arena for conflicts shifted from mesa and valley to courtroom and real estate office. America's last Indian war is being fought now, by lawyers instead of warriors; and growing numbers of non-Indians in search of room and fulfillment of the American dream, are also struggling to control the land and its precious resources.

The struggle between the Navajo and Hopi tribes for land in northeastern Arizona has been in progress for centuries, and over the past one hundred years, the United States government has been the reluctant arbitrator of the struggle for land between the two nations. The dispute revolves around millions of acres of land immediately to the east of the Grand Canyon, extending roughly east to Ganado, Arizona, a few miles west of the New Mexico–Arizona border, south to Leupp, Arizona, and west to Flagstaff, Arizona.

In 1882, the United States government thought it had solved the problem between Navajo and Hopi when it set aside some 2,472,095 acres of land through a presidential order and called it the 1882 Hopi Indian Executive Order Reservation. On paper, it was a rectangle about seventy miles long and fifty-five miles wide. The Hopis were not happy with the arbitrary line-drawing, as their ancestral homeland encompassed hundreds of miles of land from near what is now the New Mexico–Arizona borderlands, west to the Grand Canyon, and south to the Mogollon Rim. Hopi clan petroglyphs and religious shrines demarcated this area and they had settled the boundaries with their Zuni neighbors a millenium before the coming of people who were to become known as Navajos.

When the Navajos were subjugated by the United States Army in the 1860s, they signed a treaty with the Americans in 1868. Not all Navajos submitted to the foreign armies; some fled as far west as the Grand Canyon to evade capture. Others hid in canyons and mesa lands deep within the Hopi homeland. But the majority of Navajo people had to endure the hardship of a forced march and relocation to concentration camps at Bosque Redondo in eastern New Mexico. During their captivity, the federal government listened to Navajo entreaties for permission to return to their land, and set aside some 3.5 million acres of land straddling the Arizona–New Mexico border for Navajo use; Navajos considered this area to be the heart of their ancestral lands. Maps and boundary lines were not part of traditional Navajo concerns, and the returnees did not limit their settlement to within the 1868 treaty boundaries. At the time of the signing of the Executive Order of 1882, there were hundreds of Navajos living on lands the United States had allotted to the Hopis. For almost a century, Navajo and Hopi complaints against each other would be reviewed by Washington bureaucrats.

Ultimately, the Hopi took their claims to federal court. The courts established a Joint Use Area for the tribes to share, taking land from the 1882 Hopi Reservation and parts of the expanded Navajo Reservation. This land was from the heart of the Hopi ancestral claims, on farming and grazing lands surrounding the Hopi mesas and coal-rich Black Mesa, near Kayenta, Arizona. Despite the establishment of a Joint Use Area, stress between the two expanding Indian populations continued. The courts were forced to partition the Joint Use Area, separating Navajo from Hopi and causing additional hardship and suffering for both. Indians were not the only victims. American taxpayers would be forced to shoulder the burden of a $500 million price tag to move tribesmen to the appropriate side of the partition line, to build them new homes, to drill water wells for them, to develop new community infrastructures, to buy promised replacement lands, and to develop tribal relocation programs.

After the division of the 1882 area, millions of additional acres west of the former Joint Use Area, which stems from congressional expansion of the Navajo Reservation over the complaints of the Hopi and San Juan Paiute tribes, continues to be contested in federal court. The 1934 dispute is slated to be settled in 1988 or 1989. No one knows what price tag the next federal settlement will carry.

Native Cultures

There are two dominant native cultures in the Four Corners (Utah, Colorado, New Mexico, and Arizona) region: Pueblo and Athabascan. " Pueblo" is Spanish for town, and is used to describe a number of different groups who traditionally built homes with common walls and who lived settled, agricultural lives. Scattered from the Rio Grande Valley and northwestern New Mexico to northeastern Arizona, they survive today, much as they always have, by farming, raising corn, beans, squash, cotton, and tobacco. Life, land, and religion are intricately interwoven in this world. In support of their farming culture, Puebloan ceremonial life revolves around prayers for moisture and fertility. Prayer takes the form of dance, and their Gods answer them with rain and children. Hopi, Zuni, and the other Rio Grande tribes are the descendants of the ancient Anasazi and Sinagua farmers and astronomers who built the adobe complexes today called Chaco Canyon, Mesa Verde, and Wupatki. They carry the living legacy of the high cultures that flourished in this region of the country a thousand years ago.

The ancestors of modern Navajo and Apache people were no doubt influenced by the cultures of the Pueblo people, as small bands of Athabascan-speaking nomads arrived in the Southwest sometime between five hundred and eight hundred years ago. Ultimately, the Navajo were far more heavily influenced by their Pueblo neighbors than their Apache cousins; Navajo tradition has it that some of their ancestral bands watched the construction of the Chaco Canyon pueblos, but did not participate. It is also maintained by some that there was no separation between Navajo and Apache during the first Athabascan migrations into the Southwest, but that the break occurred later. Linguistically, the Navajo are related to the Hoopas of northern California and some of the great whaling and totem-carving tribes of the Pacific Northwest.

When the Navajo came to the Southwest, they were a hunting and gathering people. They quickly established a land base in northeastern New Mexico and Colorado and adapted the farming and many of the religious practices of their Pueblo neighbors. The Spanish brought horses, sheep, goats, and guns, and the Navajo adopted them all with enthusiasm. The acquisition of horses meant that the Navajo could move more freely throughout their world, more easily utilizing seasonal grazing sites for their livestock and conducting raids on their neighbors to supplement their farming and nomadic subsistence economy.

The Navajo world is bounded by four sacred mountains: the San Francisco Peaks in Arizona, Mount Taylor in New Mexico, Blanca Peak in Colorado, and Mount Hesperus in Colorado. These four sacred mountains marked the boundary of their universe. The Navajo call themselves *Diné*, or "The People," and their land *Dinétah*, "of The People." As more and more of their kinsmen came to this area, the Navajo gradually made a large piece of it their own. The federal relocation program may have accelerated Navajo movement away from their reservation, but The Peoples' westward expansion has been in progress for almost two centuries.

Navajo and Hopi as Cain and Abel

The struggle between Navajo and Hopi over land rights illustrates nothing new in human history. Herdsmen and farmers have never gotten along—in fact, much of the history of the American West is dominated by the struggle between those who raised livestock and those who farmed. In many ways, the current Navajo-Hopi land dispute epitomizes the latest chapter in an ancient epic.

The Hebrew story of Cain and Abel—in which the farmer Cain killed his shepherd brother Abel in a jealous rage motivated by God's preference for Abel's sacrificial gifts over those of Cain—can be considered an attempt to explain the tensions between nomadic, herding societies and small, agricultural city-states. The ancestral Hebrews originally were themselves herdsmen and raiders, and were undoubtedly impressed by the might of Mesopotamian cities like Ur and Uruk, whose citizens manipulated their environment through trade networks, irrigation, and farming.

In the contemporary Southwestern version, the Navajo, nomadic herdsmen who followed their sheep and cattle, moved west from their original homeland onto Hopi lands. Tradition has it that permission was requested for this move: the *kikmongwi* (the highest Hopi social and religious leader) of Old Oraibi said that this arrangement was made sometime in the 1800s, perhaps during the Navajos' flight from Kit Carson and his New Mexico Volunteers. Thinking the request was for temporary sanctuary, the Hopis gave their approval, and the Navajo and their flocks settled on the Hopi *tusqua* (Hopi word for homeland) around Big Mountain and Teesto.

In 1868, the Navajo signed a treaty with the Americans and were given a formal land grant with clearly delineated boundaries and were allowed to return to Arizona from their captivity in eastern New Mexico at Bosque Redondo. Not unlike their American counterparts, they were a fruitful and resourceful people. The Navajo considered any vacant land appropriate for occupation. As their population grew, people spread out to adjacent areas and gradually came to occupy the region around the Hopi mesas.

The Hopi, on the other hand, had never been at war with the Americans, and thus had no protected lands prior to 1882, when they made a formal request to Congress; there were only the traditional homelands, marked by boundary stones and shrines. When President Chester A. Arthur set aside land for the Hopi Reservation, he knew nothing about these markers, which went far into the Hopi past and reflected their spiritual beliefs; rather, he drew arbitrary lines and set aside the land within them for "Hopis and other such Indians as the Secretary of the Interior sees fit to settle thereon."

Almost a century later, in 1974, Congress drew another line, a partition line, in an attempt to stop the quarrels that sprang up as Navajo and Hopi populations impinged upon one another. According to the elders of First Mesa, the physical killings between Navajo and Hopi stopped in 1915, but hard feelings and occasional physical scuffles continue even today. Millions of dollars have been spent by both tribes on attorneys, lobbying trips to Washington, D.C., and media exposure. Many of the people involved have voiced concerns that this money could have been better spent on hospitals, nutrition, and birth control programs for both tribes. As attorneys and councils vie for supremacy over the opposition, the people directly involved in the relocation efforts live lives of anguish and confusion.

Participants in the Conflict

The Navajo lost an important battle to the Americans in the 1860s, when they were pursued and burned off their land by Kit Carson and his troops; rounded up, defeated and starving, The People and their leaders successfully convinced the United States to let them go home again. But by the time they were allowed to begin the long walk back, there were less than 10,000 survivors. Today, there are more than 200,000 Navajo Indians, and the tribe is increasing its numbers exponentially. Their warrior days are over, but they continue to press outward against the boundaries of their universe.

The Hopi Tribe was reduced to some 2,000 members in the early twentieth century, but has increased its population to more than

10,000 individuals. Because the Hopi had earlier yielded much of their original lands to the Navajo, they found themselves relegated to the status of a small enclave within the heart of the Navajo Reservation. The only way they can expand their land base and provide for their own increasing numbers is by regaining land lost to the Navajo and the Anglo. (The term "Anglo" is widely used throughout the Southwest in reference to Americans of European ancestry.) Because the Hopi do not have as much money to invest as do the Navajo, they have turned to the federal court system to regain their land.

In addition to the Navajo and Hopi interests in the conflict, the small band of Paiute Indians, who reside on what is now the western side of the Navajo Reservation, have an interest in the problem. The San Juan Paiutes are struggling to regain the tribal recognition they lost in 1922 with the stroke of a federal pen. The members of this group were stripped of both their identity and their homeland at the behest of American mining interests. When the industry failed to reap the mineral wealth it sought, the Navajo Tribe petitioned Congress for permission to add what had been the Paiute Reservation to their own holdings. Congress granted this petition in 1933, and the Navajo Tribe acquired the land, with the Paiutes still on it. The culturally and linguistically distinct Paiutes were officially absorbed into the ranks of the Navajo Nation. Today, the Navajo Tribe claims descendants of the San Juan Paiutes as Navajos. The Paiutes do not agree and want a separate identity. If their petition for recognition is granted by the Bureau of Indian Affairs, it may mean another Indian exodus and a further redrawing of Navajo and Hopi reservation lines.

Non-Indian Americans are also flocking to Arizona and the Southwest in search of economic stability and scenic beauty. These "new immigrants" put pressure on Indians and old Anglo and Hispanic ranching families, because there is a limited amount of water and a limited amount of arable land available for development.

Modern Tactics

The relocation program, with its replacement land program, has actually added more land to the Navajo map. Tribal acquisition of land in Winslow and around Flagstaff, Arizona, has made some Anglo ranchers and real estate salesmen nervous. The tribal council has most recently (and controversially) initiated acquisition of the Boquillas Ranch, 491,431 acres of land adjacent to the Havasupai and Hualapai Indian reservations and Grand Canyon National Park. Leaders of these two tribes, in fear of being eclipsed by the Navajo presence, have already lodged formal complaints against the purchase.

Despite complaints by outsiders, both former Navajo Tribal Chairman Peterson Zah (who engineered the purchase of some 92,569 acres of private land near Winslow and Joseph City, Arizona, and 174,000 acres of land around the San Francisco Peaks in Flagstaff, Arizona) and the current chairman, Peter MacDonald, have said that the tribe's westward expansion will continue. Since the tribe has surplus money available for land purchases from strip-mining revenues and assorted severance taxes, there is no reason to doubt their statements. The Navajo Tribe may soon become the largest landholder in the American Southwest.

The land struggle is complicated by the fact that all those involved feel a kinship with the land. Perhaps because natural resources are so scarce, the Southwest's native populations developed deeply felt religious systems that guided their daily lives. Religion became intrinsic to attitudes and practices; since land and religion were interwoven, people could survive because they considered their land sacred and they followed cycles of ceremony and prayer. The unifying theme in the struggle between Navajo and Hopi, Navajo and Zuni, Navajo and Ute, and Navajo and Paiute, is that all believe the land is sacred and is part of them, personally. Interviews with Navajo medicinemen, Navajo and Hopi residents of the former Joint Use Area, Hopi priests and kikmongwis, and Paiute, Hopi, and Zuni tribal leaders clearly demonstrate the intricate relationship between land, religion, and tribal identity.

Understanding the Dispute

The struggle cannot be reduced to a simple matter of good and evil. Rather, it revolves around the imperatives of physical and cultural survival. Each side has a different perception of land use and land ownership. Each side is tied to its sacred ground. The key to understanding the issue and how it will affect the Southwest and the rest of the United States does not lie in emotionalism and overreaction. It lies in understanding the perspectives of the combatants and how the problem evolved. The combination of faith, population growth, and limited land base, when allied with the relatively recent migration of non-Indians to northern Arizona, makes it a pressure cooker, one that will soon explode if steps are not taken to control it. The purpose of this book is to explain how the present scenario developed, the attitudes and beliefs of the people involved, and the progress being made toward some sort of equitable solution. It will examine the possible future of the people who live in this beautiful, vital, and volatile region, the House of Dawn.

1

"THIS IS HOW IT WAS"

Oral tradition is important to any understanding of Hopi or Navajo history. In the Hopi culture, the keepers of the past are the priests, kikmongwis, and men and women initiated into various religious societies. The Navajo stories are primarily told by medicinemen, but are also passed along by clan elders. The concept of time is fluid in these cultures, and incidents that happened decades ago are often recounted as if they had taken place only yesterday.

It has long been the opinion of those who have worked and lived with the Hopi and Navajo that, for too long, archaeologists and anthropologists have neglected the wealth of oral history within these groups. For example, Hopis are often amused by the scholars who search for keys to the Hopi past by digging in the ground; they find it peculiar that Anglos put themselves to so much trouble, when all they need to do to find out is to ask.

The Hopi Creation

The people now known as Hopi have lived in Arizona for centuries—they say their ancestors saw the arrival of the Paiutes, the development of the Rio Grande pueblos, and the coming of the Spanish. They regularly recount the tale of Navajo arrival and encroachment on their homeland. First and foremost, however, an understanding of the Hopi creation epic is critical to any understanding of the people themselves.

"This is how it was," the Hopi priests always say when starting a story. A long time ago, before people were really human beings, they lived in an Underworld, the Third World. For a while, all went well. All of the people who weren't fully people got along. There was peace between the First People and the First Animals. Everybody got along. There was plenty of rain and plenty of food.

But then, corruption set in and people began to quarrel. Things got so bad that the leaders of all the people called a meeting. Next, everyone was fighting. Something had to be done to protect the good people from the bad ones.

A four-day council was held. People prayed for guidance. After a long series of events, in which supernatural animal-beings assisted the good-hearted people, a reed was planted.

The reed began to grow and the people who were not quite yet fully human beings began to realize that there was another world, an Upper World above the Third World. There was a Fourth World above the Underworld.

The reed was hollow and people crawled up the reed to the Fourth World. The entrance to the Fourth World was called *Sipapu*.

Upon arrival in the Fourth World, the people encountered a frightening, yet fascinating Being who asked them what they wanted. The people explained their past problems and their need for land.

The Being told the people who had emerged from Sipapu that he was Masau-u, God of Life, God of Death, Fire, and Keeper of the Fourth World. Masau-u said that the land was his, but that the people who were coming out of the Third World could live with him on his land, provided that they did what he asked and were fully aware that they would lead a difficult life, a life of hard work and poverty.

In return for living on his land, they would have to perform rituals to provide moisture for the entire world. They would have to make a covenant with him, and listen to his teachings and abide by his rules. The people made the covenant and said that they would obey Masau-u. Masau-u then proceeded to teach them that the Secret of Life is Death.

The ancestral Hopis made a covenant with the Lord of This World that they would serve him and act as caretakers of his land. (They try to keep this covenant even to this day.)

Upon emergence from the Underworld, the first man to emerge saw a dead bear. Clan names were based on viewing certain parts of the bear and various plants and animals around the emergence scene. Thus, the clans came into being.

Upon arrival in the Fourth World, the people scattered. Eventually, the clans that were to become Hopi gathered together and settled in the mesa country east of the Little Colorado River, in what is now northern Arizona.

Each Hopi village retells a variation of this basic creation story. The point of commonality in all the emergence tales is that the ancestral Hopi emerged from the Third World and encountered Masau-u. The land they live on is his land.

In return for living on Masau-u's land, Hopis must fulfill important responsibilities. Providing moisture for the world is paramount. This is done through prayers and ceremonies, which include dancing. The ceremonies are held every year, as set in a cyclical calender, and are oriented toward the well-being of the community and the world.

Despite enormous pressure to abandon traditional ways and convert to Christian sects, the Hopi continue to fulfill their covenant. The mystical and the human world are inseparable in the Hopi view. The masked kachina dances, the famous Snake Dance, and the various planting and social dances are all manifestations of the unique way in which men, ancestral spirits, and the mystic and divine world blend together.

The Navajo Genesis

In contrast to Hopi ceremonies, which are carried out seasonally at the dictate of custom and relationship of the earth to the sun and moon, Navajos recite daily prayers and blessings and conduct their ceremonies on an as-needed basis, generally in response to a crisis. Medicinemen sing prayers and use herbs and various other remedies to restore harmony to the lives of their patients. Harmony is central to the Navajo concept of health, as they believe that all illness—physical or psychological—is due to some action that causes a disharmony in the universe. Often, this "out of balance" can be the result of something that an individual has done, and occasionally is the result of someone doing something to the individual (i.e., witchcraft).

In the Navajo world, there are specialists who diagnose the cause of a problem through a process called hand trembling or crystal gazing. Frequently, these diagnosticians refer the patient to a specialist, an individual who knows the appropriate chant to bring the patient back into balance with the universe. It takes years to learn even one chant and the recognition and use of appropriate plants and herbs. Some singers may know three or four chants and portions of other healing ways, but very few know more than that. Many healing ways incorporate sections of the Navajo creation myths and legends, calling upon the Gods and Holy People to restore harmony and beauty to the life of the patient. Creation tales and other religious stories are usually recited only in late fall and winter.

The Navajo creation epic varies slightly from area to area on the reservation, but is unified by numerous similarities. The *hatałii* (Navajo singers or medicinemen) hold the key of knowledge to Navajo origins. The following was recited in interviews with a medicineman from the White Cone area on the boundary of the former Joint Use Area; it is also prevalent among the residents of the Big Mountain region, heartland of resistance to relocation efforts.

"The Navajos went through many worlds before we came into this world," he explained. "Most of the reason we and our ancestral people went through so many worlds was because of trouble caused by evil. But," he continued, "some of the greatest evils occurred shortly after Navajos came into this world, and were caused by the frailities and jealousies of human nature.

"Some of the things I am going to tell you may sound strange to you. Other things may sound suggestive or nasty. But I am not telling you dirty things. I am telling you what we Navajos really believe so that someday, you can tell other people in other places how we Navajos really are. This is what we believe, and we believe it as the truth," he said.

"When the first Navajos came to the Southwest, they were living around Chaco Canyon; we watched Pueblo Bonito being built, but we really didn't get involved in it," he said. "We were really people then, but we had not always been real people when we lived in the lower worlds."

He explained that the ancestral Navajos had lived for a time in an island world, called the First World. There they had an insect form, but the Insect People quarrelled among themselves and sinned. The quarelling was the result of having sex with wives that were not their own wives.

The Gods of the First World became disgusted with the conduct of the Insect People, and told them that they would have to fly away to another world. The Gods sent a flood to drown the sinful, quarrelsome, and noisy Insect People.

The Insect People flew around in a panic, hitting the sky of the First World and not knowing where to go. At their most desperate moment, a blue swallow appeared and showed them a hole in the sky, the entrance to Second World.

The blue swallow and his people, the Swallow People, said that the Insect People could live in their world, as it was a big, empty place with room enough for everyone. So the Swallow People and the Insect People lived together. At first, there was peace and harmony, but trouble began when one of the Insect People made advances to the wife of one of the Swallow People.

When the husband, who was a chief of the Swallow People, heard about the sexual transgression, he demanded that the Insect People leave the Second World. All of the other Swallow People agreed, and the Insect People were forced to make a second exodus.

The Insect People had a hard time finding a way out of Second World. But Wind God told them about an opening in the southern sky of Second World, and they climbed out of Second World and into Third World.

In Third World, the Insect People met a group of people with the heads of grasshoppers. The Insect People begged the Grasshopper People to let them live in the Third World. The Grasshopper People felt sorry for the Insect People and said that they could stay. Unfortunately, within a short time, one of the Insect People made sexual advances toward one of the married Grasshopper women. When the situation was revealed, the Insect People were forced to leave Third World.

The Insect People had a hard time finding a way out of Third World, but finally, Red Wind God told them that there was an opening to another world in the western part of the sky.

As the Insect People had been going through the different worlds, they had become more and more human in their appearance and less buglike. They were still not quite wholly human when they arrived in Fourth World, which was very like the world of the Four Corners area, bounded by Four Sacred Mountains, but they were almost human.

When they emerged into Fourth World, the surviving Insect People encountered men who lived in cities. These men, the ancestors of the *Kisaani* (Hopi), called Anasazi by the Navajo, were kind to the newcomers.

The Insect People lived near the Anasazi for a while, but the Gods began to call to the Insect People, telling them to get ready for a big event and to take baths in water and get cleaned up.

After a while, several of the Gods called a council with the Insect People. They told them they wanted to make a race of people with the forms of Gods, and while the Insect People were close, there were some modifications in form that had to be made.

Four Gods brought sacred buckskins with them to the council. Inside one of the buckskins, the Gods put one yellow ear of corn (yellow is the female color) and one white ear of corn (white is the male color). The Gods placed a second buckskin on the bundle and caused the winds to blow. The winds blew life into the bundles and when the buckskins were removed, there stood First Man and First Woman. The Gods told First Man and First Woman to live together as man and wife. They had the Insect People build them a shelter. First Man and First Woman were the mother and father of the Diné. Other creatures came to be after First Man and First Woman were created. Among them were Coyote and Badger, who play important roles in Navajo religion.

First Man told everyone that the boundaries of their world were four of the Sacred Mountains: *Sisnaajini* (Blanca Peak) in the East, *Tsoodzit* (Mount Taylor) in the South, *Dook'o'osliid* (San Francisco Peaks) in the West, and *Dibe'ntsaa* (Mount Hesperus) in the North.

First Man and First Woman had many children, but after a time, they began to quarrel. First Woman accused First Man of loving her and taking care of her only so he could have sex with her.

The children began to quarrel among themselves, and after a time, the men and women decided that they did not need each other in order to live. In fact, each group felt they would be happier without the other.

"This is when the real, the biggest trouble began," he explained. "The men moved away from the women." Each group became lonely. After a while, both groups began to have unnatural sex acts. The men masturbated and had sex with each other.

"The women began having sex with rocks. Because of the women masturbating with rocks and other strange sexual acts, many monsters came into the world. These monsters almost destroyed the Diné, until two heroes came forth and made the world safer. But it was because of the sex acts that monsters and death and unhappiness and hunger came into the world. It didn't exist before," he concluded.

After a time, the women became hungry because they had no one to help them till the fields and no one to hunt for them. The men at least could hunt for themselves and they knew how to plant fields and reap a harvest, too. When the men saw the suffering of the women, they remembered their love for their wives and took them back. Men and women were reunited and each vowed that they would never leave the other again. The women admitted that they needed their husbands, and a sense of harmony was restored among the Diné.

But not everything was beautiful. The monsters that had come into the world as a result of the women's sexual misbehavior were ravaging the land, killing people and animals and demanding exhorbitant ransoms from the Diné.

Coyote, the sky-born, angered a very old monster named *Tieholtsodi* by stealing two of his children. In his anger and anguish, Tieholtsodi sent a great flood into the Fourth World. The flood approached from the east. The Diné fled to the west. Through the assistance of the Gods moments before they were to be drowned, they hid inside a huge magic reed. A number of animals and birds, who could talk to the Diné in a common language in those days, entered the reed with the people.

The reed grew up and up until it touched the sky. As in past exoduses, once the refugees found the top of the sky, they could not find an entrance to the next world. First, Hawk tried to scratch a hole in the sky with his talons. He did not succeed. Then Bear tried to tear a hole in the sky with his claws, but he did not succeed. Coyote, sky-born, tried to dig too, but he did not succeed. Bobcat also tried to tear a hole in the sky with his claws, but he also failed. Each creature tried and tried until he was exhausted, but to no avail.

While some creatures attempted to tear a hole in the sky, other animals and insects tried to find an existing opening. After a long time, Locust came back to the reed and said he had found a way into the next world, the Fifth World.

Locust took everyone to the place of emergence into the Fifth World. While the hole was big enough for Locust, it was too small for many. So Badger dug an entryway into Fifth World large enough for all to squeeze through.

Despite their escape to Fifth World, the Water Monster still sought his children. The hole that connected Fourth World with Fifth World began to fill with water, and everyone was afraid that the flood would come to Fifth World. People became worried and sought the cause of the trouble. Within a short time, Coyote's theft of the children of Tieholtsodi was discovered.

The Diné sent the children of Tieholtsodi back down to the Fourth World through the point of emergence. Then, the Diné and their friends became familiar with their new world and they set about building replicas of the sacred mountains with the help of the Gods.

First Man and First Woman said that four of the sacred mountains would be the boundaries of the Diné universe and three mountains within the interior of the universe would serve as places of worship and homes for sacred and curative plants and springs.

Sisnaajini, the Black Mountain, is the eastern boundary of the Navajo universe. It is the home of Crystal Boy and Crystal Girl. The Gods fastened it to the earth with a bolt of lightning and decorated it with white corn, white shells, white lightning, and torrential rains. A heavy downpour that rises quickly, unloads a large amount of rain, and is quickly over is referred to as a male rain by Navajos. The male rain can be compared with the ejaculation of semen during sex. A soft rain, which lasts a very long time and is beneficial to the growing of crops is called a female rain.

Tsooził, the sacred mountain of the south, was fastened to the earth with a great stone knife and was decorated with turquoise, mist, and female rain. Boy Who Carries Turquoise and Girl Who Carries Corn reside inside Tsoodził.

Dook'o'osłiid, the sacred mountain of the west, was fastened to the earth by a sunbeam. (To the Hopi, Dook'o'osłiid is the home of the kachinas). Decorated with haliotis shells, black clouds, male rain and yellow corn, Dook'o'osłiid shelters White Corn Boy and Yellow Corn Girl.

Dibe'ntsaa, the sacred mountain of the north, was fastened to the earth by a rainbow. It was decorated with black beads and mist and is the home of Pollen Boy and Grasshopper Girl. The other three holy mountains within the boundaries of the four major mountains also had special decorations and deities placed within them.

First Man and First Woman, with the help of the Gods, made the Sun and the Moon. They created the stars, but did not know exactly where to place them, so Coyote wrapped them up in a blanket and tossed them high into the sky.

Despite all the busy preparations in the new world, not all was well. The Diné were scattered by the on-going attacks of monsters, many of them the offspring of the masturbatory activities of the Navajo women. Others were monsters that Coyote had enraged by his mischievious adventures.

The clans of the Diné were suffering. People were eaten every day, and the monsters sometimes demanded ransoms and bribes of food and goods to leave the Diné alone. Sometimes, the monsters took the food and goods and ate the people anyway. The monsters were collectively called *Nay'ei*, "Enemy Gods." It was a dark time for the Diné.

The Goddesses, Changing Woman and her sister White Shell Woman, each conceived a son. The boys were fathered by the Sun. These sons were to deliver the Diné and all the world from the horrors of the man-eating monsters.

While the boys were growing up, the identity of their father was kept secret from them, but after watching the boys overcome many monsters, the Goddess Spider Woman admired their courage and told them that their father was the Sun. The boys told Spider Woman that they wanted to go to their father's house.

Spider Woman explained that the way to the House of the Sun was long and treacherous, but through their courage and with her help, they would succeed in their journey and meet and be recognized by their father.

After many trials and tribulations, and after killing many monsters, the boys, called the Hero Twins by some Navajos and Monster Twins by others, came to the house of their father.

"The various stones and the red marks on the ground that you see around Tuba City and in the Painted Desert are the bones and blood of the monsters the twins killed," the medicineman explained. "You can see it even today."

Because of their exploits, and saving the Diné from the monsters, the elder boy came to be called Killer of Enemy Gods. His brother came to be called Born of Water, since he was conceived in water when his mother was swimming.

The Hero Twins delivered the Diné from bondage to the monsters. After their labors were done, they settled along the banks of the San Juan River, where they remain even today. Changing Woman taught the Diné the proper way to live and she taught them ceremonies for healing and restoring harmony. Spider Woman taught the Diné how to weave, and her home can still be seen today on Spider Rock, in Canyon de Chelly, near Chinle.

BIG MOUNTAIN NAVAJO GENESIS BELIEFS

The people of Big Mountain have added several items to this basic creation myth. What is most important about variations in the Big Mountain area is the fact that many Big Mountain Navajos believe that they actually crawled up into this world through the magic reed with the Hopi. Other Big Mountain Navajos say that they have always had close alliances with the Hopi, especially the Third Mesa villages of Hotevilla and Oraibi. Extensive intermarriage has taken place between Big Mountain Navajo and Third Mesa Hopi for quite some time.

The Big Mountain Navajo say that Hopi and Navajo have always lived together, that the Hopi have always provided agricultural products like peaches and squash to the Navajo, and the Navajo have traded game and sheep to the Hopi. According to Navajos at Big Mountain, they have been "the defenders of the Hopis," and the "strong arms of the Hopi people."

Stanley Bahnimptewa, the kikmongwi of Old Oraibi, insists that during the 1860s, small groups of Navajos did contact the theocratic leaders of Oraibi and request permission to camp on lands around Big Mountain and Teesto.

"We thought they only wanted to stay a little while, to rest their horses and sheep and move on," Bahnimptewa said. " We didn't know that they would stay so long. But we say who goes and who stays on our land. That land is ours. We have just let them stay on there. When we tell them to go, they will have to go. But it will be our decision, not the United States government's decision."

Big Mountain leaders explain their acquisition of the land in this way.

"Navajos and Hopis crawled out of the Third World together. When they came out, they rested. Then they had a big ceremony. The Holy People had made medicine bundles, which they wanted to share with the Hopi and Navajo. A race for the medicine bundles was conducted.

Whichever runners would get certain bundles would determine who was going to live where. There was a long and a short medicine bundle. The best Hopi and Navajo runners were in the race. Since the Navajo runners had longer legs, they were the first to reach the bundles. They took the larger bundle. The Hopi runners took the shorter bundle. It was decided by the Holy People that, as a result of this race, the Navajos would have all the lands they now occupy. The Hopis would live on their mesas and farm, as they had the short medicine bundle."

Some Hopi tell a similar story, only they maintain that the Hopi were the better runners and that they won the race and allowed Navajos limited use of Hopi land. Regardless of the origins of the race story, it certainly presents the Navajo viewpoint. Hopis were destined to live on the mesas and be farmers. Navajos were destined to live off the mesas, settle where they pleased and live the way Changing Woman taught them to live, "the Navajo Way."

An important thing to remember when listening to Big Mountain Navajos recount the origin tales is not archaeological or historical evidence, but what the people say they believe happened. In the Navajo world, the perception of reality is frequently much more important than the actual facts as they happened; rumor and gossip are used as forms of social control. Incidents in history and tradition are remembered different ways by different people. Feeling, belief, and emotion combine with fact to create Navajo reality. In the turmoil relocation has brought, this is especially true. To people facing relocation, it doesn't matter whether their great-great grandparents moved west to Big Mountain in an attempt to escape Kit Carson in the 1860s or whether their ancestors emerged with the Hopi at Sipapu near the Grand Canyon.

2

CONTACT AND CONQUEST

When the Europeans came into the New World, they brought with them over a thousand years of Roman and Judaeo-Christian heritage. They perceived the world much differently than did the native peoples; to the Europeans, the world was a place to exploit, and Nature an adversary to be bested.

The Spanish colonizers were among the most aggressive of the New World's invaders. Fresh from victories over Islam in Andalusia, they felt that God was clearly on their side. As they had imposed the Catholic Inquisition on fellow Spaniards, Moslems, and Jews, they also brought it to America. There was no consideration of any religious belief except Catholicism and God, Church, and King were to be obeyed. The native populations were viewed as a crop to be harvested for the Christian God. The Spanish viewed the peoples' religious practices as Satanic— to them, the Devil and witchcraft were everywhere. Thus, they had a double obligation: They had to subdue the natural world, extracting as much as they could from its land and people—gold, minerals, labor—and they had to wrestle with Satan for control of the Indian peoples' souls. In an effort to accomplish these goals, military and religious representatives of the King of Spain made regular sweeps through the region that is known today as Arizona and New Mexico. It was a difficult challenge, one that they were never entirely successful in meeting.

Before the Spanish

Although it is generally accepted that the Navajo were in the Four Corners area by the dawn of the sixteenth century, it is less clear exactly when they entered this area. It is likely that the ancestors of the Navajo and Apache wandered into the Southwest through the Rocky Mountain corridor from what is now British Columbia. As the Athabascans began to interact with the more established Pueblo tribes, they incorporated Puebloan ceremonialism into their own religious practices and learned farming and pottery making from their neighbors, as well.

According to Spanish accounts, there were very few Navajo in the area of the Hopi mesas during the late sixteenth century. However, it may be inferred that the Spanish did not have extensive contact with the Navajo, as archaeological evidence has established that the land around the Governador and Chama rivers was occupied by the Navajos during this period.

There are two versions of the way in which the word "Navajo"came to be attached to the descendants of the early Athabascans. One has it that the Zunis called them *nabahu*, meaning "enemies"; the other traces the appellation to the Spanish, who called them *Apaches de Nabahu*, meaning "Apaches with great tilled fields."

Also open to speculation is the way in which the Navajo acquired their lands. There is evidence that raids were conducted against the Zuni and other Rio Grande pueblos prior to the arrival of the Spanish, and it is likely that the Navajo—a warrior people—were stronger than their Pueblo neighbors. It seems reasonable to speculate, then, that the land was wrested by force from the more sedentary people. It is clear, however, that the Navajo had established footholds in Hopi country and were involved with various Hopi villages for an extended period. For most Navajo, the Hopi were a convenience, a source of food and goods that were sometimes traded for, sometimes taken.

Early Spanish Contact with Hopi and Navajo

Francisco Vásquez de Coronado, in search of the Seven Cities of Cibola and their gold-paved streets, led Spanish troops into the Rio Grande Valley in 1540, and then dispatched a small westward expedition under the leadership of Don Pedro de Tovar and Fray Juan Padilla. On their trek, the Spaniards apparently encountered the Hopi for the first time. It was not a friendly meeting.

The first line of Hopi defense was ceremonial: a narrow track of sacred cornmeal. The Spanish troop crossed this line and a battle ensued near the Hopi village of Kawiokuh on Antelope Mesa (Bartlett 1943). After subduing the Hopi, who had no real capacity to resist the armed and mounted soldiers, Tovar returned to Coronado's encampment near the Zuni pueblo of Hawikuh to report on his mission. A second expedition was later sent in search of the great river that was reported by the Hopi to lie to the west of their villages. Led by Don García López de Cárdenas, this group reached the river, the Colorado as it is known today, and thus became the first Europeans to see the

Grand Canyon. They were in search of treasure, however, not scenic beauty, and returned to Coronado with their report. The Cárdenas expedition traversed through Hopiland and also included in their report the information that there were no other Indian inhabitants in the area between the Hopi mesas and the Rio Colorado.

Although the Spaniards saw no one, it is likely that there were native people in the area, as it was part of the homeland of the San Juan Paiutes. Either the Paiutes were not directly in the expedition's path, or they wisely avoided contact with the Europeans.

After these early investigations, the Spanish did not return to the vicinity of the Hopi mesas for more than forty years. Then, in 1583, Antonio de Espejo led a group to Awatobi; the villagers, unhappy at the prospect of another Spanish visit and its attendant demands, made a show of strength. There is evidence that in the forty year interval, a definite Navajo presence developed near the mesas; according to Espejo's journal, the people of Awatobi sent messages to neighboring Navajo bands requesting help in warding off the conquistadores. These warriors responded, and together, a show of strength and unity was presented. In the limited engagement that ensued, Espejo dominated because of his company's military power, and both Hopi and Navajo were forced to make peace with him.

In 1598, Don Juan de Oñate led a group to the mesas and once again, formal submission to the King of Spain was required of the Hopi; Oñate returned with the same demand again in 1604 and 1605, on his expedition to California. Each time, the Hopi people superficially obeyed these orders and undoubtedly hoped for a hasty departure for the Spaniard and his troops.

Contact between the Europeans and the native people accelerated between 1628 and 1680, due largely to Spanish proselytizing on the mesas and in the river valleys. Vigorous attempts to force Christianity into the culture of the Rio Grande Pueblo people laid the groundwork for a dramatic confrontation in 1680.

The Hopi humored the Spanish when they spoke of their Great King Beyond the Seas; they supplied food and other material requirements when they came to the mesas; they pledged loyalty when the soldiers were there with them, and tried to forget about them after they marched off. This attitude changed in 1628, when the first of the priests ordered by the King of Spain to "convert the heathen" arrived. Thirty Franciscans made the long trip from New Spain (Mexico) to New Mexico (the modern states of Arizona and New Mexico), and four went to the Hopi villages. These priests established missions at Awatobi, Oraibi, Shungopovi, Mishongnovi, and Walpi (Stephens 1964, and interviews with Terrance Talaswaima (Honvantewa) 1981/1982, and Caleb Johnson 1987).

The Spanish attempted to convert the Navajo at the same time. An interesting account of this effort was presented by Benavides in his 1630 Memorial to the King of Spain.

> Leaving this province of the Xila Apaches, one continues in the same direction along the western edge of the settlements; and advancing northward along their border for a distance of more than 50 leagues occupied by villages of the Xila jurisdiction one arrives at the province of the Navajo Apaches . . . . The Navajos are very skillful farmers, for the word Navajo means 'large cultivated fields'. This province is the most warlike of the entire Apache nation, and here the Spaniards have certainly shown their valor . . . . They (the Navajos) unite for the express purpose of coming to wage war on Christian Indians . . . . At times the Spaniards have gone there to wage war on them for murdering so many Christian Indians, and although they attacked at daybreak without the least warning, they have always found countless numbers crowded into the fields. They have their own peculiar type of underground dwelling places, as well as a certain kind of hut for storing grain and they always live in that same place . . . . During . . . September of last year, 1629, I was taking care of the . . . Friary of Santa Clara in the Pueblo of Capoo . . . . It was most frequently the victim of attack from the Navajo Apaches (Benavides 1945).

It is unlikely that the Navajo attacked the "Christian" pueblos solely because of their religion; more realistically, they were continuing the raiding behavior that had been established before the incursion of Spain's representatives.

Spain enslaved the pueblos of the Rio Grande and forced a superficial acceptance of Christianity and the rigors of the Spanish Inquisition upon their people. The "civilized" Spanish Christians brutally tortured Pueblo religious leaders who were found practicing their own religion, and often burned people alive, those who continued to follow traditional teachings, as an example to other recalcitrants.

THE GREAT PUEBLO REVOLT

Within fifty years after Benavides' memorial, Hopis, the Pueblo people of the Rio Grande Valley, and some Navajo bands united and rose in rebellion against Spain. What has been called the Great Pueblo Revolt took place in 1680 and under the leadership of a Tewa Indian called Popé, who was from the San Juan Pueblo in New Mexico, they drove out the Spanish invaders. Those whom they did not kill, they pursued from the Rio Grande Valley to El Paso. The revolt started on August 10, and within a month, Spanish towns in New Mexico were abandoned and Spanish missions were in flames. It was over a decade before the Spanish ventured back into the House of Dawn.

Not much is known of the life of Popé. It is known that he was a member of a priestly society and that, along with other traditional leaders, he was imprisoned and tortured by the Spanish for his beliefs. It is said that after the decision to drive out the Spanish had been made, runners set out from San Juan Pueblo to all the Rio Grande Valley villages, Zuni, and Hopi. The runners carried knotted cords which were untied one knot each day, until the last knot was untied. That day signalled the beginning of the uprising, and the beginning of twelve years of freedom from Spanish rule for the people of the Four Corners.

In Hopiland, the four resident missionaries were killed and their missions destroyed. Many Hopis who had converted exclusively to Catholicism were killed as well.

Today, the revolt is remembered by Hopis as the days when kachinas and Gods came down and drove out the invaders. The children learn the story from their elders; at the 1980 Hopi Children's Art Show, children drew out the story in commemoration of the tricentennial of the Great Pueblo Revolt. In their depictions, Gods, warriors and avenging kachinas come to the mesas, killing black-robed Spanish monster priests and throwing their bodies over the cliffs. It is a celebration of deliverance from the bonds of spiritual and physical slavery.

Navajo and Hopi sources have recounted the tale of the destruction of Awatobi, a ruined Hopi city on Antelope Mesa that serves as a reminder of the price Hopis were willing to pay to honor their contract with Masau'u and maintain righteousness and sanctity. Most Hopi are reluctant to discuss the story, because it is holy and also because it is a painful reminder of a bitter time.

Historical records indicate that the destruction of Awatobi occurred around 1700 or 1701. Traditional Navajos from Big Mountain say that Awatobi was destroyed because its people became too corrupt. Caleb Johnson of Old Oraibi has said that the Chief of Awatobi decreed that his own village should be destroyed, not strictly because of the Christianity but because of the wicked deeds of its people.

Johnson said the destruction of Awatobi occurred sometime within twenty years after the Great Pueblo Revolt, and that many Anglo historians claim that the conversion to Christianity was the sole cause of the destruction; he stressed however, that the corruption of the people and the Spanish priests were the foremost contributing factors.

As it is told, certain residents of the village of Awatobi had converted to the "Jesus Way" at about the time of the revolt. To forsake traditional teachings was to forsake the contract with Masau'u. Awatobi had become *ka-Hopi*, the opposite of Hopi, the opposite of all that is good and righteous. To become ka-Hopi was to be against all nature, to become anti-human. But most importantly, it was a violation of the covenant between Masau'u and the Hopi people.

Hopi from all three mesas met to decide what to do about Awatobi. Because the transgressions, the corruption and the immorality were so great, it was decided that the village must be destroyed, along with the converts and their Spanish priests. Although not every Hopi village participated in the attack on Awatobi, an attack was jointly planned and executed.

According to Navajo sources, when Christian Hopis were attacked with their Spanish priests, all the men were in a kiva. The priests and the male converts were sealed in the kiva and suffocated by having burning, hot ground chilies poured through the roof opening. The women and children were carried away to other Hopi villages. Navajos say that the surviving inhabitants of Awatobi ran away to neighboring Navajo bands living south and east of Awatobi. They were taken in by the Navajos and founded the Tobacco Clan of the Diné. (Medicineman Miller Nez July 1981; Colbert Daizy May 1982; Peggy Scott of Teesto June 1986; confirmed by Hopi Museum Curator Terrance Talaswaima June 1984, and Caleb Johnson June 1987).

Despite the limited involvement of Navajos in the Great Pueblo Revolt, it is unlikely that any true unity existed between Navajo and Pueblo. The Spanish had not been able to establish a firm foothold in Dinétah, but they had infringed upon further Navajo expansion into New Mexico, had led slave raids against the Navajo, and had forced Navajos to be baptized into the Jesus Way. On occasion, members of various Rio Grande Pueblos helped the Spanish in their raids against the Navajo (this could explain why few Navajo got involved in the revolt). When the revolt began, the Spanish were too busy defending themselves to protect their holdings of cattle, sheep, and horses, and it is likely that some Navajo, like their Pueblo neighbors, saw an opportunity for revenge against the slavers and also an opportunity to collect valuable goods.

After the revolt, the Spanish governor of New Mexico made a weak attempt at reconquest in 1681; he was unsuccessful. It was twelve years later that Don Diego de Vargas led the Spanish back into New

Mexico on a mission of reconquest and revenge, inspired by the concern that other tribes might entertain similar ideas of freedom if the New Mexico province was allowed to remain free.

The tale of the *Reconquista* is bloody and brutal, full of cruelty and barbarism. One cannot help but wonder who the truly civilized people were after reading accounts of Spanish behavior during the reconquest. Nothing any Navajo or Pueblo war party had ever done compared with the mass destruction and senseless slaughter wreaked by the Spanish. One example occurred after the seige of Acoma. The people of that pueblo resisted a lengthy Spanish seige with courage and valor; after the Spanish conquered the village, they cut off the left foot and hand of every adult male and sold many of the women and children into slavery. Refugees from New Mexico fled to Dinétah and Hopi. The Navajos took in many Pueblo people, and some of the Navajo clans trace their origins back to the horror of the Reconquista.

Hoping for a miracle, desperate for freedom, the Rio Grande pueblos revolted again in 1696. This time, they were easily crushed. Anticipating repercussions, the Hopi moved some of their villages to even more remote areas atop First and Second mesas. Additionally, a group of Tewas from the Rio Grande were invited by the village of Walpi to relocate from their homes to First Mesa. The Hopi needed the services of the Tewa to aid in their efforts to repel the Ute, Apache, Navajo, and Spanish, and since the Tewa were nervous about the return of the Spanish, they accepted the offer. Their village on First Mesa came to be called Hano, and as time went by, more and more of their clan members and other relatives emigrated west from the Rio Grande to the new enclave.

A redoubled effort was made early in the eighteenth century to bring the Hopi into the Christian fold, and if the Spanish could not do it with priests, they would do it with soldiers. In 1701, Governor Cubero "invaded the Hopi country" (Bartlett 1934); once again, the Hopi submitted on the surface only.

By this time, the raiding activities of the Navajo had increased; due to Spanish pressure, some Navajo bands had moved west, and as they did so, the level of raiding on Hopi pueblos escalated. The Navajo established dominion over Dinétah, and were unafraid of engaging in battle with the Europeans, especially once they were mounted on Spanish horses and armed with Spanish weapons.

By 1757, the Hopi people were so desperate for help that they sent a delegation to Santa Fe to the Governor and Captain-General Don Joachin Codallos y Rabel, begging for protection. They also asked Father Escalante to intercede on their behalf with the governor.

Population and food supplies seriously decimated, the Hopi needed assistance. But Santa Fe was a long way from Hopiland, and authorities did little or nothing to help the pueblos.

Intertribal Conflict

A typical intertribal conflict has been described by Big Mountain Navajo elders: When the Navajo were hungry, they went to Hopi country. The Hopi would treat them well and feed them. Then, when the Navajos had eaten, the Hopi would sneak up behind them, hit them over the head, and throw them off the mesa. In revenge, the Navajo would organize a war party. After the attack, the Navajo would go home, and the Hopi would prepare a counterattack into Navajo country. Then each party would consider itself satisfied and a treaty would be made until another Navajo was thrown over a mesa or another Hopi was killed in the cornfields.

Almost twenty years later, the situation was basically unchanged: "We were told . . . that they were now at fierce war with the Navajo Apaches, who had killed and captured many of their people" (Espinosa 1976). Navajo raids against the Pueblo people and the Spanish continued until the end of the Spanish Period in 1823.

UNDERSTANDING TRIBAL WARFARE

Both Navajo and Hopi have pointed out that despite the constant state of warfare that existed between the tribes from the Spanish period through the conquest of the Southwest by the American army, human life was viewed as a sacred thing; the taking of a human life was not something done lightly by warriors of either tribe. To Americans raised in a world where millions of lives can be taken at the pressing of a button, the concept of tribal warfare may seem archaic, alien, and brutal. But tribal warfare was a mechanism to establish and hold clan and tribal boundaries and territories. It was not a method for the wholesale destruction of nations.

Hopis have pointed out that warriors had to go through elaborate rituals before and after killing. After taking human life, a Hopi's immortal soul was in danger of never being reborn if proper ceremonial cleansing was not quickly done. Navajos in the past and today live in mortal fear of haunting by the ghosts of the dead, called *chindi*, through some intrusion, either deliberate or inadvertent. Even contact with a dead body or an object that belonged to a dead person can cause a haunting called "corpse sickness," and lead to nightmares, insanity, and death. This is especially so if the Navajo has been the direct cause of a person's death. Killing of enemies may sometimes be neccessary, but it is equally necessary to cleanse the warrior after the killing has been done. A religious rite called the Enemy Way is conducted to ritually cleanse a person after he has killed.

Intertribal warfare between Navajo and Hopi was not intended to totally destroy the enemy. In some ways, it was a hit and run type of casual warfare, a vendetta of honor or revenge. If Hopis had killed someone from a Navajo clan, his relatives would come to the mesas seeking vengeance. If a Hopi had been carried away in a Navajo raid, the village warriors would seek the captive and bring him home again.

The last battle between Navajos and Hopis from Oraibi is an interesting illustration of intertribal warfare, and accounts of it by Navajos and Hopis capture a feeling for tribal war and serve to point out different interpretations of the same incident, showing the gap in crosscultural understanding. As the history of both people is kept alive through oral tradition, an account of the raid by a Navajo friend of W.W. Hill and a retelling of the story by an Oraibi Hopi gives insight into both cultures. Particularly interesting in the comparative accounts are the contrasting attitudes toward the role of women (Navajo women had more influence and freedom within their society than Hopi women, who were supposed to stay at home, cook, raise children, and take care of their husbands); the fact that even though the Navajos were victorious over the Oraibi warriors, they did not go in and wipe out the village; and the role that magic played in the marital conduct of both sides. It is also interesting that the raiders were from far-away Lukachukai, not Navajos living close to the Hopi mesas.

Details of the last Navajo raid on Oraibi were given to W. W. Hill by a man who was part of the raiding party. The story was told to Hill in 1936.

> [The night before the raid on Oraibi], they were forbidden to build a fire. One of the men in the party could talk Ute fairly well [probably Paiute]. He walked back and forth all night. The Oraibi were great friends of the Ute, and when their spies heard this man talking Ute, they went back and said, "it is just the Ute who are [sic] coming to trade." However, during the night the Oraibi became suspicious and prepared themselves. The next morning when the Navajo got within two or three miles from the village, they could see a party of men coming down the mesa; all were dressed in white . . . . The Navajo vanguard rode up, made a circle and led the Oraibi away from the village. The Oraibi followed these men back to the main body of the Navajo. One Oraibi had an arrow feathered with the feathers of the "Monster

Eagle." He attempted to shoot this arrow over the whole group of Navajo but failed. If he had succeeded, the Oraibi would have been victorious.

There was a young woman among the Navajo. She was on a very fast horse and rode right into the center of the Oraibi. She called to the Navajo to come on and give all they had. The Navajo encircled the Oraibi and started to slaughter them. They chased those who broke through up to the back of the mesa. There were dead Hopi lying about for over two miles. What was left of the Oraibi ran for their houses . . . . The leader then called off the Navajo war party. He said that they had done enough damage and that they had better leave. They gathered up the plunder, took some of the pottery and broke the remainder. When they were leaving, the few surviving Oraibi came out on their house tops and you should have heard them wail . . . . When the Navajo were six miles from the village, they drew a line in back of them. That was a mark over which no enemy could pass.

When they returned home with the plunder, they were serenaded in front of the hogans. The warriors threw out to the serenaders the sheep and the plunder they had secured (Hill 1936).

Oraibi Hopis remember the battle, too. They say it happened just prior to the arrival of Kit Carson in the 1860s. They remember it as a defeat, but have added some details that point out a Hopi perspective. Oraibi people remember the Navajo heroine who road into the thick of battle to encourage a Navajo victory. They say they do not view her as a heroine, but as a "loose woman who had slept with a lot of men. When she rode in, she said to the men, 'all of you who know me, follow me,' and her lovers were bound to do so. She is a hero to the Navajos, but she is not a hero to the Hopi people." Hopis also stress that more damage was done to the Navajos than they realized at the battle, because the Oraibi had dipped their arrows in rattlesnake venom and "Navajos continued to die for days after the battle."

Intertribal warfare as a means for Navajos and Hopis to establish and hold territory and avenge slights on one another did not cease voluntarily. It only happened when a stronger group forced them to stop fighting with each other. What the power of Spain could not accomplish, the expanding United States did. The Navajo would be subjugated in their own land, and the Hopi, too, would soon come to be treated as a conquered people.

The Mexican Period

From 1823 until 1846 is considered by historians to be the Mexican Period in the Southwest. During this time, the power that controlled New Spain, or Mexico, was lost by representatives of the Spanish King and transferred to the revolutionary Mexican leaders, many of whom had served in the army of the King. The change in authority did little or nothing to improve the lot of the native people to the north. The power of Spain was gone, and the Navajos incorporated the animosity that had been directed toward their former enemies into a new form of tribal warfare. They continued to raid the pueblos and also attacked the Mexican haciendas and rancheros. As they had been enemies of Spain, they were now enemies of Mexico.

Both Navajo and Hopi were subject to raids by Mexican slavers. These individuals used Santa Fe and the New Mexican rancheros as bases of operations. A young Navajo brought the equivalent of $60 to $120 on the auction block, and Indians were thus considered to be yet another cash crop by the raiders. Additionally, the Catholic Church implicitly condoned the activity, in that the Church insisted that slavers baptize their captives and thus bring more heathen souls into the fold of Christianity. The slavers not only made a profit from the sale of human beings, they also gained heavenly merit.

The American Period: "The New Men"

When the Americans marched into Santa Fe on August 18, 1846, the yoke of Mexican rule was forcefully removed. Word that a new type of man had come to Dinétah swept the region, and the Navajo hoped that they could exist harmoniously with the Americans and that the two groups could share domination of the land they both claimed. It was also important to the Navajo to solicit the help of the Americans to return their captive brothers and sisters from the slavers.

Navajo aggression took the form of raiding, land acquisition, and settlement. The concept of slavery as the Americans practiced it with Black Africans was unknown to the Navajo. Children taken in raids would be incorporated into Navajo families, and women would become wives or concubines; any children resulting from these unions would have full clan rights and responsibilities. Many Navajo clans can trace their origins to captives from other tribes and from the Mexican population. People were viewed first as people, then as whatever their cultural affiliation dictated. Slavery as a demeaning institution, with racial or cultural roots, did not exist in the Navajo ethos.

Further, the concept of land ownership by an individual was foreign to the Navajo (and to other tribes as well). Land acquisition was made by right of conquest and settlement. Whoever could hold the land owned it, but selling, parcel by parcel, was another alien idea.

Navajos operated on a band-by-band, clan-to-clan system, government by consensus, and pure clan democracy. No one band or clan leader, or area nataani, could make decisions binding upon the totality of the Navajo people. Certain land areas in Dinétah were the traditional use areas of particular clans, and generally, people moved freely, with kinship ties the controlling factor over where a person lived. Intraclan harmony was not always present, however. Some Navajos, working in conjunction with the New Mexicans, preyed upon other Navajos, selling them as slaves.

The Americans represented a blossoming, expanding republic, full of ideas from the Age of Reason, flexing its military muscle, and interested in acquiring the entire North American continent for itself. Government was not by consensus but by elected representatives. The rights of men were an issue, and the country was on the verge of a civil war that would determine whether states' rights or federal rights would prevail. Navajo and American agendas were poised on the brink of collision and there was little hope that one would or could comprehend the needs of the other.

Navajo hopes for cooperative rule over their own land and that of the Pueblo people were dashed when the American commander, General Stephen W. Kearny, proclaimed that the United States was annexing all of present-day New Mexico and Arizona (which was the Territory of New Mexico until 1863, when the Territory of Arizona was created by Congress). Kearny went on to say that by virtue of this annexation, the enemies of the New Mexicans were now the enemies of the United States Government as well. Since the native people had had an adversarial relationship with those of European descent since the time of the Spanish, Kearny's sentiments effectively set the Navajo among the opposition.

When the Americans initially annexed the Territory of New Mexico, the Navajos were cooperative about captive exchanges. For the most part, they returned both people and livestock that had been carried off, and then waited for the New Mexicans, under American direction, to do the same. A few women and children were returned, as well as some of the stock, but the bulk of both people and animals were not sent back to their rightful place, and the Americans did not seem inclined to enforce the directive. Consistently disappointed, the Navajo ended any cooperation.

Within two years of their initial contact with the New Men, the

Navajo came to view the Americans with the same contempt and loathing they felt for the Mexicans. Unfortunately, they did not realize that they were facing the most significant threat to their survival within human memory. Within twenty years of American annexation, Dinétah was successfully invaded and most of its people were forced into captivity. The enemy was no longer a poorly organized, poorly supplied group with tenuous ties to its government, but rather, the highly trained and experienced United States Army. Kearny sent troops into the field against the Navajo, and as the Americans routed Navajo warriors, treaties were made with individual bands. No one agreement bound the entire Navajo population, however, and the separate treaties were generally ignored.

NAVAJO IMPERIALISM MEETS AMERICAN MANIFEST DESTINY

Prior to the American conquest of New Mexico, the Navajos had been in a state of warfare with the Spaniards for almost two centuries. This situation was the result of at least two things: the decimation caused by the slave raiders and the expansionist tendencies implicit to the Navajo.

The Navajo world is bounded, but not necessarily limited to, land within the Four Sacred Mountains. In the "old days," they roamed more or less freely within these boundaries. In order to establish ownership, they built hogans and challenged anyone who disputed their ownership to fight for the land. Eventually, the various Navajo clans were able to claim specific areas as their own.

When the Navajo realized the numbers and strength of the New Men, and realized that they could not hope to defeat them, they sought to establish peace and a sharing of territory with them. But the Americans, motivated by the political and philosophical theory historians have designated as Manifest Destiny, had no intention of sharing anything. The native people, such as the Navajo, were merely annoyances, impediments in America's march to the Pacific Ocean. Through their total disregard of the cultural dynamics of the region, the Americans ensured that conflict between the larger nation and the indigenous population would erupt.

The Navajo and Apache were the only real hinderances to American expansionist goals. Both Athabascan groups were active in the Southwest, and were, on the whole, fierce antagonists. They fought wars of attrition against the Spanish and the Mexicans, and were prepared to do the same against the Americans.

When it became clear that they could not hope to prevail over American troops, the Navajo met with them in 1846. Colonel Doniphan of the United States Army and Diné leaders assembled at Bear Springs, near what is now Fort Wingate, New Mexico. Doniphan told the Navajo that the United States had taken military control of New Mexico, and his government had promised protection to its citizens. This meant all the residents of New Mexico—whether descendants of the Spanish, Mexicans who had elected to remain in the region, Pueblo villagers, or American citizens. He also said his government wanted to enter into a treaty of peace with the Navajo and pointed out that the U.S. now controlled Navajo land as well as New Mexican land.

Further, Doniphan said that if the Navajo wanted to continue fighting Mexicans, they could join the Americans as allies and fight alongside the troops in Chihuahua. The army commander added that if the Navajo did not choose to make peace with the United States, he had orders to prepare for a war against them.

The Navajo were not particularly interested in fighting Mexicans in Chihuahua, since their primary enemies and those who were stealing their children lived in the recently acquired American territory of New Mexico. Nor were they overcome with pleasure at the prospect of being incorporated into the jurisdiction of the United States. They were lords of the earth—how could they accept American rule? They saw themselves as equal to the American force, not subservient to it. They wanted what they perceived as justice, and they wanted to continue their dominance of the region.

A young Navajo war leader, Nataalith (also known as Zarcillas Largo) stood up during the November 22, 1846, meeting and through a translator, delineated his tribe's position.

"If New Mexico be really in your possession, and it be the intention of your government to hold it, we will cease our raids and refrain from future wars upon that people; for we have no cause to quarrel with you and do not desire to have any war with so powerful a nation. Let there be peace between us," Largo said (McNitt 1972). He also pointed out that the Americans were newcomers to an arena of long-standing conflict between the people of the Southwest: Navajo, Pueblo, Spanish.

Violence between the Hopi and Navajo accelerated during the period as well. In a report to the Bureau of Indian Affairs, the first American governor of the territory summarized the situation in the following manner:

The Moquis [Hopis] are neighbors of the Navajos and live in permanent villages, cultivate grains and fruits and raise all the varieties of stock. They were formerly a very numerous tribe in possession of large flocks and herds but have been reduced in numbers and possessions by their more warlike neighbors and enemies, the Navajos. The Moquis are an intelligent and industrious people.

> [The Navajos] have no permanent villages or places of residence, but roam over the country between the San Juan on the north and the water of the Jila on the south . . . . They have in their possession many of the prisoners, men, women and children taken from settlements of this Territory whom they hold and treat as slaves (Abel 1914).

Problems constantly arose between the Navajo, the Hopi, and the Americans. In Indian Agent Calhoun's report for 1849-50, Hopi complaints against the Navajo were emphasized. In his August 1851 report, Calhoun stated that a delegation of Hopi from several villages had come to him and asked for help against Navajo raiders, whom they said were driving them to starvation.

From 1850 to 1858, the United States conducted several vigorous campaigns against the Navajo. By 1852, Fort Defiance, near what is now the Arizona–New Mexico border, was established. The military presence in the heartland of Dinétah ameliorated the overt violence, but did not end it. Tensions remained, and by 1858, a state of total warfare existed between the Navajo and the Americans. For the first time in their history, the Navajo were fighting a foe stronger than themselves.

The conflicts escalated through the winter of 1861. A "scorched earth" campaign was launched against the Navajo; great numbers of cattle, sheep, and crops were destroyed, and Americans and their New Mexican allies burned down hogan after hogan. These cruel tactics effectively subdued the Navajo until spring.

By 1861, the Civil War occupied Washington, D.C.'s military minds; and American troops were withdrawn from the Territory of New Mexico in July. Full-scale raiding was then resumed by the Navajo and their targets were, once again, the Pueblo, Anglo, and Hispanic settlements. The raiders were largely unchecked until 1863, when the New Mexico militia initiated a campaign to combat the depredations.

The Hopi memory of this campaign gives some insight into their perspective. "The Navajos were pests to everyone. They stole our children. The Americans finally brought in Kit Carson because they were tired of being pestered by the Navajos. He rounded them up and took them to New Mexico" (Talaswaima interview 1982).

The campaigns of 1863-64 were conducted under the command of Brigadier-General James R. Carleton. Carleton instructed Colonel Christopher (Kit) Carson to destroy the Navajo; he was urged to kill every Navajo man, but could not bring himself to follow through on that directive. Even so, the most horrible chapter in Navajo history was written by the hand of Kit Carson and the New Mexico Volunteers.

Carson led a regiment of New Mexico militia in a relentless round-up of the Navajo nation. Mindful of old tribal hostilities, Carson employed Hopi and Zuni men in his campaign against the Navajo. Some Hopi, however, continued to aid and support the Navajo. During the campaign of 1863, Carson learned from informed sources that the Oraibi Hopi had formed an alliance with some of the Navajo people who lived near the village. In a dispatch to Santa Fe, Carson noted that "Before my arrival at Oraibi, I was credibly informed that the people of that village had formed an alliance with the Navajos, and on reaching there I caused to be bound their Governor and another of their principal men and took them with me as prisoners."

After discussing the situation with these leaders, Carson released his captives, noting that "Hopi and Navajo were at odds over some injustice perpetrated by the later." Carson then recruited Hopi from every other village except Oraibi to join his war party.

"My objective in insisting on parties of these people accompanying me was to simply involve them so far that they could not retract; to bind them to us, and place them in antagonism to the Navajos. They were of some service and manifested a great desire to lead us on in every respect" (Grant 1926).

In other dispatches, Carson recommended that some form of relief be granted the Hopi, as their environment was "quite barren . . . entirely destitute of vegetation. They have no water for the purpose of irrigation, and their only dependence for subsistence is on the little corn they raise when the weather is propitious, which is not always the case in this latitude" (Grant 1926).

Neither hunted nor hunter got much rest during the winter and summer of those two years. For the first time in their experience, the Navajo were pursued month after month across the mesas and desert recesses of their homeland. After this endless chase, during which time more hogans were burned; more sheep, cattle, and goats were destroyed; and hundreds of people were killed, small bands began to surrender. Larger groups followed, and finally, hundreds of Navajo surrendered to Carson, to be driven, cattlelike, to Bosque Redondo. These proud people were broken and disheartened.

Despite Carson's persistence, not all Navajos were captured. Some fled west into the Grand Canyon; others hid with Hopi friends and relatives; still others hid in the canyons around Big Mountain. Hopi religious leaders gave some of the Navajo bands permission to stay on Hopi land during the roundup, but anticipated that they would leave once the emergency was over (Bahnimptewa interview 1986). The roundup of the Navajo brought some relief to the Hopi, but raids continued from the Utes, Apaches, and Mexican and New Mexican slavers. Some Navajo bands, those few not captured by Carson, also resumed raiding after the soldiers left.

In 1868, successful in negotiating their return to Dinétah, the Navajo were allowed to leave the Bosque Redondo. The People returned to Dinétah, accompanied by each individual's allotment of sheep and goats, and this further stressed the already fragile environment. As the Navajo population increased over the next few decades, they moved closer and closer to the Hopi mesas. The Hopi, whose numbers by this time were down to about two thousand, were unable to mount any significant resistance to the intrusions; they complained to the American authorities, who did little to halt the migration.

A Hopi man explained that "the trouble between the Navajos and the Hopi really escalated after the Navajos came back from New Mexico. Because when the Navajos came back from New Mexico, the Americans told the Hopi chiefs that the American army would keep the Navajos away from us. Before that, our Hopi warriors would go and raid the Navajo camps whenever they got too close. We kept them in check that way . . . . But [the army] didn't keep [them] away; they moved in on us with their camps, their sheep, and their goats. Some had permission and others didn't. They moved in on us and they are still here today."

The violence between the tribes continued well into this century. Ethel Mahle, sixty-four, Walpi kiva keeper and head of a Hopi Women's Society, discussed the period of Navajo and Hopi warfare quite willingly one afternoon on the causeway connecting Walpi with Sichomovi and Hano on First Mesa.

"The latest thing that the Navajo and their friends are doing is telling people that the Navajo and the Hopi got along in the past as good neighbors and that we never had problems. But that isn't true. We Hopi have always had problems with the Navajo; we even used to fight and kill [each other].

"See over there, way over there." Mrs. Mahle pointed to the northeast, across a vast plain. "If you go about twelve miles that way, you come to a small mesa. We call it Meat Mesa. That is where the people of Walpi had our last battle with the Navajo.

"We saw them trying to sneak up on our mesa and kill us and steal our food and our children. So our warriors went out and we fought and we killed them. We killed them all; only one horse got away alive. That is the way it was, and it wasn't even that long ago. It was in 1910."

3

THE HOUSE OF DAWN TODAY

The struggle for land and resources in the House of Dawn escalated with the coming of the twentieth century. In addition to Navajo and Hopi fighting over land, an increasing number of non-Indians have moved into the region, putting pressure on larger tribes and smaller tribes alike. Due to the intervention of the United States government, Navajo and Hopi have been forced to fight with each other to expand their land bases in order to support growing populations. In addition, traditional governing structures have been undermined and Indian societies have been placed under enormous stress. The struggle between the Navajo and Hopi in the 1882 and 1934 reservation areas (to be discussed in the following chapters) has received much attention from federal bureaucrats, but other factors involving outside pressures contribute to the complicated mosaic of the House of Dawn today.

What happens between the tribes and just how far tribal land bases will be allowed to expand ultimately will be determined by the non-Indian members of the dominant society, who are pouring into the Four Corners region in the biggest migration in southwestern history. Caught in the middle between the Navajo-Hopi struggle and the Anglo-American migrations are smaller Southwestern tribes, especially the San Juan Paiutes, the Hualapai, and Havasupai, who also have growing populations and deep religious ties to the land.

Navajo Tribal Scenario

The Navajo Tribe currently controls approximately 17 million acres (the size of West Virginia) of land in New Mexico, Arizona, and Utah. The land supports some 200,000 people and it holds valuable timber and energy resources necessary to provide a sound economic base for a growing nation. In 1985, the tribe started utilizing its sovereign right to impose severance taxes on energy companies operating on the reservation. As a result, the tribe has a $45 million surplus in its savings account.

Since 1985, the tribe has involved itself in extensive land-buying, using its power of taxation, mining revenues, and the recent acquisition of 400,000 acres of replacement land (given to the tribe as one of the provisions of the 1974 Navajo and Hopi Land Settlement Act) as springboards for financial and territorial expansion.

When compared to the limited resources and small populations of other American tribes, it appears that the Navajo Tribe has become the most influential and powerful tribe in the country. On the surface, it seems that the Navajo are doing well. But appearances can be deceiving. Life is not easy for members of the nation's largest tribe.

Currently, more than 55% of tribal members are under age twenty-five. The average education level is sixth grade. Approximately 60% of the population is bilingual in Navajo and English, and less than 50% of Navajo people live traditional farming and ranching lifestyles. The average cash income of tribal members is $2,000 per year.

The unemployment rate on the Navajo Reservation is 30.4% (CANDO 1988). Two-thirds of reservation jobs are in state, tribal, and federal agencies. The BIA employs approximately six thousand Navajo, but all governmental jobs are subject to changes in administrative policies, cutbacks in the federal budget, or a change of tribal administration. Employment on the reservation is not a dependable thing. There are better employment opportunities off-reservation, but many Navajos do not have the basic skills to get and keep jobs in the non-Navajo world. Despite an uncertain economic future, most Navajo choose to remain on their homeland for clan, family, and religious reasons, though most could find better jobs elsewhere.

Navajos with college educations are frustrated in their attempts to find reservation employment. There is no viable private sector on the Navajo Reservation; what limited private sector there is consists mainly of service and restaurant work. Some educated Navajos take jobs with Peabody Coal on Black Mesa, or other mining projects, but most people working in the mines do not need a higher education. Many Navajos with college degrees are forced to move to cities like Los Angeles, Albuquerque, and Phoenix to work in their chosen fields, creating a Navajo "brain-drain" of sorts.

In many ways, the Navajo Nation represents a developing state within the dominant American state. A Third World scenario dominates Navajoland.

NAVAJO EDUCATION

Most Navajo are undereducated, despite tribal programs to promote high school education and to provide financial assistance on the college level. One of the stipulations of the Treaty of 1868 was that the Navajo would allow their children to be educated by the Americans. Until recently, most Navajo children were sent off to boarding schools, far away from their homes, families, language, and culture. At the beginning of the education programs in the 1860s, many Navajos resisted exposing their children to alien ideas and sending them so far away from home. Resistance to education continued through the 1950s, when some families would hide their children from government Indian agents and keep them at home to teach them the right way to live, "the Navajo Way." Resistance to American education has given way, however, to a desire for better education in recent years, as Navajo leaders and their people began to realize how American education could assist their nation.

Former Navajo Tribal Chairman Peterson Zah heads up an entire office dedicated to higher education, The Navajo Education and Scholarship Foundation. Prior to becoming tribal chairman in 1982, Zah was head of the largest Indian legal service group in the country, Navajo People's Legal Services (DNA) and worked as an advocate for education through that office. Peter MacDonald has led the tribal council in a move to revoke the foundation's independent status and place it under tribal council control, but both men agree that higher education is necessary to the future of the Navajo Tribe.

Schools have been established on the reservation, and many Navajos have become teachers. Bilingual education programs have been incorporated into many curriculae, and American education is no longer something to be feared. Despite improvements, education levels remain low.

THE EMPLOYMENT PICTURE

Much of the Navajo work force is seasonal and underemployed. Despite attempts by both the MacDonald and the Zah administrations to improve the employment picture, and meeting after meeting with federal problem-solvers and private sector executives in an effort to improve the economic picture, the outlook remains grim.

In the summer of 1987, Navajo Tribal Chairman Peter MacDonald hosted a five-day economic summit at Tohatchi, New Mexico. He invited corporate executives, United States Senators and Congressmen, over a hundred reporters, and various state leaders in an attempt to attract business to the reservation. Despite the excitement of a media extravaganza, few businesses have taken steps to relocate to Dinétah and employ Navajo people at a living wage as a result of the economic summit.

MacDonald also established a tribal Commission for Accelerating Navajo Development Opportunities (CANDO) as a result of the economic conference, in an attempt to cut bureaucratic red tape and help small and large businesses move to the Navajo Reservation. MacDonald has tried to set up regional business-development boards on the reservation, to encourage development of a Navajo business sector. He also established a $30 million fund for industrial development in an attempt to attract factories to Navajoland. According to tribal reports, several small plants ranging from an auto parts assembly line to a food-processing company are slated to open in 1988.

The tribe has been working to promote tourism for the past decade, and progress in that arena has been slow but steady. In an unusual move, MacDonald contracted with fashion designer Oleg Cassini to develop a "world-class resort" in Navajoland. It is unclear when or where that project will open, and it may be difficult to find recreational developers willing to build such a resort because of the tribe's past history with resort development. (Zah had negotiated a working plan for development of a resort on Lake Powell's Antelope Point, near Page, Arizona, on tribal lands in 1985. The development company had put up money and materials and had established a working relationship with both tribal and LeChee chapter officials, when Zah lost the 1986 election. MacDonald subsequently cancelled all plans for the development and as a consequence of that cancellation, the developer has filed a lawsuit against the tribe. Potential investors have voiced concerns about this precedent.) Perhaps an increase in revenues from the new lands, energy development, and tourism will help to ease the tribe's economic burden. But the challenges facing the Navajo people remain formidable.

THE GROWING BIRTH RATE

One of the biggest contributing factors to problems in Navajo employment, education, and an adequate land base is the growing Navajo birth rate. According to traditional Navajo beliefs, life is sacred and children are a blessing from heaven. Therefore, birth control and abortion are traditionally anathema in Navajo culture. Consequently, one of the biggest problems facing today's Navajo Nation is a geometric population growth, and despite attempts by Navajo Nation Family Planning and the Indian Health Service to educate women about birth control, the rate continues to rise.

In traditional times, Navajo men could have more than one wife, and frequently, sisters were married to the same man or to a man and his brother to consolidate families and land use areas. There are some families who continue this practice today, but most polygamous marriages are among older Navajos living in the remote recesses of the big reservation.

Children are born into the mother's clan, and while a child may be "born for" the man's clan, he or she belongs (is "born to") to the mother and her clan. In the Navajo Way, a woman can increase her importance by producing many children. Therefore, children are more important than marriage and whether or not a child is born in wedlock is secondary.

Modern Navajo culture is caught in a double population bind. In traditional times, deformed, abnormal, or retarded children were left to die of exposure, so as not to be a burden to family or clan. This was one form of population control. But with the coming of Christian missionaries and American law to Navajoland, such behavior was no longer accepted or legally permitted. So in addition to normal population growth, there has been the addition of abnormal genetic pools to the population. Retarded or deformed children are viewed as an embarassment by their families, and these children are generally sent to homes subsidized and run by the tribe. Occasionally, they also have children and add more people to the general population. What traditional limits there were to Navajo population growth have been undermined by modern practice and standards.

Evidence of the boom in population growth has been clearly documented since the Navajo returned from the Long Walk. Navajo population was reduced to approximately 8,000 people as a result of the Long Walk and the horrors of internment in the Bosque Redondo concentration camps. After their return to Dinétah, the tribe grew more and more fruitful and multiplied. By 1960, less than a century after the Long Walk, there were 60,000 Navajo; by 1970, there were 120,000 Navajo. The number had grown to 175,000 by 1980. In 1987, the tribal population broke the 200,000 mark. With the bulk of Navajo population under twenty-five years old, more and more Navajos will continue having children. They will need land, food, and employment.

The traditional Navajo world is disappearing and the future world is being created. Much of tomorrow's picture depends on what the Navajo tribal leadership does today. The fate of a few thousand Navajo relocatees may sometimes appear insignificant to Navajo leaders and many Navajo people when striving to encourage the survival and prosperity of an entire tribe. Current growth projection statistics show an estimated 300,000 Navajo by 2007. But recent changes in the Indian Health Service (IHS) policies regarding birth control may make that projection unrealistic.

Despite general resistance to birth control among Navajo women, one modern method became accepted by many in the 1960s: the intrauterine birth control device (IUD). The IHS promoted the device and many women responded favorably. But in recent years, as a result of a stampede of lawsuits against IUD manufacturers, IHS physicians were ordered to stop prescribing and inserting the devices. (As a result, if even a small portion of Navajo women who would have used IUDs become pregnant, there may be twice as many Navajos by the year 2007 as there are today. That would mean some 400,000 people.)

In the United States as a whole, fear of lawsuits has caused all but one IUD manufacturer to remove their product from the market. According to IHS statistics, the IUD has been the most popular form of Navajo birth control for twenty years.

"Approximately three thousand Navajo women were fitted with IUDs every year," Navajo Nation Family Planning Corporation Consulting Physician Alan Waxman explained. "That means for every three women who chose the birth control pill, four Navajo women preferred the IUD."

Waxman said that the ramifications of a change in the preferred method of birth control could be serious. He expressed concern that a mini-Navajo baby boom is imminent, and that such an increase in births would further complicate the problems of a nation already bursting at its land boundaries.

"Many women do not want to use the birth control pill or other alternative contraceptive options," Waxman explained. "If one-third of those 3,000 women who get IUDs in one year become pregnant, the result is going to be 1,000 new births per year. That's a 25% increase in our birth rate."

According to IHS statistics, in 1985 there were 4,699 babies born in the Navajo service region. At that time, Navajo population was estimated at 175,000 people. An additional 25% increase in an already high population growth area could have drastic impacts on the Navajo future.

"Such an increase in birth rate would stress the health care systems, social service systems, the tribal assistance systems, and the schools," Waxman said. "The land is already over-taxed. The snowball effect and the ramifications of this are potentially very serious."

Sterilization is currently the most popular form of birth control in mainstream American society, but such an option is not culturally acceptable for Navajo people. Fecundity is highly valued, and a woman's status is partially gauged on fertility. Even among modern Navajo, it is one thing to chose not to have children, but to be forever unable to have them is quite another.

In a society with very little privacy, options like birth control pills, foams, or other birth control devices are not easily accepted. "The IUD required one insertion and no further worrying. It was excellent for privacy, where you have large families in the hogan or the trailer or house; you don't have to worry about hiding your birth control method," Waxman explained. "[The IUD] was not subject to personal error, as forgetting to take a pill might be. As a result, the health care providers and the patients were very happy with the IUD and providers told providers and patients that this was a great form of birth control. The result by the 1980s was that when Navajo women would come to us requesting contraception, a large percentage of them would come in requesting specifically the IUD."

Waxman said that as a result of the IHS withdrawal of IUDs from their clinics in 1986, there is a great deal of anger and confusion among Navajo women. He said that women become frustrated when they ask for the IUD and are told that it is no longer available through their clinic. Many Navajos do not have the money to go to a private clinic or doctor for the device, so they are forced to choose another birth control method.

Waxman said that women respond in one of three ways after being told that the IUD is unavailable. One group, especially the younger women, decides that the birth control pill is an acceptable alternative. He said a second reaction is refusal to use the birth control pill out of a fear of side effects; this group usually resorts to barrier methods such as the prophylactic or diaphram.

"The third group says 'if I can't have my IUD, I won't use anything,' and this is the group we are most concerned about," Waxman explained. "This is the group most likely to cause a thousand new births per year—the Navajo baby boom."

Whether or not the projected baby boom occurs, Navajo people are going to need more land, more opportunities for employment and education and more input in helping to develop their own future if the nation is to prosper. Navajo tribal development officers have said that their reservation is already stretched to the limit by providing for the existing population. Growth trends will continue, and the tribe will be forced to look for new ways to provide for its members.

The Hopi Tribal Scenario

The Hopi Tribe today consists of some 10,000 people and it controls some 1.56 million acres of land. A good portion of that land was gained as a result of the 1974 land partition, which added 910,833.37 acres to the reservation map. The tribe received no replacement land for land it lost to the Navajo Tribe during partition of the Joint Use Area. Most Hopi tribal revenues come from royalties paid by Peabody Coal mined on Black Mesa, and some money comes in from the federal government for social services, education, and administrative programs. The average Hopi income is approximately $5,000 a year.

HOPI POPULATION GROWTH

Hopi population has also grown since the 1860s and 1880s. According to government records, it was approximately 5,000 people in 1868, but smallpox, famine, raiders, and drought brought Hopi numbers down to 3,000 in the 1880s (Nequatewa 1936; Stephens 1964). After the turn of the century, Hopi population began a steady recovery. By the 1950s, there was a full recovery and there were 5,000 Hopi. By 1980, population was on the rise and there were 7,500 Hopi. Today there are over 10,000, and the population continues to increase. Current tribal estimates indicate a growth rate of 2% per year since 1982.

As a result of such rapid population growth, approximately 54% of Hopi people are under 20 years old. A Hopi baby boom is projected within the next 20 years, as today's children become tomorrow's parents. If present population trends continue, there will be 12,500 Hopi by the year 2000, and 44% of the population will be under age twenty. Currently, there are approximately 3,000 Hopi under age twenty, and the reproductive population is projected to increase by 50%, to some 4,700 people by the year 2000. This will have a great impact on the Hopi land base, and the reacquisition of lands formerly occupied by Navajos will play an important role in the Hopi future. Hopis will need land, jobs, and a strong economic base to support their people, and they are looking to the Hopi partition lands (HPL) as a source for future tribal survival.

Traditionally, the Hopi were farmers and traders. The idea of culling and selecting the best seeds for crops was utilized by the Hopi, and they applied similar concepts to population control. The Hopi developed numerous birth control methods through herbs and medicinal plants. In traditional times, abortive herbs were occasionally used by Hopi women, and while today most Hopi women prefer preventive birth control measures, abortion is not uncommon. They were and are a monogamous society.

For centuries, Hopi lived in small and concentrated cities. They lived in a controlled world, where villages could not support large populations. The concept of an ordered, limited universe, one with clearly defined boundaries and limits, is characteristic of Hopi thought. The Hopi were forced to concentrate on mesas during the old raiding days, but now that Hopi population has grown and more peaceful times have come to the mesas, more and more Hopi people have returned to the plains of their ancestral homelands. Hopis say they view this return as nothing new, but as a continuation of ancient land use patterns.

HOPI POPULATION DISTRIBUTION AND HOPI PARTITION LAND

Currently, the Hopi population is primarily distributed among twelve villages. A little over 60% of the Hopi population lives in the five villages of Moencopi, Hotevillla, Kykotsmovi, Shungopovi, and Polacca. Many village families live in tight, crowded conditions, and many people have applied for home sites on the recently acquired Hopi partition land. Over 20 families have moved out onto the land, and there is a list of over 300 families waiting to move there.

Young Hopis have pointed out that until the tribe took formal possession of the land in 1986, the prospect of getting married and setting up housekeeping with the mother, aunties, and uncles in the same house was grim. They also have said that even though farming conditions were getting crowded, they are looking forward to farming, as well as setting up ranches and developing businesses on the recently acquired land.

In July 1987, the tribe presented a preliminary land use plan for the combined reservation and the Hopi partition land. Tribal officers and council representatives are soliciting input from the villages on how they would like to use the land, and a final development plan is due by 1990. The preliminary plan explains that the Hopi Reservation has more than doubled in size since the addition of the HPL, and it analyzes Hopi need for land, farming, pinyon- and herb-gathering, new housing and economic development, and access to and protection of religious shrines and holy places.

Key policies in the plan revolve around balancing the Hopi need for an extended land base with the traditional respect for land and resources that sustain religious, agricultural, economic, and recreational activities. Throughout the plan, the rights of villages, kikmongwis, and clan authority are recognized. The incorporation of traditional means of problem-solving and land use along with modern needs for land as a result of population growth is stressed.

Hopis have said that the partition land is vital to their cultural and economic survival, and essential to their continuation as a people. They feel that they have merely reacquired land that had been forcibly taken from them by the United States and the Navajo. Some Hopis have also pointed out that they have no intention of stopping with the acquisition of 1882 lands, but also want to regain as much land as possible in the 1934 expanded boundary land of the Navajo Reservation.

HOPI EDUCATION

The median education level among Hopis is twelfth grade. Many young Hopi now graduate from high school and college, and the education level among them will likely increase with the advent of the first Hopi high school in the mesa country in 1986.

Hopis did not eagerly embrace the American system of education when the United States government ordered them to have their children educated by Americans in the 1880s. Even today, Hopis recite the horrors and humiliation that their great-grandparents were subjected to in the past. Even though the Hopi never signed a treaty or were defeated by the United States, they were treated as a conquered people. The government decreed education for Hopi children, and would send troops of soldiers to round up children and drag them to the nearest boarding schools. Parents who resisted the round-up would be whipped and were frequently forced into involuntary servitude to Indian agents or the Americans "educating" the children.

In time, some of the kikmongwis came to realize that it would be best for Hopi youth to learn how to deal effectively with both the American and the Hopi world. So, American education eventually came to be accepted and encouraged. Today, Hopi are among the best educated of American Indians.

Despite the levels of education and the likelihood that more Hopi will receive university degrees, opportunities for employment and professional achievement are currently few and far between on the Hopi Reservation. There are some thriving small businesses on the reservation, and there are limited opportunities for tribal employment, but there is no strong private sector. What employment exists outside the tribal administration is with the BIA or in service industries. Like the Navajo, most university-educated Hopi are forced to move to major urban centers to pursue their careers.

Young Hopi want to stay close to their homes and not relocate off-reservation for employment, and in response, the tribe is trying to develop on-reservation employment. Some progress has been made through joint ventures with American and South Korean businesses, but much remains to be done.

Both Tribes Need More Land

From an outsider's point of view, there is more than enough land for
Navajo and Hopi. With Navajo living on reservation lands the size of
West Virginia, Hopi living on almost a million acres of land, and a combined population of less than half a million people, an outsider might
well wonder why there is a problem at all.

The key to understanding why tensions exist is in understanding
how the two groups utilize the land and how growing populations
have affected land use. Until recent years, Navajo herded sheep as a
primary means of economic support. Sheep need great amounts of land
to forage. Traditionally, Navajo clans set up clan areas and settled
largely within those lands; in more recent years, grazing permits and
grazing districts as well as chapters (political units) were organized.
With herding as the focal point of life, land and water resources came
to be highly treasured and retained within certain families and clans.
If too many sheep or too many people tried to live within an area,
tensions resulted. In some cases, families packed up and headed west
to freer lands. The government expanded Navajo Reservation lines to
accommodate the population movement several times up through the
1930s. The finalization of reservation boundaries in 1934 restricted
Navajo movement, however, and until the acquisition of 400,000 acres
of new land as a result of the 1974 land settlement, Navajos fought
with Hopis for land. The tribe did not have a large financial surplus
with which to buy land until recent years.

Even before the Hopi acquired sheep and cows, they had marked
their land boundaries. They did not use the land in the same way as the
Navajo, but they knew what land belonged to what clan and which
kikmongwi was responsible for each region. Hopis had always been
farmers, and when they acquired sheep and cows, the equation became
more complicated. As Hopi population grew after the difficult years
between 1700 and 1900, Hopi ranches became more common on the
flatlands. The mesas still remained the ceremonial homes for the Hopi,
but practical daily existence came to be lived farther away from the
mesas. Hopi farmers and ranchers began to come into direct competition with Navajo farmers and herdsmen. Both populations were growing and neither had any way to gain more land except by taking it from
the other.

When the Hopi Reservation was established in 1882, Hopis lost most
of their ancestral land, and when the federal government expanded
the Navajo Reservation in 1934, Hopis started to feel boxed in. By the
time the Hopi Tribe took the Navajo Tribe to court in the 1960s, the
need for land as a result of population growth had reached critical

dimensions. Hopis felt that they were fighting for their very survival as a people, and the only way they could expand and survive was to take land from the Navajo. The Navajo felt that their existence was also under attack, and they could not understand why the Hopi had become so aggressive.

Settlement of the 1882 land issue by partition and relocation did not solve the stress between Navajo and Hopi. Both tribes are preparing legal cases to support their claims in the 1934 expanded Navajo Reservation, and another group of Indians, whose very existence has been affected by the struggle for land in the House of Dawn, has asked to become party to the 1934 legal case as well.

THE STORY OF THE SAN JUAN PAIUTES

The absorption of the San Juan Band of Paiutes (also called the San Juan Band of Southern Paiutes) into the Navajo Nation is an interesting case study in how Navajo come into contact with non-Navajo and their land and how they can acquire both land and people. As illustrated in the Navajo creation epics, Navajos have a long history of coming into contact with other cultures; absorbing what they feel is important in that culture; and incorporating land, people, and elements of the alien culture itself in a uniquely Navajo way. What is important about the absorption of the San Juan Paiutes is that it happened in modern times and has been clearly documented.

The Paiutes once lived in a triangular section of the Four Corners area, bounded roughly by Navajo Mountain (also known as Paiute Mountain), Monument Valley, and the Grand Canyon. Navajo Mountain is sacred both to the Navajo and the Paiutes, and lies in Utah, east of Page, Arizona, near the Arizona state line.

Prior to 1922, the San Juan band had its own reservation, comprising land from the Colorado River on the Utah-Arizona boundary line to the middle of Monument Valley. The reservation was established in 1907, and the Paiutes were recognized as an established tribe by the federal government. Both land and federal recognition were withdrawn by the government in 1922, however.

"They lost the reservation because of mining interests," Pam Bunte, anthropologist and co-author of a book *(From the Sands to the Mountains)* about the band explained. "When the miners learned there wasn't anything worthwhile there, they lost interest." Miners may have lost interest in the land, but the Navajo, pressed by the need for more room for their growing human and sheep populations, petitioned the federal government for it, and their petition was granted by the government in 1933. The San Juan Paiutes still occupied the territory as Navajo families moved onto their former reservation.

As the years passed, many Paiutes accepted Navajo census numbers and became integrated into the Navajo Tribe. Census numbers were part of a program developed by the federal government in the 1920s in an attempt to enumerate indigenous American populations. Not every tribe participated in the program, but the Navajo did. When the Navajo tribal government was reorganized in the 1930s, the tribe took over administration of the identification program on their own reservation. Included in the administration were Paiutes who had taken census numbers.

According to Paiute testimony, many felt they had been forced to accept the numbers. As Indians, without proof of being part of a federally recognized tribe, regardless of tribal background, they were not acknowledged as indigenous people with established treaty rights. Without proof of recognition there was no access to federal food programs, no medical care, no land, and survival was difficult. So many Paiutes accepted census numbers as a way to survive. Gradually, Paiutes with Navajo census numbers came to be viewed as members of the Navajo tribe.

"They had census numbers and it was assumed that they were Navajos" Bunte explained. "Some people assumed this, but not the Paiutes." Paiutes maintain that they were forced to join the ranks of the Navajo first by dispossession and then by desperation.

Navajo tribal leaders tell a slightly different version of the absorption story. They say that they helped the Paiutes by giving them census numbers and accepted them freely into their tribe. Navajos say that the Paiutes asked for Navajo protection and admission into the tribal ranks.

"We helped them. When they were weak and needed our help, they wanted to be part of our tribe," Willie Greyeyes, a Navajo politician, tribal council delegate, and member of the Navajo Mountain Chapter (in which many Paiutes live) explained. "But now all they do is complain and say they don't want to be Navajos anymore. But they are Navajos just the same." Greyeyes' analysis of the situation fits within the general framework of the Navajo perception of the Paiute bid for separate tribal recognition. The consensus in the Navajo tribal council is that the Paiutes are really Navajos who have been politically frustrated and want to break away from the main part of the tribe. As a result, the Navajo Tribe officially opposes Paiute claims of a separate identity. Members of the tribe concede that at one time the San Juan Paiutes were separate, but stress that they have been incorporated into the body of the tribe in much the same way as many other Navajo clans (like the Nakai [Mexican] and Zuni clans).

Whatever the motivation for the move to regain federal recognition, the San Juan Paiutes have gone to great lengths to regain their lost tribal identity. The band numbers about 300 people who live in isolated pockets of the western portion of the Navajo Reservation. The Paiutes have stated that they are different from Navajos and have a different language and a different culture. The band has presented a formal petition to the BIA to regain the tribal recognition they lost in 1922. They have received preliminary recognition, but the BIA has asked the Navajo and Hopi tribes to comment on the Paiute status, as their official recognition by the federal government could affect Navajo and Hopi land claims in the 1934 land dispute case.

In 1984, a federal judge in Phoenix gave the San Juan Paiutes permission to pursue their land claims in the 1934 area. Land the Paiutes currently inhabit is part of the Bennett Freeze Area, which Congress designated as part of the Navajo Reservation in 1934. If the Paiute receive formal recognition and petition the federal courts for land to go with that recognition, it may mean yet another Indian relocation program.

It is easy to see why Navajo and many non-Indians view the San Juan band as part of the Navajo tribe. Although many San Juans speak Paiute, all of them speak Navajo. They have been surrounded by a dominant Navajo culture, and they have assumed the material trappings of that culture. Paiute women wear the flounced skirts and velveteen blouses of the Navajo. Paiutes farm and raise cattle and sheep like the Navajo. Some even live in hogans. Many have intermarried with Navajo people, and their children could conceivably grow up confused about their tribal identity.

Despite the outward similarities, Paiute leaders have stressed that they cannot deny their traditional identity. In their quest to regain their tribal recognition, they have turned to attorneys and anthropologists.

"Look at me, do I look like a Navajo?" Evelyn James, the appointed spokeswoman of the San Juan Band asked during an interview in a Tuba City legal office. "No, I don't. I am not a Navajo and neither are my people. That is why we are doing all of this with attorneys, that is why we have asked others in to document our history." The band has retained attorneys with the Native American Rights Fund in Denver, Colorado, to fight for their federal recognition and look after their interests in the 1934 dispute.

James, a widow, was once married to a Navajo. She stressed that despite what may be similarities to the casual observer, Navajo and Paiute are quite different from one another. She said that despite her marriage, she was never integrated into Navajo culture, and that neither she nor her people want to be or ever will be integrated.

"My husband was a Navajo . . . . He noticed the differences. His family and my family noticed the differences. Our families had different attitudes," James explained. "He used to say that after a visit with his family, when he came back to me, it was like coming into a different world. When I would go to visit his family, it was like another world for me. We would go in between, and we would both get confused and go through a culture shock . . . . I can't do the Navajo way of things. I am a Paiute and I am not used to it. My people want to be recognized for what we are. We are not Navajos. We are Paiutes."

James further drove home the point about outward appearances being deceiving. "I drive a pick-up and wear blue jeans and speak English, but that does not make me an Anglo. I can't change what I am. We cannot change what we are. We are Paiutes and we are not ashamed of it."

James disputes the claim that Paiutes are just another Navajo clan. "Paiutes never make decisions for the Navajo Tribe, nor do they participate in Navajo chapter meetings. We are not involved in Navajo community stuff . . . . Paiutes have a very different feeling about themselves than Navajos. I don't like it when someone tells me that I am a Navajo because I don't know anything about Navajo culture. . . ."

James said that more than anything else, her people want recognition as Paiutes, with access to federal health care and benefits as a separate tribe and their reaffirmation as a sovereign nation. "We don't really want our old reservation back and we don't want to make more trouble between the Navajos and the Hopis by having a piece of land of our own out here," James explained. "We just want to be known as Paiutes."

HOPI SUPPORT FOR PAIUTE CLAIMS

Despite Navajo claims of similarities and absorption of the San Juan band, anthropological evidence and Hopi and Paiute oral traditions point to a number of factors that separate Paiutes from their Navajo neighbors. Linguistic history, ethnobotany, and archaeological evidence all support Paiute claims. Paiutes speak a language in the Shoshonean family, linguistically related to the Hopi language through the Uto-Aztecan superfamily; Shoshonean languages can be found from northern Canada south into Mexico. Anthropologists use language distribution as a tool in determining how long a group of people have lived in an area, and linguistic and archaeological evidence combined demonstrate that the San Juan band has lived on the Colorado Plateau for at least a thousand years.

The Hopi say they don't need scientific evidence to support Paiute claims; they claim that the Paiutes have been their neighbors much longer than the Navajo and support the San Juan band in their struggle for a separate identity.

"The Hopis were here first," former Upper Moencopi Village Governor Roy Tuchawena explained. "Then the Paiutes came in and set up farms. At first, we didn't get along with the Paiutes and we fought with each other. But then, after a while, we realized that we spoke the same language and we stopped fighting and started trading. After the Paiutes had been around a long time, the Spanish showed up, then a few Navajos and then, at about the same time, some white [Mormon] settlers."

Both Hopi traditionalists and members of the tribal council remember the Paiutes, and support their claims in the 1934 area. "We do not feel that they are a threat to Hopi in any way," Hopi Tribal Chairman Ivan Sidney explained. "We would like to see them regain what is rightfully theirs. They were victims of aggression by both Navajos and in-coming Anglos. Congress and the BIA took away their identity and then the Navajos took away their land."

CURRENT STATUS OF THE PAIUTE CASE

The documented combination of language difference, widespread distribution of Shoshonean-speaking Paiutes, archaeological evidence, and the San Juan knowledge of medicinal herbs and plants on the Colorado Plateau, coupled with Hopi and Paiute oral traditions, make a strong case for separate Paiute identity and land claims in the 1934 dispute. A federal aside giving more strength to Paiute claims is the wording of the 1934 law itself. This law expanded the Navajo Reservation for Navajo and "other Indians living there." According to Paiute interpretation of the law, it is clear that Paiute, Navajo, and Hopi were on the land and that the Paiute were a separate cultural component.

Attorneys for the Navajo Tribe have presented a motion in the 1934 land dispute case to try the Navajo and Hopi claims in federal court in 1989. They do not want the San Juan claims to be considered together with the Navajo and Hopi because it would further burden Navajo case discovery. Attorneys for the Hopi Tribe have said that they want both Hopi and Paiute claims considered in the same trial. Paiute tribal attorneys have supported the Hopi position regarding the proposed trial date. Much of the Paiute future is tied to whether or not the BIA and Congress approve their claim for tribal recognition. But the final determination of any Paiute land claim in the 1934 area, and how that will affect Navajo and Hopi claims in the region, lies with a federal judge.

How the Dominant Society Affects Tribal Futures

How far Indian tribes are allowed to expand and how extensively tribes will compete for land and resources will largely be determined by members of the dominant Anglo-American society. In projecting the future of both Navajo and Hopi people, as well as smaller tribes, the inroads of the current non-Indian migration to the Southwest must be considered. Indians may well be permitted to struggle with each other for land, but if tribal expansion presents a threat to the growth and financial well-being of the dominant society, the struggles may be quickly quelled. Indian expansion will go only as far as the American government allows it to go.

When the United States took the Southwest from Mexico, it took over many populations in addition to Indian groups. These populations included New Mexican Spanish families, Mexicans, and American traders. Non-Indian populations have expanded as more and more people crowd into the region every year. If the struggle between Navajo and Hopi has created a national uproar, one can only imagine how land struggles will intensify for all people in the region as the biggest migration in Southwest history continues.

Today there are over 8,370,672 non-Indians in the Four Corners region (U.S. Census 1980). Arizona's population alone has almost doubled in the past decade, and Utah, Colorado, and New Mexico have steadily increasing growth rates as well. Over 400,000 people move into the House of Dawn every year. Over 100,000 people leave other parts of the nation and move to Arizona annually (U.S. Census 1980).

The non-Indian population boom in the Southwest is a comparatively recent thing. When the first non-Indian population census was done for New Mexico in 1850, some 61,540 heads were counted. An 1850 Utah census counted 11,380 people. The first Colorado census was not done until 1860, and 34,277 people were counted. An Arizona census was not done until 1870, when 9,658 non-Indians were counted.

Non-Indian populations grew slowly in the House of Dawn until after the Second World War. The region's remoteness, the lack of economic opportunities, and harsh extremes of weather made the House of Dawn unappealing to most Americans. That has changed with the development of air-conditioning and the decline of American industry, however. As the Industrial Age gave way to the space and computer ages, American population centers in the Northeast and Midwest started to diminish. Business has developed an interest in the Southwest, and American populations are shifting to the Sun Belt and the Southwest as the eastern cities lose their appeal and their economic viability.

American society is moving westward, seeking fulfillment of financial and material dreams, while at the same time, seeking a more attractive living environment. On the move, searching for better jobs and more lucrative regions to exploit, many Americans look to the West, and their car caravans arrive daily in the House of Dawn.

As the Americans have flocked to the region, their need for land, water, and other resources have squeezed the dominant tribes and almost eliminated many of the smaller tribes. Arizona has borne the brunt of the latest migrations because many industries have chosen Phoenix as a base of operations. According to statistics of the United States Department of Commerce, Arizona and Florida will be the nation's two biggest growth states by the year 2000, as the American population ages and retirees search for warm and sunny places to live. Indigenous populations will undoubtedly continue to be affected by the migrations.

Americans have been competing with native populations for the best water, the best grazing lands, the most scenic locations for over a hundred years. At the end of the last century, the United States government transported smaller tribes like the Hualapai, Yavapai-Apache, and Havasupai to concentration camps in harsh desert regions, another shameful chapter in American history. Despite the debacle at Bosque Redondo and the suffering Navajos endured there, both Navajo and Hopi were more fortunate than many other Arizona tribes. Smaller tribal populations were decimated. Some, like the Hualapai, were marched from their homes along the rim of the Grand Canyon, 500 miles south to La Paz; their numbers dwindled from 5,000 to less than 800 people after their lands were discovered to be attractive to ranchers and miners. They were able to regain a small portion of their lands and return, but today they number only twelve hundred (Walema interview 1987). Recent purchases of land by the Navajo tribe, adjacent to Hualapai and Havasupai reservations concern tribal leaders; they worry that their numbers and development plans may be eclipsed by the Navajo presence. Many Apache bands, linguistic and cultural cousins of the Navajo, were relocated to New Mexico or as far away as Oklahoma, but their numbers, too, are slowly increasing.

Isolation limited Anglo-American interests in Navajo and Hopiland until the discovery of many valuable minerals in the mid-twentieth century. By the time of the discoveries, the tribes had achieved enough sophistication to better defend their land and interests. It is likely that isolation and the rugged terrain of their homelands saved both Navajo and Hopi from the fates of smaller tribes.

To Americans, land is not sacred. Americans, with their European and Judaeo-Christian religious values, seek to dominate and exploit the natural world. They believe that their God created Man in his own image, and established him as ruler of the world. There is no concept of harmony, no divine contract of stewardship. American Christians seek to accumulate wealth in this world and look for a spiritual reward in the next. Indians, with their ties to the land, their "strange, pagan" ideas and "barbarous" cultures are viewed by many as an antiquated group, Noble Savages who are largely in the way, an obstacle to civilized development. Many Americans residing in the Southwest have little contact with indigenous people, and there are those who support the abrogation of all Indian treaties and the absorption of reservation lands into private allotments and land parcels. Others have unrealistic ideas and expectations about Indian people and their culture. They are part of another kind of migration, and they have added an interesting dimension to the Navajo-Hopi land dispute.

Other Influences

It happens every spring in northern Arizona. Bands of colorfully dressed people wander the streets of Flagstaff, talking about "the struggle" and the need "to give support" to Navajos and Hopis resisting relocation (most do not realize that the Hopi have moved off the partitioned lands). In their enthusiasm, many either do not recognize—or choose to ignore—the facts of relocation and work instead from a basis of insufficient information. Hopi, Navajo, and many local residents view the visitors with a mixture of amusement and annoyance.

Another more formal entity is the Big Mountain Legal Defense/Offense Committee (BMLDOC), a Navajo-advocacy group organized by Boston attorney Lew Gurwitz in 1982. A descendant of this organization, now called the Big Mountain Legal Office, is currently based in Flagstaff, Arizona. The group operates in a systematic and highly organized way to focus attention on relocation and works to repeal laws that affect the relocation issue; it also accepts selected legal cases, those that affect Navajo relocatees and potential relocatees.

Peabody Coal Company, a major corporation and mining presence in the Four Corners states, is representative of yet another level of interest in the relocation scenario. Peabody Coal operates "two large coal surface mines in northeastern Arizona," as noted by Robert H. Quenon, president of Peabody Holding Company, headquartered in St. Louis, Missouri, in a statement prepared July 1986. Quenon further noted that Peabody had no part in the development of the legislation that led to relocation and had no position on the issue. "It's a matter between the tribes and the government," Quenon concluded. Howard Williams, president of Peabody Coal, has also stressed that the company will never mine coal from Big Mountain.

Finally, there has been an element of involvement by native American activist groups such as the American Indian Movement (AIM) and some Plains Indian individuals.

These outside influences have had definite impacts upon the already emotionally charged situation, and are certainly critical to any comprehensive discussion. For the most part, their primary accomplishment is the focusing of national and international attention upon the problem. Reporters from throughout the world have taken an interest in the dispute, and the story of relocation has appeared on the front pages of newspapers world-wide.

THE WANNABES

As Capistrano is blessed by swallows, the Southwest is blessed (or plagued, depending upon perspective) by the return each spring of the Wannabe tribe. The group's annual migration begins sometime around Easter, when the bitter winter temperatures begin to ease; it reaches its peak in early July, and steadily wanes as cool autumn nights commence in September. The largely unwashed masses stream through Flagstaff, stop downtown for supplies and "authentic" Indian jewelry and herbs, visit advocacy and government relocation offices, and then wander north toward the Hopi mesas and the Big Mountain region.

The term "Wannabe" was coined to describe the hordes of painfully hip people who flock here, mesmerized by the "holy Hopis and Navajos who live so close to the earth." They frequently give themselves names such as White Pony and Earth Bear, and try very hard to live as they perceive native Americans to live. They "wanna be" Indians, hence the name.

Many Wannabes appear to be leftover from the 1967 Summer-of-Love generation. Many are Anglo or Hispanic, most come from outside of the Southwest, and most know nothing substantive about the dispute between Hopi and Navajo. They are simply fascinated by any aspect of what they think of as authentic "Indian" life.

Wannabes gather regularly at the offices of the federal Navajo and Hopi Indian Relocation Commission in Flagstaff to protest relocation. Beating drums and carrying signs with slogans such as "Relocation is Genocide" and "Stop Relocation," they parade up and down the streets of downtown Flagstaff, expressing their opinions. Conversations with the protesters indicate that they believe that the Navajo and Hopi have always lived in peace and harmony, and that the dispute was engineered by the federal government. They voice a belief in something called Navajo and Hopi unity, and are sometimes ardent followers of Thomas Banyacaya, a Hopi traditionalist.

Banyacaya was appointed as a spokesman for a number of Hopi religious leaders in the 1940s; he and three other Hopi men who could
speak English were asked by the kikmongwis to carry their messages
to the world. All of the leaders who originally appointed Banyacaya
have died, as have the other three spokesmen. The majority of Hopis
asked about Banyacaya have explained that Banyacaya's duties ended
with the death of the last of the religious leaders whom he represented,
and he is part of an internal Hopi disagreement involving a variety of
"traditional" and "progressive" philosophies within the tribe.

Wannabes who have embraced Banyacaya's ideas feel that he is a
holy man, and they listen intently to his words against nuclear war, the
mining of uranium and coal, and the dangers of the land dispute. In the
summer of 1986, Banyacaya took his message to Los Angeles and was
a media sensation. During a press conference that he shared with Hol-
lywood celebrities Jon Voight and Elizabeth Taylor, Voight said that
through his time with Banyacaya, he had learned that Hopi Indian elders would reveal the solution to the continuation of human existence
and it was time for white society to listen to Banyacaya's message. Banyacaya also told Voight that the last phase of Hopi prophecy would be
revealed at a late-summer meeting on the Hopi Reservation. Voight,
voice cracking with emotion, read his own statement about the importance of understanding the Hopi message.

Banyacaya's Los Angeles efforts did not receive a warm reception
from Hopi kikmongwis or the tribal council. Outpourings of opinion
swept through the Hopi mesas. Chairman Ivan Sidney; Vice Chairman
Clifford Honanie (now deceased); Caleb Johnson, a Third Mesa Hopi
and spokesman for the kikmongwi of Old Oraibi; and a number of
priests from throughout the mesa country publicly expressed their
concerns about Banyacaya's activities. Members of various religious societies became worried about the possibility of exploitation of Hopi
ceremonial dances to raise money, and the Antelope and Snake priests
closed a Snake Dance at Shungopovi that was originally scheduled to
be open to the public. In interviews, Banyacaya defended his actions,
saying that he was appointed to act as a spokesman for several religious
leaders, and stressed his concerns about the future not only of the
Hopi people, but of the entire world.

Another aspect of the Wannabes that disturbs Navajo, Hopi, and
other northern Arizona residents is the cultural arrogance that many
bring with them. Wannabes have a certain perception of native Americans and their lives and they expect the Navajo and Hopi to conform
to it. One idea that many share is that the "poor Indians" of the former
Joint Use Area are in desperate need of their help. Without Wannabe

help, they seem to feel, the energy companies and the federal government will surely destroy the Navajo and Hopi cultures.

THE BIG MOUNTAIN LEGAL DEFENSE/OFFENSE COMMITTEE

The Big Mountain Legal Defense/Offense Committee was founded in the summer of 1982 by Indian Rights Attorney Lew Gurwitz. Gurwitz was asked to look after Navajo rights by Navajo elders from the Big Mountain area. The first legal office was founded in Flagstaff and was staffed by Gurwitz and various volunteer law clerks and non-Indians concerned about the relocation issue. As the years have passed, several activist attorneys have worked with the program.

Gurwitz and his supporters successfully organized BMLDOC into a vast information-distribution network and fund-raising machine, with offices from San Francisco to New York City. Funding has come from the Capp Street Foundation, the National Lawyers Guild, and a multitude of private donations. Prior to the July 6, 1986, relocation deadline, the group was extremely vocal about their concerns for possible violence on deadline day. It was almost anti-climactic when nothing happened—reporters from throughout the country came to the former Joint Use Area in search of an exciting story, and left without one.

PEABODY COAL COMPANY

Peabody Coal Company signed its first mining lease with the Navajo Tribe in 1964. Later, in 1966, both Navajo and Hopi officials signed leases with the company. Mining operations began on Black Mesa in 1970, and each tribe receives over $2 million a year in royalties from JUA coal. Not all of the land Peabody extracts coal from lies in the JUA, most lies on the Navajo Reservation. There was a relocation of Navajo families from the area slated for mining, and there is no record of any formal tribal protest regarding that relocation. Those involved appear to have simply accepted their new homes (built at the coal company's expense) and moved.

The idea of a "coal conspiracy" has been widely discussed both in the media and among individuals involved in the relocation controversy. In a handout from the Big Mountain Coalition in Defense of Sacred Lands, a headline announces "Relocation of 13,000 Indians in Order to Stripmine—Hopi, Navajos and King Coal." The page-long broadside alleges that Indians in the Joint Use Area live on top of 19 billion tons of coal, and that 13,000 people are slated for relocation due to an energy conspiracy between Congress and energy and development corporations. It also states that Peabody Coal Company is an active participant in this process.

However, despite the hundreds of newsletters full of accusations, Peabody officials have repeatedly denied the charges; no documents have been brought to light that support the allegations. Peabody officials have repeatedly denied any conspiracy and any intention to mine in the Big Mountain area. Peabody Coal attorney Greg Leisse has frequently stressed that during the partition, only the surface of the Joint Use Area was divided; the mineral interests remained jointly owned and managed by both tribes.

An internationally known broadcaster, Paul Harvey, repeated the conspiracy theory on his September 6, 1986, radio show, and later retracted his statements. In the first case, he said that America, a country so willing to right the wrongs of other nations, was committing a dastardly deed in coalition with coal and uranium companies by the partition of the JUA and the relocation of Navajo and Hopi families from the area. In an October broadcast, however, he said, "The media have been guilty· of a hit-and-run and I have been a party to it . . . .You have heard that Public Law 93-531 requires partition of three thousand square miles of Indian tribal lands north of Flagstaff, Arizona. And that is so. You have heard that thousands of Navajo and Hopi people are to be removed and that is the truth . . . . You have heard that Peabody Coal is mining just outside of this area, and that is the truth. But this led to an inference that the big coal company was in cahoots with the government and tribal councils to 'rape for profit,' the Big Mountain area once the Indians are chased out. On the contrary . . ."

Harvey went on to explain that Peabody Coal operates more than fifteen miles away from Big Mountain and has no leases in the Big Mountain area, nor was it seeking any. He pointed out that 85% of the workers at the mine are native Americans, most of them Navajo and many from the Big Mountain region. He also pointed out that any mining done by Peabody on Black Mesa and any further expansion must be done with the consent of both the Navajo and Hopi tribes, and both would receive equal payment on any coal sold.

Finally, he said that "Peabody has demonstrated that there is a difference between the 'development' and 'exploitation' of mineral land . . . . [Peabody] has spent $80 million reclaiming the mined-out land for agriculture, leaving it more productive than before . . . . Some of us remain resentful of the mismanagement of American Indian affairs, but 'industry' in this instance is not the carpetbagger."

When asked why the conspiracy story is so persistent, Peabody representatives have said that it survives because strip-mining coal companies are popular villains and this helps enlist support among environmentally conscious groups. Officials stressed that in order to continue working with the tribes, they needed to maintain a positive relationship with the people and dispossessing families does not make for a good situation.

Attorney Leisse has said that the value of the minerals makes it possible to understand the genesis of a conspiracy theory. "There are some things that have to be acknowledged. At least in the non-Indian culture, whenever people are involved in a land dispute or any struggle over property, what is on and what is in that land will play a part in how strongly they assert their position to that land. So I don't know that the minerals in that land have not been a factor that both tribes have weighed in their decision-making process when deciding to fight for the land . . . . Those are objective facts that cannot be disputed or ignored . . . . But Peabody had nothing to do with the problems between the two tribes or the development of relocation.

"There is a real desire on the part of people who have taken on the relocation issue to discredit the relocation process. They have reached the conclusion that if you can show that there was a different purpose underlying the relocation, other than just resolving the inequity of the land situation as existed, if you can discredit it, maybe you can change the law," Leisse explained. "I think the opponents think that they can possibly get Congress to revisit the issue and reconsider some of its decisions. I think the strategy of some of those people has been to try and make it an energy issue, which it is not."

OTHER NATIVE AMERICAN GROUPS

Many traditional Navajo and Hopi have been deeply upset by the Northern Plains Sun Dance that was brought to Big Mountain in 1982 by undoubtedly well-meaning Lakota and Cheyenne people. Sun Dances are performed in a four-year cycle, so the concluding dance wound up the week before the deadline day in July 1986. Every summer between 1982 and 1986 saw dancers and hordes of Wannabes flocking to Big Mountain.

The Sun Dance, a sacred Plains Indian ceremony, entails not only dancing and prayers but also blood-letting and self-mutilation. In Northern Plains terms, nothing shows more devotion than the offering of the self to the Mystic. The Sun Dance, with its ritual piercing of the pectoral region and connection to a central dancing pole with a long strip of rawhide that is tied through the flesh, is, to the Plains people, the ultimate manifestation of courage, devotion, and self-sacrifice.

All of this is noble within the Plains tradition, but self-mutilation and blood-letting are anathema in both Pueblo and Navajo beliefs. Not only is it not done, it is taboo. Even in the old days, when Hopi and Navajo were at war with one another, ritual cleansing had to be done after battles to cleanse the blood from the warriors hands. The Navajo Enemy Way, also called the Squaw Dance, is a survival of such a cleansing ritual.

Apparently, the American Indian Movement (AIM) people and others who brought the Sun Dance to Big Mountain were unaware of the stress they created among the people they sought to help. While many of the younger Navajos who were involved with AIM also accepted Plains Indians practices, their elders most decidedly did not. Nor did the Hopi priests. Traditional Hopi and Navajo alike rejected the pan-Indian AIM movement, and the Sun Dance was particularly offensive to this group.

A Navajo lady from the JUA explained that she understood that the Sun Dance people meant well, but she was saddened by the blood, and was more than a little frightened by it.

"The Sun Dance was basically brought here by the Lakota people from South Dakota," a young Navajo woman from the disputed area explained. "It's not Diné people's religion, it is Lakota people's religion. They brought it to Big Mountain. I guess the Lakota people felt that this is one way they could help the Diné with their struggle, through the Sun Dance, through their ceremonies. It's a unity in support of the Diné."

Several Hopi have explained that they have respect for the Plains religion, but that to bring it into the Hopi homeland was a disservice to everyone.

"We respect people's religion, but certain things should be practiced where they originate and that Sun Dance is one of those things," Tribal Chairman Sidney commented.

Implications

In litigation on relocation issues, Navajos have often been presented as having difficulties in handling their financial affairs, particularly regarding mortgage and tax payments. While some relocatees, especially ones for whom English is a second language, have encountered problems and have had problems in the off-reservation world, others have successfully made the transition. Some have sold their relocation homes at a profit, obtained on-reservation homesite leases, and moved back to the land with which they are familiar. Organizations such as the Relocation Commission and the Flagstaff-based Native Americans for Community Action have developed counselling and orientation programs to assist relocatees, but critics have said that more needs to be done.

Letters are another result of outside involvement. Dianne Fernicola, federal Navajo and Hopi Indian Relocation Commission administrative assistant, estimates that the commission has received hundreds of thousands of letters during the years it has been in operation. She says that the volume of mail from Europe is far higher than from the United States. "I'm sure that some people are really convinced that something horrible is going on with relocation, but they are badly misinformed," she comments.

Relocation commission Research and Statistics Analyst Dave Shaw-Serdar stressed that most letter writers have been convinced that the program is the result of the fabled energy conspiracy. "These people are very concerned, but at the same time, they are misinformed. You have to respect their sincerity, but you begin to wish that they would do some of their own research and get their facts straight."

Letter writing reached the point of harassment for wives and families of Peabody Coal employees and executives during the summer of 1986. The letters reportedly accused the executives of being involved in a genocidal conspiracy and compared them to the Nazis in Germany.

Some who had previously supported anti-relocation efforts have changed their opinions. A concerned westerner wrote his Congressman in 1987. In his letter, he urged the senator not to reintroduce S2545, a relocation "moratorium bill" (a modified repeal bill). "In the past, I have supported the repeal of PL 93-531, but conditions have changed and repeal or moratorium of the process would result in greater psychological stress and economic hardship to many Navajo relocatees and resisters," he wrote.

Further, he pointed out, "the debate has now shifted from control of land and resource development to an esoteric dialogue of 'traditional' versus 'progressive' values. I don't believe [any outsider] . . . would be able to either legally or intellectually enter into this kind of conflict . . . . What little I have learned so far gives me the feeling that 'traditional' values are the basis of the problem in that the concepts of overpopulation and overgrazing are precluded in the thought world of traditional spiritual tenets . . . . All of us should have high respect for these people, even though some of them may be doing things we may disagree with . . . ."

The sometimes-distorted understanding of Hopi and Navajo cultures is particularly evident in the Wannabes. An instance of this occurred at the San Francisco Press Club in 1986, when kikmongwi Stanley Bahnimptewa went there to discuss relocation and what it meant; his audience was largely composed of members of the Berkeley Big Mountain Support Group and the media. He arrived dressed in contemporary clothing and just before entering the pressroom, put on his headband and turquoise beads. A young male Wannabe in the audience saw Bahnimptewa preparing for the meeting and shouted in outrage, "He can't be a real religious leader! Look at him, he doesn't even wear real Indian clothes except to come on stage! Unbelievable!"

Apparently, this young man felt that time should stand still for native cultures. Picture-book people, no doubt wearing buckskins and feathers, would have been more "real" to him.

A similar incident occurred in Boulder, Colorado, in November 1986, a few weeks after Peter MacDonald's election as Navajo Tribal Chairman. MacDonald and Ivan Sidney presented their respective tribe's views on relocation and the sanctity of land at a forum at Colorado State University. Nona Tuchawena, a Hopi tribal council delegate, had finished explaining the importance of land in the Hopi world and the concept of religion as a very personal thing. After she opened the floor for questions, a young man dressed in what appeared to be an Afghani outfit asked her what he could do to join a Hopi religious society. He asked this after completing his own ten-minute oration on readings that indicated that certain Hopi priests could fly through the air during ceremonies.

"You cannot join a religious society because you are not a Hopi," Tuchawena replied.

"What, you can't mean it! That's discriminatory. I have my rights," the outraged Wannabe said. "That's discrimination," he muttered again as he relinquished the microphone.

Many Wannabes claim to admire traditional Indian cultures, but they have difficulty understanding that static cultures become extinct. Human societies do not exist in a vacuum, and time has not stood still among American Indians. Realities have displaced non-Indian fantasies about life among the tribes.

Although there are a variety of attitudes at work in this issue, there are many individuals who come to the Southwest with a sincere desire to learn and understand. These people may have notions about the land issue prior to their arrival, but they are able to set them aside. These sorts of people are always welcome in all types of societies. They recognize a very important fact: truth is not found on one side or another of a partition—it lives on both sides.

4

TRADITIONAL GOVERNMENT
AND THE TRIBAL COUNCILS

Traditional Navajo and Hopi government was much different from the modern tribal council systems. Modern council systems were adopted after the advent of the twentieth century as a vehicle for dealing with the federal government. In the case of the Navajo Tribe, the system was developed and accepted by the Navajo people. In the case of the Hopi, a constitutional system was developed by non-Indians and controversially imposed on the villages. Despite decades under siege, traditional governing systems survive among both tribes today, but the United States government recognizes only the legitimacy of the tribal councils.

It is important to remember that prior to the American incursion into the Four Corners region, there was no concept of a unified Navajo Tribe or a unified Hopi Tribe. Governing among the Navajo was based upon family, clan, and group consensus. The Navajo developed a genuine democracy, where problems were discussed and input was sought from all involved prior to a decision being reached. The Hopi evolved a theocratic system, with priestly leaders and fiercely independent villages bound not by common government, but by common culture and religious beliefs. The Navajo have accepted the concept of a unified tribe, or small nation-state, much more quickly than the Hopi, who still maintain their traditional village theocracies. Decision making by consensus survives on the Navajo family and chapter level, but even traditional Navajos look to their elected leadership in Window Rock as a definitive means of problem solving. The idea of a Hopi tribal chairman and tribal council is still controversial among the Hopi people, although more and more Hopi are slowly becoming involved in tribal bureaucracy and government.

Traditional Hopi Government

The struggle between theocracy and the Hopi tribal council is a continuing point of stress among the Hopi people, despite attempts by Ivan Sidney and other Hopi leaders to bridge differences. The basic problem is that there are two styles of government in Hopiland, and the two forms compete with each other. Traditionally, Hopi villages were ruled by established clan theocracies. The High Priest of a village was (and is) called the kikmongwi and served as father of the village. The kikmongwi usually appointed at least one spokesman to make his wishes known to the outside world, and to serve as a source of information about that world. Various Crier Chiefs, Kiva Chiefs, and other leaders formed the village government; clan relationships usually dictated who would receive specific ceremonial and governing positions; and each Hopi village was autonomous, with various villages having special clan and religious relationships with one another. Therefore, traditional Hopi government was not democratic. It is true that the priests, religious leaders, warriors, and kikmongwis would listen to various opinions before making decisions, but government was not necessarily by consensus.

Boys and girls were initiated into religious societies at some point between the ages of ten and fourteen. Each society had specific religious rites and secrets that no society member would discuss outside of the society. The religious societies and the theocracies continue today, although many clans and societies have become extinct, and in some cases the succession of the kikmongwi has not continued in the strict traditional manner.

Whenever dissent within a village reached a boiling point, it was not uncommon for the disgruntled group to break away from the home village and found a satellite settlement. There is evidence that when populations grew too great, or other stresses arose, priestly leaders would conspire to cause a split and create new villages (Nequatewa 1936; Whiteley 1988).

At some point in the late 1500s or early 1600s, the Walpi theocracy asked Tewa warriors from the Rio Grande Valley to move to First Mesa to act as protectors of the Hopi. The Walpi leaders promised the Tewa their own village on First Mesa and they promised to treat them well in return for protection. Some Tewa responded to the Hopi invitation, and after the Great Pueblo Revolt of 1690, many of their clansmen, anticipating the Spanish return, joined them. When the Tewa came to Hopi, they brought their own language and ceremonial traditions and established Tewa Village (also called Hano) at the eastern tip of First Mesa. Their descendants still speak Tewa, though many have intermarried with the Hopi and speak Hopi and English as well.

CONSTITUTIONAL GOVERNMENT COMES TO THE HOPI

Traditional Hopi culture was not the culture of an embryo nation-state, as each city was autonomous. The closest thing Western European civilization has to compare with the village theocracies are the Hellenic Dark Age Greek city-states. Like the early Greeks, Hopi society was held together by ties of common language and religious beliefs. Each village was independent, however, and strove to protect its independence. There was no unifying concept of "Hopi"—a person was from Walpi, or Awatobi, or Oraibi. Each village had different customs and villages valued their autonomy. The word "Hopi" denoted a culture, a philosophy, and a way of life. It did not identify a governmental entity.

Hopi life revolved around the ceremonial calender. Priesthoods and women's societies all worked to provide the world with moisture so crops could grow, people would have enough to eat, and the Hopi could continue to honor their covenant with Masau'u. Farming and trading were mainstays of Hopi life, and Hopi warriors vigilantly looked after their people, protecting them from marauding tribes.

When the tribes of the Southwest were absorbed by the United States, challenges to traditional government arose. The Americans could not understand the intricacies of Hopi tribal government, and so appointed Hopis with whom they were familiar as spokesmen for their villages. The kikmongwis tried to educate American representatives about their perspectives and about Hopi government, but very few Indian agents listened. Tensions reached fever-pitch in the 1930s, when Oliver LaFarge, the Hopi agent, drafted a Hopi tribal constitution. LaFarge told the Hopi and federal officials that he was concerned about what he perceived as the fragmentation of Hopi culture. He thought that a tribal constitution would strengthen Hopi government. What he did not realize was that the establishment and imposition of constitutional government on the villages created a government outside the world of Hopi tradition. The idea of a constitutional government was foreign and divisive, and cultural scars from the imposition of such a government on the Hopi are still visible today.

LaFarge's constitution developed a structure similar to a one-house legislature, with elected village delegates, a tribal chairman, and a vice-chairman. Established in 1935, the constitution divided Hopi society, as many theocrats opposed it and many kikmongwis refused to recognize its legitimacy. Many Hopi refused to vote for or against a constitution, leaving those few Hopi who supported the idea to carry the vote. Because of theocratic opposition to the council, the first Hopi tribal council was not elected until 1955. (Some conservative villages still do not accept the authority of the Hopi tribal council, and villages like

Oraibi and the residents of Lower Moencopi have loudly voiced opposition to tribal council negotiation of energy leases and tribal involvement in the 1974 Navajo and Hopi Land Settlement Act.)

The idea of a tribal constitution and a tribal council has not been well received among the Hopi because the impetus for establishment of the ideas did not come from the Hopi themselves. A complication contributing to Hopi refusal to accept the 1935 constitution and refusal to certify council delegates until 1955 was the Indian Land Claims Commission. According to Chairman Sidney, the federal government offered the Hopi Tribe approximately $5 million in an attempt to settle Hopi land claims for lands Americans outside of the 1882 reservation taken from the Hopi by the Americans. Details of the land settlement plan were outlined in a report to the Hopi kikmongwis (Indian Law Resource Center 1979), and the theocracy soundly rejected the offer. Sidney has stressed that neither he nor the tribe will accept the money. "Hopi land is not for sale, whether it be to Navajos or to Anglos, and this dollar settlement further made the Hopi suspicious of American plans revolving around tribal councils, so there was a delay in seating the council until 1955."

Despite opposition from many Hopi, and rejection of the constitution and council by Hotevilla, Oraibi, and Shungopavi, seven other Hopi villages produced support for the concept, and by 1955 there were enough council representatives for a quorum. In a concession to the authority of the kikmongwis, the tribal constitution stated that tribal council members must be certified by religious leaders of their village, and the Hopi tribal chairman must act as an intermediary between the village theocrats, the council, and the Hopi people. A tribal chairman cannot make independent decisions binding on the tribe without approval of the council, and he must work within the framework and limitations of the tribal constitution.

The tribal government has slowly gained legitimacy in the eyes of younger Hopi in the past two decades, but despite a growing level of participation in tribal government, the establishment and legitimacy of the Hopi tribal council remains a bone of contention among the Hopi. Despite consistent attempts to make the Hopi conform to the American world view, including the years of brutality from 1882 through the late 1930s (when American soldiers marched into Hopi villages and took Hopi children from their parents' arms, dragging them off to Anglo-run boarding schools), and the numerous Indian agents who punished Hopis for continuing traditional life, as well as the stampede of Christian missionaries to the mesas since the turn of the century, Hopis have consistently resisted attempts to become Americanized.

While it is true that some Hopi have embraced Christianity and some have adopted the trappings of American culture, the Hopi in general have refused to become fully integrated into American culture and they have not yet internalized American values. Some Hopi have tried to integrate what they perceive as the positive aspects of American culture, while at the same time retaining their own Hopi-ness. Other Hopi have rejected the idea of integration and have also rejected any authority other than their own theocracies.

The federal government and the Bureau of Indian Affairs are aware of the tensions between traditional Hopi government and the established tribal council, but because of the difficulty in dealing with so many villages, the United States government has accepted the Hopi tribal council as the voice of the Hopi people. In the early days of the council, many council representatives were so-called "progressive Hopis," a number of whom were Mormon converts who appeared to have forsaken traditional Hopi ways.

But much has changed since the 1950s, and today, many tribal council members are initiates of Hopi religious societies, seeking to walk the thin line of cultural compromise. Ivan Sidney is an initiated member of one of these societies; he dances the ritual dances and farms and raises livestock in addition to his official tribal duties. Sidney is now into his second term as tribal chairman, and in his re-election campaign of 1985, he stressed the survival of Hopi traditions as part of his platform. Many older Hopis who had never registered to vote in a tribal council election signed up to vote for the first time as a result of Sidney's campaign promises.

In his attempted integration of religious theocracy and tribal government, Sidney has regularly consulted with religious leaders about tribal decisions. Despite attempts to meld the two systems, there are only 2,125 registered Hopi voters. Out of a total population of 10,000 Hopi, the registered voters seem a small percentage, but according to tribal election officials, it is the largest number of registered voters in the people's history. Getting Hopis involved in the electoral process has been a long, hard climb, but it appears that the tribal council system is slowly gaining acceptance.

The Hopi Resistance Movement

Despite the slow inroads the constitutional system has made since the 1955 revival of the tribal council, a militant traditionalist sector has developed on the mesas.* These individuals consistently refuse to recognize the authority of the United States government in Hopi affairs; they oppose energy development and tribal council approval of mining leases and they do not recognize the authority of the federal government to partition their Hopi homeland or any other Indian homeland. The Traditionalist Movement of the twentieth century is a continuation of the Hopi resistance developed in the nineteenth century by leaders like Youkioma and Tewaquoptewa who struggled to promote the survival of Hopi theocratic government and resisted the Americanization of the Hopi people. The roots of the modern resistance can be traced back to 1947, after a Shungopovi clan leader announced that when a gourd full of ashes fell from the sky, he was bound to explain his religious teachings, Hopi prophecies, and Hopi traditions to all who would listen.

After several meetings of various religious leaders, it was collectively decided that the gourd of ashes could be nothing other than the atomic bombs the United States had dropped on Hiroshima and Nagasaki in 1945. At an inter-village meeting at Shungopovi in 1948, a religious leader named Katchongva appointed Thomas Banyacaya as his personal spokesman. Three other young men were appointed spokesmen for other village chiefs, and each spokesman was ordered to carry the Hopi Traditionalist message to the outside world. In a way, it was the birth of an official movement which would proclaim the message of Hopi cultural survival and Hopi resistance to Americanization to the world.

The movement sought to revitalize traditional Hopi culture and increase initiates into religious societies. The movement's goals were clearly outlined in a 1949 letter to the president of the United States. Although the movement's leadership has changed through the deaths of many of its founders, the goals of the movement remain basically the same today.

In the letter to President Truman, hereditary chiefs and priests from Hotevilla, Shungopovi, and Mishongnovi and one from Shipalovi point out that "the Hopi form of government was established solely upon the religious and traditional grounds. The divine plan of life in this land was laid out for us by Great Spirit, Massau'u. This plan cannot be changed. The Hopi life is all set according to the fundamental principles of life in this divine plan . . . ." (Clemmer 1978).

The kikmongwis point out that, "This land is a sacred homeland of the Hopi people and all the Indian Race in this land. It was given to the

---

*As a result of the birth of this resistance movement, there are two types of traditionalists. In the usual reference to traditionalist, one who practices traditional life and religion is the subject. In the word Traditionalist, one who is involved in the political movement is the subject. The two are not necessarily mutually exclusive.

Hopi people the task to guard this land not by force of arms, not by killing, not by confiscating the property of others, but by humble prayers, by obedience to our traditional and religious instructions and by being faithful to our Great Spirit Massau'u. We are still a sovereign nation. Our flag still flies throughout our land (our ancient ruins). We have never abandoned our sovereignty to any foreign power or nation. We've been self-governing people long before any white man came to our shores. What Great Spirit made and planned, no power on earth can change" (Clemmer 1978).

The chiefs pointed out that the Hopi have kept stone tablets which record the Hopi boundaries, and that Pahana, the White Brother who emerged at Sipapu with the Hopi, had identical tablets that, when put together with the stone records of the Hopi leaders will prove to the whole world what land belongs to the Hopi, and will also prove that Pahana is a true brother to the Hopi. "Then the white brother will restore order and judge all people here who have been unfaithful to their traditional and religious principles and who have mistreated his people" (Clemmer 1978).

The chiefs then proceeded to point out why they cannot accept any money from the federal Land Claims Commission. They stressed that they cannot and will not file any claims because they will not ask anything from the federal government. "We will not ask a white man, who came to us recently, for a piece of land that is already ours . . . neither will we lease any part of our land for oil development at this time. This land is not for leasing or for sale. This is our sacred soil . . . ." (Clemmer 1978).

The Hopi kikmongwis said that they understood that over ninety million dollars had been appropriated by the BIA to repay the Navajo and Hopi Indians for lands they had lost, but they said they did not want the money. "We are still poor, even poorer because of the reduction of our land, [due to the creation of the 1882 and 1934 reservation lands] stock, farms, and it seems though the Indian Bureau or whoever is planning new lives for us is now ready to reduce us, the Hopi people, under this plan . . . . We do not need all that money and we do not ask for it . . . . We are self-supporting people. We are not starving . . . maybe the Indian Bureau is starving . . . ." (Clemmer 1978).

The letter condemns a proposed federal plan which would terminate reservations and make Indians full tax-paying citizens. It also condemns the American role in development of the North American Treaty Organization (NATO). The kikmongwis state that they will not bind themselves to any foreign nation at this time, "Neither will we go with you on a wild and reckless adventure which we know will only lead us to a total ruin . . . . We have met all other rich and powerful nations who have come to our shores, from the early Spanish Conquistadors down to the present government of the United States, all of whom have used force in trying to wipe out our existence here in our own home. We want to come to our own destiny in our own way . . . . What nation who has taken up arms ever brought peace and happiness to his people" (Clemmer 1978).

The chiefs further point out that "all the laws under the Constitution of the United States were made without our consent, knowledge and approval, yet we are being forced to do everything that we know are contrary to our religious principles and those principles of the Constitution of the United States" (Clemmer 1978).

Basically, the Hopi priests wanted the United States to respect their sovereignty and stay out of Hopi affairs. It must be kept in mind that the Traditionalist manifesto was a reaction to almost a century of contact with the Americans: a reaction to the American carving up of the Hopi homeland and American limiting of the Hopi religio-political world by the imposition of the 1882 Hopi Reservation boundaries; the imposition of grazing districts and stock reduction on the Hopi (and Navajo) people; to the creation of expanded reservation boundaries for the Navajos by an act of Congress in 1934. These factors, coupled with the constant pressure of American missionaries, the involvement of Hopi youth in the Second World War, and the mining of uranium to support the development of the atom bomb all combined to make the priestly leadership assume an aggressive stance.

In the years since the manifesto of the Hopi Resistance, the group has seen water levels drop and the radioactive contamination of both Navajo and Hopi lands (presumed to be the result of coal and uranium mining), and they have seen the erosion of Hopi theocratic government as the tribal council slowly gains more acceptance. As a result of these problems, the kikmongwis have condemned the Hopi tribal council's involvement in coal and water leases with Peabody Coal Company operations on Black Mesa and in the former Joint Use Area, where both the Navajo and Hopi tribes share revenues resulting from mineral extraction. They view the mining and the loss of millions of gallons of water every year as a result of mining operations dewatering as a violation of the Hopi covenant with Masau'u. Resistance members have also condemned the partition of the former Joint Use Area (which they perceive as Hopi land), and have opposed Public Law 93-531.

Much ado has been made by non-Hopi opponents to the relocation law about the Traditionalist resistance's position on relocation. Many opponents to relocation misunderstand the motives behind the Hopi resistance. The traditionalists oppose the law, not because it removes Navajos from Hopi land, but because it does not do enough to restore the Hopi homeland; further, it is felt that Congress did not consult with the kikmongwis prior to mandating partition and relocation. Hopi religious leaders stress that the boundaries of the Hopi homeland were laid out by Masau'u and they recognize no other authority. Followed to its logical conclusion, this means that all land from Lupton, on the Arizona-New Mexico border northwest to the Grand Canyon, west to Williams, Arizona, and south to the Mogollon Rim, is Hopi land. In the Hopi view, everyone else—Navajos, Hispanics, Anglos, and all the people in all the cities built on the land since the advent of the Europeans and the Americans—are intruders.

The Navajo-Hopi Unity Committee

During the 1970s, a woman was acting in a regent capacity for the kikmongwi of Old Oraibi. Her name was Mina Lanza, and she was a sister to the current kikmongwi, Stanley Bahnimptewa. Mina was a leader of the Traditionalist resistance, and she was the de facto chief of Oraibi. Very concerned about mining on Black Mesa, Mina did not approve of the relocation law. She felt that she had been slighted by the federal government because she had not been consulted about relocation, and she was convinced that there was a connection between energy development and federal interference in Indian affairs. She was also concerned about the fate of both Navajo and Hopi relocatees, and as a result of her concern, an organization called the Navajo-Hopi Unity Committee was founded and officially incorporated in 1974.

Under Mina's guidance, Navajos (including medicinemen) from the former Joint Use Area and Hopi members of the Traditionalist resistance met to strategize on how to change the relocation law. The single most important point that members of the committee agreed on was that the federal government had no business interfering in Indian affairs. After the founding of the organization, non-Indians occasionally attended meetings.

"Mina Lanza was very concerned about the relocation of the Navajos," Caleb Johnson, Lanza's advisor and the spokesman for the current Oraibi kikmongwi, explained. "The main focus of the unity committee was to repeal the relocation law. Mina was concerned about the well-being of all people because as chief, all the people were her children . . . . Also, since the tribal council was involved in the partition and she did not recognize the tribal council, she opposed it just on principle. Also, I think she believed that the Hopi tribal council was being used by the energy companies and the government. She publicized the use of the words, 'Mother Earth', she was concerned about the ripping up of Mother Earth and the dewatering due to mining. We founded the Unity Committee in an attempt to repeal the law. But Hopi involvement in the Unity Committee stopped when Mina passed away and Stanley came back. It is still incorporated as an entity, but we are no longer active in it."

Even when Hopis were involved with the Unity Committee, there was no question in the Hopi mind as to whom the land belonged. It was unquestionably Hopi land. All Hopis stand unified in stating that the disputed land is Hopi land, whether it be in the 1882 area or the 1934 area. The kikmongwis maintain that some Navajos made agreements long ago with some Hopis, and asked permission to stay on the land, and that part of the agreement was that the Navajos would move if and when the Hopis told them to move. Even Thomas Banyacaya, a Hopi well known to the outside world as an opponent of the relocation law, has stressed that all the land in the 1882 area is Hopi land, and that the Navajo requested permission to come onto the land. "The law is a bad law, and we do not support the law," Banyacaya explained, "but the land is Hopi land."

Traditional Navajo Government

Traditional Navajo government was based on kinship and clan ties, with people of wisdom and experience leading various family, band, and clan groups. People of experience and wisdom were (and are) called *nataani,* or "respected elders." During times of war or raiding, warriors of experience and prowess would lead their local war parties. Families joined together during ceremonial times of need when a relative would get sick and require a ceremony or "sing," as the healings were called. Religion as a separate cultural entity was never recognized as independent in any Indian society, but was incorporated into every aspect of life. Traditional Navajos incorporate prayer into daily life, but major ceremonial gatherings are only held in response to a crisis or in time of individual need. This is in contrast to the Hopi, who follow elaborate religious cycles and perform specific rituals at specific times dictated by the ceremonial calender.

No one family, band, or clan could make decisions binding to all Navajos, and government was largely by consensus. Once a decision was made, all involved in the process would honor the decision. Individual feelings and needs were always considered to be important, and decision making, binding the band or clan, could be a lengthy process.

"Traditional decision making came down to your kinship, it came down to the local families, it came down to the local clans. And it was the kinship/clan system that had everything to do with the way decisions were made and it was done through a consensus," former Navajo Tribal Chairman Peterson Zah explained. "Back in those days, the Navajo people really knew the traditional way of life. And the traditional way of life was that you didn't necessarily have to punish anybody to get what you need or what you want. You didn't have to physically punish anyone or psychologically punish anyone to get to where the local families or tribes wanted to go. It was something that was done with understanding. It was something that was done with love and a great respect for each other . . . . [Navajo people used to] have a pure, a genuine democracy. It was done through talking with each other, pleading with each other in resolving some of the most complicated issues. It was probably a real, genuine democracy at work. And it is just really sad, really, really sad and sometimes it just bothers me that we are beginning to float away from that."

Traditional decision making survives today on the family, clan, and chapter levels. In various meetings at the Big Mountain Community Hogan from 1981-85, rule by consensus was practiced. Such decisions as to whether or not to allow an anthropologist to document the importance of land and religion to the Navajo people in the area, or how to respond to BIA stock impoundment could take days, weeks, or months. In many cases, if a consensus was not reached, no action would be taken. When meetings were held, Navajos from all around the area—many related to each other through family or clan ties—would gather early in the morning. Meetings usually broke up a couple of hours before dusk so that people could go home and take care of their livestock. On weekends, if a decision had not been collectively reached, the meeting resumed the next morning; some lasted weekend after weekend for months on end. People sat patiently, quietly, and respectfully while each concerned person rose and said his or her piece.

The desire for consensus still predominates at Navajo Tribal Council sessions, even those affecting energy leases and coal renegotiation leases; but consensus is not always practiced among the councilmen and the tribal chairman. The Navajo Tribal Council and the chairman of the Navajo Tribe have acquired policy development and decision making powers that were once the realm of the nataani, medicine people, and war chiefs. The council has more power over Navajo lives than traditional leaders held—the tribal chairman can make decisions binding the entire nation and holds a power over the Navajo people unprecedented in their history.

THE NAVAJO TRIBAL COUNCIL

The concept of a Navajo Tribal Council was developed by the Navajo people themselves and was initiated in 1923, when the tribe incorporated as a business organization in order to negotiate mineral leases with the outside world and the federal government. Roughly, the council took the form of a typical state government, with a one-house legislature and a chairman elected at large, like a state governor.

Today, the tribal council consists of eighty-eight members elected from one hundred and nine certified chapters. The chapter is roughly politically equivalent to a county, and chapters have their own locally elected chapter officers. The chairman and vice-chairman are popularly elected every four years. The Navajo have no constitution delineating the power of chairman and council, and thus power has gravitated toward the executive branch, which has largely been left to define its own role and responsibilities.

For over fifty years, there has been talk among the Navajo people of developing a means of making council representatives and the chairman and vice-chairman accountable to the Navajo people, and the movement for some type of document defining the powers of council, chairman, and the Navajo courts has been gaining more momentum in recent years. A group called the Dineh Rights Association is working to build grass-roots support for a tribal constitution. But some Navajos, especially members of the older generations, view the idea of a constitution with suspicion.

"I think the Navajo people need some kind of a principle of statements from the local people that would say 'here's how we want our government and government officials to behave'—some ways that will tell people that get elected, whether it's me, or Mr. MacDonald, or somebody in back of us . . . what they can't do and what they can do. Something of that nature is needed. Some people like to call that a constitution. It just so happens that on the Navajo [Reservation] there is a stigma attached to the word constitution and I don't know if the Navajo people who have such a negative attitude towards the word will ever accept any arguments that anyone can put forth about the need for a constitution because it was identified with the livestock reduction," Peterson Zah explained. "It was identified with people like John Collier, way back in the old days, because the federal government sent all of those representatives out here and they were pushing livestock reduction, and then as soon as the Navajo people were devastated by the livestock reduction, the next thing they did was push really hard for a constitution, so therefore [older Navajos say] 'we are going to reject it.' "

Zah said that the push for a constitution has taken place off and on since 1925. "It's interesting, it is something that comes out and then it dies. The discussion of a constitution on the Navajo Reservation is like a roller coaster—it comes and it goes and then it comes up and it goes down," Zah explained. "Way back when they were fighting with John Collier over the livestock reduction, there were a lot of discussions about a constitution then, but it narrowly got defeated. And then Raymond Nakai came along back in the 1950s and revived it. He revived the issue and put some more breath into it and really won the Navajo tribal election saying we need a constitution and then he didn't do anything the first four years in his term, and then as he was getting ready to leave office, he had his lawyer . . . draft a constitution which was a verbatim constitution from the United States Constitution. Raymond Nakai gave it to the tribal council and they tabled it and that's where it died. That was back in the 1960s, and we haven't revived it since then. Now you have the Dinéh Rights Association who's advocating for adoption of a constitution by the tribe. So it is something that comes and goes and I think the Navajo people have to really put their minds together and decide whether or not they want it. They have to make up their minds. If they say we need something like that, then they ought to work very hard on it . . . ."

Zah said that the only way that something like a constitution could be developed by the Navajo would be if the idea took root first at the local level. "You can't have the chairman of the tribe advocate for it, because then it would be coming from the top to the bottom and the guy who is doing all of that would be imposing his own values on the people. The only way for it to happen is to have the concept come from the local people. It has to come from the schools, it has to come from the families. It has to come from the younger generations. It has to then work its way into the chapter houses, it has to go to the agencies and then it has to work itself into the council. That scenario is something that is needed. That kind of building up a case for something like a constitution is what is needed . . . ."

Zah said he was not necessarily an advocate of a tribal constitution, but he did not necessarily oppose the idea. He said that he felt some guidelines were necessary for tribal leaders, and some type of plan should be developed to make elected officials accountable to their constituents. But at the same time, Zah emphasized that there was a need to remember traditional ways of government and to try and better integrate ideas of consensus and democracy in contemporary Navajo government.

"The last tribal election was so divisive," Zah said. "And I am worried that dividing the Navajo Nation will hurt our peoples' future. Our past government—the government of consensus and democracy—was a real strength for the Navajo people, and if we're beginning to float away from that, what it really tells me is that we don't know our own strength. Democracy and consensus—that was our strength—it has helped us survive all these many years. When the Navajo people are floating away from their own strength—from consensus, from the Navajo language, from the Navajo culture . . . people are going to have identity crises within themselves. If you don't know who you are and if you don't know where you come from, you are going to have problems. You better look at yourself in the mirror each morning and say, "I know who I am. I am this person. I am unique, yes, I look different. I may not like everything that is on my face, but that's me. It's unique and God made me this way—for me to be different.' To me, that is really, really important. And we have to continue to function as a nation that way. That is why one of the things that I always push is education . . . . I taught clan relationships at Window Rock High School and I really love doing these things. [The kids] really listen when you talk about clan systems, about Navajo culture and about Navajo lifestyle and it's something that I think the Navajo tribe should continue pushing—those are our strengths. If they are our strengths, then we should teach them in school. Navajo democracy—genuine, true democracy—it was so good to the Navajo people that it has enabled us to live as long as we have as a nation. Then why should we give it up? Why should we just throw it out the window and say forget about it, we're going the modern way? There's no room for those kind of actions if we are to survive."

Honoring Traditional Agreements

Despite the existence of a congressional act officially solving the land issue on paper, many traditional Navajos and Hopis have voiced the hope that they should sit down with each other and work out the problem in a traditional Indian-to-Indian way. Traditional and political leaders of both groups have pointed out that before American intervention in the region, they were able to work out problems and negotiate treaties and make commitments to each other. Zah and Sidney have both said that they would be willing to sit down and discuss alternatives to the total relocation of Navajos from the former Joint Use Area. In 1983, the two tried to negotiate alternatives for 1882 and 1934, but the talks broke down. Sidney and Navajo Tribal Chairman Peter MacDonald have addressed forums on relocation together, but since MacDonald's election in 1986, no active chairman-to-chairman negotiations have been pursued. But both tribes have referred to traditional agreements about the disputed lands. What were the understandings the two tribes had with each other in the past and what is the likelihood of a traditional settlement to the complicated problem?

In a 1977 interview printed in a Hopi newspaper, Duke Pahona, then seventy-four years old and the last Crier Chief of First Mesa (a member of the Sand-Snake Clan), explained the details of an agreement made between the Hopi and some Navajo bands in the Kit Carson era. Pahona and his family were the keepers of the symbols of that covenant, the *tiponi,* or "chief's medicine bundle" (*Qua' Toqti* 1977). It is an authority symbol to the Navajo, a symbol of the Mother of the Navajo Nation. Many clan and religious leaders from the mesa country have discussed the various arrangements made with the Navajos, and the belief that someday the Navajo would leave Hopi land voluntarily.

"Then there is the Navajo—he who made certain [land] claims. He still looks to those declarations. It is said that in the beginning ears of corn were laid out. The first ear was perfect, the remainder less perfect in their order," Pahona explained. "The Navajo laughed to himself and said 'You poor Utes, Hopis. I will take the best and claim it for myself. My people will yet multiply. No one shall deny me the maidens or women. So that is exactly how he conducts his life. He has really done us wrong" (*Qua' Toqti* 1977).

Navajos from Big Mountain insist that they had clear agreements with the Hopi leaders and they had permission to settle the land. They describe an ancient footrace between Navajo and Hopi runners, with the winner freely choosing the area his people would settle. "The Navajo won because he had longer legs," a Navajo elder explained. "So he said he would take the land around Big Mountain and the Hopi could stay on their mesas and farm in their canyons, the way that they always have."

Hopi traditional leaders have stressed that they oppose congressional involvement in Navajo and Hopi affairs because they want to work out the problem in a traditional way. Some traditionalists have said that they are glad that the Navajos are leaving, but they don't like to see anyone being forced to relocate; they would have preferred that the Navajos move voluntarily away from the Hopi homeland.

The Oraibi kikmongwi, Stanley Bahnimptewa, has stressed that he views the land dispute as childish and silly. He has pointed out that neither the American Congress, the Navajo Tribal Council, nor the Hopi Tribal Council have the right to fight over land entrusted to the Hopi priests to protect. The kikmongwi explained that his ancestors gave shelter to the Navajo when they needed help, and that the Navajo formally asked permission to rest on Hopi land. Bahnimptewa admitted that the Navajos have stayed on the Hopi *tusqua* much longer than anybody had anticipated that they would, but it was up to him and the other kikmongwis to decide how long the Navajo would stay and when they would be forced to move. He added that he had not asked the Navajo to leave, and if anyone was to tell them to leave, it would be him as kikmongwi and not the United States government.

"This is my land. I have to take care of it, and I haven't asked them to leave yet," Bahnimptewa said. "The Navajos need to remember who their religious leaders are. They need to decide who they are and they need to send their religious leaders to me. They need to come and talk to me and together, we will decide what is to be done about the whole matter."

Johnson further explained his kikmongwi's views on the land issue. "Chief Bahnimptewa has a very different perspective on the land dispute from other people," Johnson said. "For one thing, he feels it is like two children quarreling over something they don't have a right to quarrel over. The [Hopi] tribal council and the Navajos don't own the land. They are arguing over something which they don't have the right to argue over. The kikmongwi has the land; he is the keeper of the land by contract with the Creator. He isn't arguing with anybody about that. He is the individual that has the guardianship responsibility, not the Navajos or the chairman of the [Hopi] tribal council . . . . It hasn't gotten to the point where Chief Bahnimptewa wants to boot them off of the land."

The theme of Navajos coming and talking to Hopi religious leaders is often repeated among the Hopi. Traditionally, it has been up to the non-Hopi to come to the Hopi theocracy to make requests, to develop alliances, and to consult on matters of state. This is one key reason why the traditionalists do not recognize congressional authority—Congress had not come to consult with them about the land issue.

Both theocratic and modern political leaders have collectively voiced a desire for the Navajo political and religious leadership to come to them and work out the land problem in a traditional way. "If the Navajos would come to us and talk it over with us, and ask permission to stay after acknowledging that the land they live on is Hopi land, we would seriously have to consider their request," Sidney explained. "But is seems as if the old Navajos are reluctant to do that, and the young Navajos don't know about our ancient agreements, so they don't know that they should come and talk to us."

Zah stressed that a traditional solution could possibly be worked out if Navajo and Hopi would be willing to sit down and talk, treat each other like human beings, and prepare themselves to make realistic concessions. "I think a comprehensive solution for both the 1882 and the 1934 case should be worked out," Zah explained. "And I think the key to all of these elements in the comprehensive solution is in recognizing each other as human beings. The Navajos for many years didn't want to recognize Hopi rights. Hopis . . . essentially did the same thing. If you don't recognize each other's position, if you don't recognize each other as a person, or even to recognize their rights, you are not ever going to get anywhere. To me, the Navajo-Hopi situation is the same way. As long as the two didn't recognize each other and didn't respect one another and their position, there was never any kind of discussion . . . . The Hopi Tribe and Hopi individuals are human beings. So are we . . . . We are always going to have to live side by side together. They are not going to move away and we are not going to move away, so we are a neighbor and we have to coexist. Those are facts that we can't evade. Those are situations that we can't run away from, we can't escape those situations . . . ."

Zah said that Navajo and Hopi leaders, as well as individual members of the tribe, will have to put aside pride and egos to work out a settlement, but he lives in hope that it will be done, if not for the 1882 area, at least for the 1934 area. Zah's hopes for Navajo and Hopi reaching a settlement are not unique. The kikmongwis have stressed that the matter should be decided on a human level as well.

"If the Navajos would go to the Chief [Bahnimptewa], there would be justice. The Chief does not look at people as Navajos or Anglos or Blacks. He looks at them as people first. If the Navajos would go to the Chief with their problems and their needs, he would consider them first as human beings with human needs. He would study all solutions and all aspects of the problem. He would render a fair decision and justice would be done," Caleb Johnson said. "But such things can take a long, long time, and I don't know if the federal government has any patience left for settling things in a traditional manner. The relocation process has started. The process has gone on for such a long time and government actions have a way of moving on. The relocation law is already in place and it is difficult to stop the process at this time."

The kikmongwis maintain that they will dispense justice if the Navajo come to them, but Navajos have not gone to the kikmongwis. Some Navajos have said that they are reluctant to go to Hopis for assistance; others have said that the partitioned land was theirs by right of conquest, and they shouldn't have to go to the Hopis for anything. Russell Means, a founder of the American Indian Movement whose members have played a large role in Navajo resistance to relocation, said that he believes hope for a traditional solution is slight.

"The Navajos will never go to the Hopi religious leaders and make petition to them," Means said. "The Hopis hold all the cards. It is

Hopi land, and the old Navajos know it. They are afraid that if they go to the Hopis, in light of all the past history of trouble, the Hopis won't let them stay. So they will never go to the Hopis."

Means's analysis and Johnson's realistic assessment together with the fact that Navajo and Hopi struggled for over a century to work out the land problem in a traditional way, while at the same time consistently asking the United States government to help them in the fight, bring up an important point. How realistic is it to expect support from the federal government if the tribes came up with a settlement plan? Hawley Atkinson, one of three commissioners who heads up the federal Navajo and Hopi Indian Relocation Commission, has said that the government would support any alternative plan that both tribes develop. Ross Swimmer, the head of the BIA, has said the same thing. But the settlement act and the partition remain public law, and relocation continues as the tribes prepare to do legal battle in federal court over the 1934 area.

5

NAVAJO-HOPI TENSIONS REACH A BREAKING POINT

The congressional law mandating the relocation of thousands of Indians from land partitioned between the Navajo and Hopi tribes was enacted in 1974. Ironically, the roots of Public Law 93-531 lie in the massive relocation of Navajos to New Mexico in the 1860s. The period of American raids, forced marches, and captivity at Bosque Redondo in New Mexico is remembered as "The Long Walk" by Navajos.

Navajo children growing up today listen to stories of the captivity from their grandparents and great-grandparents. The story has been passed down from generation to generation for over a century. Because of the Long Walk and the suffering it brought to their people, the very word relocation strikes a note of fear in the Navajo heart.

After five years of captivity, the United States government listened to Navajo entreaties to go home to Dinétah. The expense of keeping eight thousand people in relocation camps, coupled with the compassion of the American army for its captives, convinced General William Tecumseh Sherman and the Indian Peace Commission to allow the Navajos to go home. Sherman agreed to set boundaries for a reservation in the heart of Dinétah. He set aside some 3.5 million acres (roughly the size of West Virginia) straddling New Mexico and Arizona. On the morning of June 1, 1868, twenty-nine Navajo nataani and war chiefs pledged peace and obedience to the United States in the Treaty of 1868. They marked x's on the paper and prepared for their return to the Land Between the Four Sacred Mountains. The People were so happy at the prospect of going home that it is doubtful if they really understood what they were signing, or the fact that their free-roaming and raiding days were coming to an end. They probably would have signed anything if it promised them a return to their homeland.

"When we saw the top of the mountain from Albuquerque," Navajo War Chief Manuelito reportedly said, "we wondered if it was our mountain, and we felt like talking to the ground, we loved it so, and some of the old men and women cried with joy when they reached their homes " (U.S. Congress, House, Executive Document 263, 49th Cong., lst session).

Among the treaty terms to which the Navajo had agreed was their confinement within reservation lines and a cessation of all raiding of any sort. They also agreed to have their children educated by American citizens at the expense of the federal government. It is doubtful that any traditional Indian people could have understood that their world was limited by lines drawn on a piece of paper. Maps, boundary lines, and American-style education were totally alien concepts to the Navajo. When the Navajo returned to Dinétah, they set up housekeeping on their traditional clan lands, and as their population grew, they established settlements beyond the 1868 treaty boundary lines, unaware that they had violated any agreement with the United States. The basic thrust of their settlement was westward, toward the Hopi mesas, although some families moved south and southwest into Zuni country.

Importance of Treaty Rights and the Hopi Land Problem

Because the Navajo had been at war with the United States, they gained the protection of a treaty with the federal government. True, they were a conquered people, but a treaty had been made between the Americans and the Diné on a nation-to-nation status; there were rights, restrictions, and guarantees made to both sides. More importantly, the Navajo had a land base recognized by the federal government. The Hopi, on the other hand, had never been at war with the United States. They had no treaty protection and no recognized reservation. By not having federally recognized land claims, the Hopi had no official federal status. The stage was set for another century of strife between Navajo and Hopi due to this situation.

Because the Hopi had no reservation, there was little that that United States Army or appointed Indian agents could do to protect them. Apparently, the United States was ignorant of Hopi traditional boundaries and had its hands full with the Navajo treaty and Reconstruction after the Civil War. Agents were appointed for both tribes, but the United States would wrestle with the thorny Hopi boundary problem for twenty years before attempting a resolution.

Stress between Navajo and Hopi populations became evident within one year of the Navajo return from captivity. According to reports filed by United States Army Captain A. D. Palmer, the first American Indian agent appointed to the Hopi, some Navajos had resumed raiding Hopi villages and cornfields during his first year as agent (Palmer Report to Commissioner 1870). In addition to Navajo raiders, Apaches continued raiding the mesas. Palmer was worried about the Hopi condition, and stressed the need for a binding treaty between Navajo and Hopi. In studying ways to protect the Hopi from raiders, Palmer considered the relocation of Hopis away from their mesas, but concluded that they were happy with their homeland and ultimately recommended that the United States arm the Hopi. The recommendation to arm the Hopi was apparently made at the Hopi request, after their allies, the Zuni, had received three hundred rifles from the Americans and proceeded to drive a number of Navajo squatters off of their traditional territory.

The Hopi received guns from the Americans, further escalation-flict between Navajo and Hopi. In the musical chairs of Navajo and Hopi Indian agents from 1870 through 1910, consistent reports of murder and thievery between the two tribes were forwarded to Washington, D.C. In some reports, Navajos were killed by Hopis while trying to steal livestock from their villages; in others, Hopis were killed by Navajos during waterhole confrontations.

By 1873, when William S. DeFree became the Hopi agent, the idea of relocating the Hopi from the mesa country to land along the Little Colorado River or Oklahoma was under serious consideration in Washington, D.C. When DeFree brought up the possibility to the Hopi, their reaction was predictable. The Hopi vowed to resist any relocation plan. In their perspective, their physical and ceremonial ties to the land and their contract with Masau'u made removal to any other part of the world impossible. DeFree traveled around Hopi country from Walpi to Moencopi, and recommended that Washington, D.C., establish a separate Hopi Reservation.

The American government was trying to cope with a complicated problem. American agents saw the decimation that raiding and fighting between Navajo and Hopi was causing, but without determining the extent of the Hopi homeland, there was little that could be done to solve the problem. In 1874, an agency was established for the Hopi at Keams Canyon. One of the key assignments given to the Hopi agent was to determine Hopi land boundaries. Hopi agents studied Hopi land boundaries until 1882, when traditional boundaries were ignored and arbitrary reservation lines were drawn by Americans.

Future problems could probably have been averted had the Americans consulted directly with the Hopi theocracy and the Navajo nataani and learned the traditional Hopi boundaries and what the Navajos would accept as Hopi boundaries in 1874. If Americans, Navajos, and

Hopis had worked out acceptable boundaries, Hopis say that there would never have been a need for Public Law 93-531. The federal government would have been able to save millions of dollars in relocation costs, and possibly Navajo and Hopi would have been able to work out their differences in a traditional way. But apparently, the ignorance of the American government about traditional problem solving among Hopi and Navajo, exacerbated by a growing Navajo population and expansion into Hopi territory, made such a settlement impossible.

Many Navajos perceived the Hopis as farmers living perched on mesas who liked to live close together and were only interested in their ceremonies and their cornfields. Unless there was clear evidence of Hopis living in a certain area, Navajos would move in and establish a camp. If no one challenged their move, Navajos assumed that the land was theirs.

Hopi clan lands and farms extended all around the mesas, however, as far south as modern-day Leupp and as far west as Moencopi, fifty miles west of Oraibi. Moencopi, a satellite farming community of Oraibi, was established in the 1870s, but Oraibi people had farmed the area for generations prior to establishment of the village. Some Navajos were aware of Hopi traditional boundaries and asked permission from the Hopi priests to move into certain areas. Other Navajos, either ignorant of traditional boundaries or simply ignoring them, moved onto the land anyway. Navajos moved onto Hopi lands in increasing numbers, and the harried Hopi started to asked Washington, D.C., for assistance in keeping the Navajo and others out.

The Navajo were not the only invaders moving into Hopi country. Mormon settlers, in search of their own Promised Land, had begun to colonize Hopi lands, in what is now Winslow, Holbrook, and the Tuba City–Moencopi area. Opinions in Washington, D.C., about what to do about the Navajo and Mormon encroachments were mixed. Some bureaucrats felt that the Hopi should be left to fend for themselves; there was even talk of abolishing the Hopi agency. But Hopi Indian agents consistently pointed out that the United States had an obligation to protect Hopi interests. Hopi agent W. B. Traux eloquently pled the Hopi case to Indian Commissioner Smith in 1876.

I am deeply impressed with the conviction that this agency should not be . . . abolished . . . . It would be similar to the abandonment of a family of children by their parents and leaving them in the midst of dangers. The Navajo Indians would very soon drive them from their best agricultural and grazing lands on the East and in various ways impose upon them. They have for some time manifested a disposition to this, but have been restrained by the presence and influence of the agent. The Mormons are also encroaching upon them on the West and Southwest. About five hundred of them have settled not far from the lands claimed by the Moquis, [Hopi] and as they are a peaceable, inoffensive tribe . . . their rights will be invaded with impunity, unless protected by an agent. They would soon drive these Indians to the wall (Traux to Smith 1876).

Despite Traux's concerns, the Hopi agency was briefly suspended in 1878, and the agent for the Navajo assumed responsibility for the Hopi as well. Both tribes were administered from Fort Defiance for approximately eighteen months. It was during the administration of Navajo-Hopi agent Alex G. Irvine that the need for a protected Hopi homeland was taken seriously in Washington, D.C. Irvine recommended setting aside a reservation of fifty square miles for the Hopi, which would include the heart of the Hopi mesas and Keams Canyon on the east. The Hopi were unimpressed with the recommendation.

Finally, while Anglo agents continued coming and going to Hopiland, Commissioner of Indian Affairs E. A. Hayt asked for an assessment of Navajo encroachment. He also asked the approximate size of the original Hopi homeland (Hayt to William R. Mateer, Field Papers, Moqui Agency 1879). After years of study and federal hand-wringing, and years of Hopi complaints against Navajo and Mormon intrusions, in 1882, Indian Commissioner Price drafted an Executive Order setting aside lands in Arizona "for the use and occupancy of the Moqui Indians and such Indians as the Secretary of the Interior may see fit to settle thereon."

Price sent the draft to the President with an explanation as to why the Hopi needed protected boundaries.

. . . Having no vested title to the lands they occupy—which in fact it seems is well understood, they are subject to continual annoyance and imposition, and it is not difficult to see, that it is only a question of time, when, if steps are not taken for their protection they will be driven from their homes and the lands that have been held and cultivated by them for generations, if not centuries, will be wrested from them, and they left in poverty and without hope . . .

President Chester Arthur signed the Executive Order creating the Hopi Reservation on Dec. 16, 1882. Out of the millions of acres of ancestral homeland the Hopi had claimed for over a thousand years, they received an Executive Order reservation of 2.5 million acres, rectangular in shape for the convenience of mapping. It was about seventy miles long in its north-south dimension and about fifty-five miles wide in its east-west dimension. It completely isolated the satellite village of Moencopi in the west, cutting it off from the main reservation by twenty miles.

At the time the order was signed, there were at least three hundred Navajos living on the designated Hopi Reservation. They were not ordered to move out, so they stayed. The seeds of the land dispute had been sown.

Contrary to federal hopes, the creation of a Hopi Reservation did not ease tensions between the Navajo and Hopi tribes. Eventually, the federal government forced the Mormons living near Moencopi and other areas to relocate; they even gave them some cash to make the move. But Navajos were not ordered to leave land on the Hopi Reservation after the signing of the presidential order. Navajos ignored the established 1882 boundaries and traversed the land; from the Navajo perspective, no one was clearly living in the area, so they saw no reason why they could not graze their flocks in unoccupied areas, build their hogans, or plant their corn.

Once Navajos move into an area and build their hogans, a blessing dedication is done and the house, land, and everything around it become sacred, according to the Navajo Way. "Navajos are uniquely tied to the land where they are born in that once a child is born, his or her umbilical cord is buried and a young tree is planted there. Thus, a person is tied to the land from the beginning," Navajo Tribal Chairman Peter MacDonald explained in a 1982 interview. Such ceremonialism, tying a person to the land from birth and making house, land, and all creatures it encompassed sacred, is a logical adaptation for nomadic people in that it helps establish real and justifiable links to new settlements.

In addition to vast cultural differences, one of the fundamental problems between Navajo and Hopi was a difference in the perceptions of land use and land ownership. In the Hopi view, Hopis are stewards and they must fulfill certain obligations in this role. Hopis perceive an ordered world, of which they and their lands are the center point. Boundaries in the Navajo world are far more nebulous. In the old days, family groups roamed within the boundaries of the Four Sacred Mountains. In more recent times, legal boundaries have not had much authority; in fact, these lines have continued to shift as the Navajo expanded the reservation to accommodate an ever-growing population.

Population pressure was another key factor in the tensions that continued between the tribes from 1882 through the enactment of the land partition and relocation mandate outlined in 1974. The Hopi have felt surrounded since 1882, when the Navajo moved west because they needed more space to support their sheep-herding economy as well as their human population. The Hopi had acquired sheep, goats, and cattle and practiced limited herding, too, but they were tied to the land by their covenant with the Mystic and by their farming. The land fight was a natural outcome of population growth and contrasting life-styles. Conflict and a struggle for control of land and water was the inevitable result.

The American conquest of the region also plays a direct role in crea-tion of the problem. Prior to American interference in the Navajo and Hopi cultures, both had practical and effective solutions for land and population problems.

Before being boxed in by imaginary lines, drawn by non-Indians to determine the extent of reservation lands, Hopis had set up clear clan and land boundaries. Even so, Hopi villages did not lead static lives. As populations grew, stresses developed within villages. The kikmongwis and other village leaders would solve growth problems by fomenting a village spilt (Nequatewa 1936; Whiteley 1988). When a split oc-curred, dissidents would move away from the home village and found a new village. The ancestral Hopi apparently moved a lot, as is evi-denced from the large number of ruined pueblos in northern Arizona. But solving population problems or intravillage conflicts by fabricating a quarrel and moving away was no longer a viable option after Ameri-cans forced formal boundaries on the Hopi. There was only a limited amount of land, and room for only a limited number of splinter villages.

When Navajo encroachment became obvious to the Hopi kikmong-wis in the early 1880s, Hopi leaders from all three mesas met to discuss a colonization plan to found villages away from the mesas and onto land they feared would be taken by the Navajo (Nequatewa 1936). Trying to solve the land problem before the Navajo could become more firmly entrenched, the Hopi reacted in a traditional manner by founding splinter villages.

When the United States government created new boundaries for the old Hopi tusqua in an attempt to act as a champion and arbitrator for both tribes, they interposed the federal presence in a way that almost guaranteed even more conflict. Despite good federal intentions, by not fully understanding either Navajo or Hopi culture and settlement pat-terns, a great disservice was done to both.

The Era of Segregation Investigations

News of intertribal conflict continued to reach Washington, D.C., after the creation of the Executive Order reservation. After the turn of the century, the focus of the conflicts shifted from raiding and establishing territory to actual land settlement by Navajos and periodic feuding between Navajo and Hopi at water holes and especially at sheep dips.

In the early 1920s, L. A. Dorrington was dispatched from Washington, D.C., to Arizona to review the situation, and his final report was sent to the commissioner of Indian affairs on January 7, 1925. After an extensive tour of the 1882 Hopi area, Dorrington concluded that the two tribes should be completely segregated and that the Hopi should be given exclusive use of some 1,200 miles, and other lands should be given to the growing Navajo tribe. According to Dorrington's analysis, Navajos had continued to push Hopis off of their lands, and were moving onto it themselves. Dorrington said that the Navajo had driven Hopi stock from the best range and water, and concluded that the Hopi were not receiving their fair share of their own reservation (Dorrington 1925).

Initially, the idea of separating Navajo from Hopi and making one group move off of lands technically given to the other was not viewed favorably in Washington, D.C., where decision makers were heavily influenced by the recommendations of E. K. Miller, who was the Hopi agent at that time. In a letter dated February 27, 1925, Miller stressed that he believed Dorrington had been misled by the Hopi, and had taken a position that was unfair to the Navajo.

> . . . So far as my experience here is concerned and from what I can learn from others who have been here many years, I am inclined to the belief that to establish boundaries such as suggested by Mr. Daniels and Col. Dorrington would not only be unfair to the Navajos but would cause more trouble and friction than has ever been evident between these people, for it is unreasonable to suppose these Navajos would peacefully give up lands they have occupied and improved for years without having a part in such an arrangement and being promised at least something good in return.
>
> It is my opinion that the matter should be carefully investigated by disinterested and outside officials before any action is taken and that the Navajos' side should be as completely and thoroughly considered as that of the Hopis. The Navajos should be allowed to present and protect their interests. It appears to me that such a thing should not be considered unless there is really trouble of more consequence than at present or there is a concerted movement toward a division of land made by both tribes (Miller 1925).

Miller pointed out that he believed Hopis had put the Navajos on the defensive in recent years, and were expanding out, pushing Navajos off of land:

Twenty years ago Navajos occupied many places such as Tall-hogan, which are now occupied by Hopis. In the last twenty years Navajos have given way to Hopis. I was here in 1906 and know something of conditions at that time. I know that the Hopis have both prospered and spread considerably since then. They are all much better off in every way than during that period. Many of them have moved out away from the mesas, establishing small communities and ranches, controlling farming, gardening and grazing sections. Additional numbers each year are doing this and we have also a number now living among Navajos in peace and prosperity . . . there is always trouble here over range, stock and crops; both between the two tribes and members of each tribe. None of this trouble seems serious. We promptly adjust these troubles, which are bound to arise as long as these Indians have to graze, to farm and run stock without adequate fencing. To me it is very astonishing they get along as well as they do and find there is not more trouble of this nature (Miller to Commissioner of Indian Affairs 1925).

Miller stressed that the most serious problems between the tribes occurred at sheep-dipping vats where Navajo and Hopi alike had to take their sheep every year. In a land with few springs and little water, the dipping vat was a natural stress point. Miller admitted that most sheep dips were located on Hopi land, and that Navajos would sometimes "too freely use water and grazing lands against the Hopis' protests. They have, also, at these times, caused friction and trouble by stealing vegetables, fruits, etc., from Hopi gardens and orchards" (Miller to Commissioner of Indian Affairs 1925).

Despite the predictable water problems and occasional thefts, Miller stressed that the government should be cautious about any land partition or separation of Navajo and Hopi populations. He said that establishing any partition line would cause both Navajo and Hopi to be "dispossessed of homes they have maintained for years" (Miller 1925).

In his letter to the commissioner of Indian affairs, Miller admitted that he respected the adaptability and industrious nature of the Navajos, and that he believed the expansion of the Hopi on the 1882 reservation was the work of young Hopis, eager for farmlands and interested in the possible development of coal and oil deposits that may be discovered in the region. He said the Hopis were deliberately agitating to get rid of the Navajo in order to acquire additional acreage for their own reservation. He viewed these aggressive Hopis as "undesirables."

Miller was suspicious of the Hopi ties to ritual and said that he felt much more comfortable with the Navajo. He certainly appeared to be more sympathetic to Navajo needs than to Hopi needs.

"The Hopi have always had the same opportunity here as the Navajo," Miller wrote. "This is their pagan persistence in putting ceremony before prosperity and living in places from where it is impossible to extend self-supporting agricultural activities to large areas. If these people danced less and emulated the Navajo woman more, their condition would be better, for it is really the Navajo woman who has made that tribe prosper as it has "(Miller 1925).

Despite his sympathy for the Navajo people, Miller stressed that he wanted to give "a square deal" to both tribes, and recommended that an outside committee review the situation. He emphasized that any land division would hurt the progress and welfare of both tribes.

Initially, Miller's recommendations were heeded in Washington and segregation of the tribes did not occur in the 1920s. But in 1927, Miller reversed his position. In a letter dated November 19 of that year, he advocated the separation of the tribes and an extension of the Hopi land base:

> Four years' careful study of the situation here makes me feel that the thing will have to be done, and as it will take some time to do, the time now seems right to start the work.
>
> The Hopis are branching out far more than I had anticipated under encouragement, and this brings more friction and trouble between them and the Navajos. Something will have to be done to protect them during this and, at the same time, make the Navajos understand they may keep within proper limits of personal action and territory.
>
> It will be a delicate, important work and only the most reliable disinterested persons should be put at it (Miller 1927).

Miller explained that his high regard for the Navajo, and his belief that suffering to both Navajo and Hopi would result if boundary lines were redrawn, had not changed, but he said he realized that if both tribes were to prosper equally well, there must be a separation of Navajo and Hopi interests, and definite land boundries must be established for the proper administration of the two.

"Since writing the letter of February 27, which covered my views at the time, the Hopis have spread out so much and we have located so many so far afield—and at such distances from their mesas—in new territories, that additional friction and misunderstanding has developed, and more determined opposition from the Navajos has been encountered," Miller explained. "This we are unable to control under the present conditions, where there is an absence of definite boundaries" (Miller 1928).

The Flagstaff Conference

The federal government has sent investigators to study the Navajo-Hopi situation for decades. Some investigators would recommend segregation, others would say it was not necessary. In 1930, federal bureaucrats decided that it was time to consult Navajos and Hopis about the best solution for the problem. It was decided that delegates from both tribes would convene in Flagstaff, Arizona, to settle the problem once and for all.

The same complaints were consistently levelled between Navajo and Hopi. Hopis would say that Navajos had stolen corn, cattle, or fruits from them or that Navajos had allowed their sheep and cattle to trespass onto Hopi land; counter-allegations would be levelled against Hopis, claiming that Hopis allowed their cattle to trespass onto Navajo grazing areas. Each side accused the other of trespassing onto grazing lands belonging to the other in order to save their own. Over-grazing by both Navajo and Hopi sheep and cattle had become a major problem on reservation lands. In the old days, Navajos would have moved into other areas and Hopis would have founded new villages in fresher lands. Those options no longer existed, so Hopis were forced to struggle for expansion onto lands Navajos had established claims to, and Navajos continued grazing on lands their fathers and grandfathers had settled.

After reviewing the allegations, H. J. Hagerman, a former governor of New Mexico and the leader of a BIA investigative team sent to appraise the situation, and C. L. Walker, then superintendent of the Western Navajo Agency at Tuba City, announced that it was time for Navajo and Hopi to sit down and resolve their differences, with the federal government acting as arbitrator. E. K. Miller also attended the conference. Flagstaff was chosen as the meeting place because it was far from the disputed territory and Hagerman thought it would be a neutral location.

The Flagstaff Conference was convened on November 6, 1930. The Navajo had eleven delegates, and the Hopi had thirteen: five Navajo from Hopi lands and six Navajo from the Western Navajo Agency met with ten Hopi from the 1882 reservation area and three from Moencopi.

In opening the meeting, Hagerman stressed that the government was concerned about repeated complaints and problems between Navajo and Hopi. He pointed out that the conference was an opportunity for both tribes to hammer out a resolution to land, grazing, and water problems. Hagerman said that the government was anxious to protect the rights of both Hopi and Navajo, and he wanted to find out what could be done to define the rights of the Navajo and the Hopi to the areas in question.

"Before asking you to speak, I simply want to emphasize again the fact which I have already tried to bring out, that the lines of the Hopi reservation so-called as now drawn, are simply arbitrary, administrative lines; that these lines are likely to be changed at any time," Hagerman said (Survey of Conditions of Indians in the United States: Navajos in New Mexico and Arizona 1932).

Both Miller and Hagerman were frustrated by the behavior of the Hopi delegates. Because of cultural responsibilities and the fact that they could not make any binding decisions for their tribesmen without consulting village leaders, the Hopi representatives had difficulty carving out land boundaries and making final decisions. Kotka, a Hopi leader, pointed out that "the Hopi Indians are not willing that our boundaries which include the [1882] Hopi reservation should be lessened" (Survey of Conditions 1932).

The Navajo delegates stressed that they were interested in establishing and maintaining clear claims and title to land. Maxwell Yazzie, the chief spokesman for the Navajos at the conference, expressed Navajo concerns when he said, "Of course, with the Navajos it is a land question all the time. We are trying every way possible to get a foot of land here and an inch of land over there and . . . we are not in a position to give any more than we have to " (Survey of Conditions 1932).

It is unclear how the Hopi and Navajo delegates were selected for the conference. Some were acknowledged tribal leaders and village spokesmen. Others were apparently acquaintances of the Tuba City agency head and Miller. Some delegates were given only forty-eight hours' notice before the conference convened. How any delegate could have been in a position to enforce conference decisions is an open question. Apparently, the meeting was a sounding board for federal mediators rather than a serious parley for land boundaries.

In a November 8, 1930, summary of the conference, Miller made the following analysis:

Hopi delegates said they would not commit themselves on any boundary matter, but insisted they wanted a separate jurisdiction and an agent for Hopis only. Would not get together with the Navajo delegates on any questions or footing. Said they could and would not act for tribe. Kotka said that his people could not get together on any proposition of this nature. The conservative element said little; the Bolshivik element took control of the speaking. Otto Lomavita and Joe Sekakuku doing most of the speaking. It was the usual outcome when Hopis try to do anything collectively.

Navajo delegates tried hard to get the Hopi delegates to do something—to take a prominent part in the conference to get some results satisfactory to the two tribes and the government. They tried to meet with the Hopis and arrange with them for some proposal on the boundaries between the tribes. Their speakers urged the Hopis to act in this matter to the end that the friction between the two tribes be ended once and for all. They accused the Hopis of making the reports and fomenting the trouble and insisted now they show their hands and the Navajos would go the limit to please them. The Navajos said they . . . thought that the separate agent and reservation should be a solution (Miller, Memo about the Flagstaff Conference 1930).

In retrospect, some Hopi today say that the Navajo promised to agree with whatever the Hopi would determine appropriate as a "show for the Americans. After all, all of them were already living on our Hopi homeland. They had nothing to lose" (Sidney interview 1986).

It is further recalled that Miller had taken a personal dislike to some Hopi delegates because they were seeking more economic development for their people, and he preferred the Navajo to the Hopi. "He didn't like some of the Hopis who were advocating energy development. Because he didn't like them, he called them Bolshiviks," one Hopi explained.

Nothing was finalized or settled at the Flagstaff conference. Despite the failure to resolve inter-tribal differences, Hagerman said in his dispatch to the commissioner of Indian affairs that the meeting was not a total waste. He said that he felt that since the Hopi had been asked to come to the conference table, and were actually being consulted by the federal government about the land problem, that they would be forced to come to a workable agreement with the Navajo, or at least submit the matter to arbitration and settlement by the United States government.

Hagerman was dismayed by what he perceived as Hopi stubborn-ness. He stated that "the Hopis have been misled by over-zealous friends and by the working of the proclamation creating the present [1882] Hopi Reservation into believing in a vague and indefinite . . . nevertheless stubborn way that they are entitled to the exclusive right not only to the area comprised in the present so-called Hopi Reserva-tion, but to a much larger country outside it" (Hagerman 1930).

In what was likely a misinterpretation of Hopi history, Hagerman pointed out that until recently, Hopi had confined their land occu-pancy for agricultural and grazing purposes to a "comparatively lim-ited and quite definitely defined area surrounding the Hopi mesas and to a small area in and around Moencopi Wash" (Hagerman 1930). He also stressed that if segregation was imposed, "it will be quite out of the question to secure from them as a tribe, agreement with or consent to any specific area or areas which may be set aside for their exclusive use. This is because they are congenitally indisposed to reach conclu-sions and because even if they were so disposed, they cannot come to formal agreement upon themselves. They have no tribal organization. There is a different chief for each village now, as there has been for the past 300 years, and it is going to be very difficult, even if it were desir-able, to change this system of theirs" (Hagerman 1930).

The most important conclusion that federal arbitrators reached as a result of the conference was the realization that unless a definite solu-tion was offered, equitable to both tribes and enforced by the govern-ment, relationships between Navajo and Hopi would continue to dete-riorate, and conflict would inevitably result. "It is clearly the duty of the government to act promptly," Hagerman wrote.

AFTER THE CONFERENCE

After the Flagstaff conference, the government continued to investigate problems between the tribes; studying the feasibility of separation and relocation for almost another fifty years. No action would be taken on such ideas until after lengthy court battles and congressional enact-ment of the 1974 Navajo and Hopi Land Settlement Act. It is possible that the massive relocation effort would never have been necessary, had both Navajo and Hopi utilized negotiation opportunities in 1930, but cultural differences led to a predictable negotiation impasse and the relocation law did come to pass.

Apparently, neither Navajo nor American understood how the Hopi viewed land tenure, while the Hopi didn't understand Anglo or Navajo perspectives on land acquistion. Hopi have consistently pointed out that the only reason their forefathers spent so much time on the mesa tops from 1700 through the 1900s was because of enemy raiding. They have also noted that lands radiating out around the mesas were part of the Hopi homeland and many Hopi farmed great distances from their mesas. Even though Hopi clans and families might not actually live on the flatlands, allotments had been made according to clan and theocratic tradition. When it became clear that Navajo encroachment was a problem, Hopi leaders developed an extensive village development and resettlement plan. The Hopi say that this plan was merely a reinforcement of settlement patterns prior to the difficult raiding days of the eighteenth and nineteenth centuries.

Navajos see it somewhat differently. The Navajo view of land acquisition and settlement is more comparable to the American view: if land appears empty, settle on it and wait to see what happens. Hopis view this as aggressive exploitation; Navajos and Americans view it as homesteading.

The government took no action on segregation recommendations until after the Hopi had won several federal lawsuits in 1974; as Hagerman had predicted in 1930, relations between the tribes deteriorated and emotions became more heated. In 1934, Congress further expanded Navajo Reservation lines and the tribe's boundaries in Arizona were firmly established. Congress set aside land for Navajos and "such other Indians as are already settled thereon." These included Hopis at Moencopi and some Paiutes.

Collier's Stock Reduction Campaign

As Navajo and Hopi herds expanded, overgrazing resulted and an arid land started to become desertified. John Collier, the commissioner of Indian affairs from 1933 to 1945, became concerned about the damage the herds were doing to the land. He became concerned about the impact overgrazing would have on both Navajo and Hopi survival. Millions of acres had been damaged by resulting erosion as sheep and goats ate away the protective mantle of ground vegetation.

A 1935 survey of Navajo and Hopi reservation lands showed that the range could support about 560,000 sheep units (a "sheep unit" is the measure of forage eaten by one sheep). When the Diné returned from the Long Walk in 1868, the government provided them with sheep and goats, and their flock represented about 20,000 sheep units. By 1928, Navajo flocks measured more than 1 million sheep units. Collier felt that a crisis was at hand, and decided that strict measures needed to be imposed to save the land and the people. Steps toward stock reduction had been taken earlier, but Collier made it mandatory and enforced it. In 1937, land management and grazing districts were established, and by the end of the year, Collier mandated an across-the-board reduction of 10%, after meeting with the Navajo Tribal Council and receiving their approval. Both Navajo and Hopi herds would be affected by the reduction.

In setting up grazing districts, a large portion of the Hopi Reservation was included in what was called District 6, some 6,631,194 acres of land intended strictly for Hopi use. The number of Hopi sheep, too, would be reduced.

To the anguish and horror of both Navajo and Hopi, all their herds suffered the 10% reduction. To a people who measure wealth by the numbers of their flocks, reduction was a cruel and bizarre thing. Even though government officials bought the stock for cash, to Navajos and Hopis living on a barter economy, cash was not adequate compensation. The era of stock reduction is remembered with revulsion by members of both tribes, and has had a direct impact on resistance to relocation and Public Law 93-531 as well.

The Court Case—The Coming of Partition and Relocation

Tensions between Navajo and Hopi tribesmen were played out in their respective tribal councils. The Hopi were adamant that the 1882 reservation was meant for their use only, and they wanted Navajos off of the land. More and more Navajos had moved onto the 1882 area, and the Hopi were upset by the increasing numbers of Navajo moving onto their ancestral homelands in what had become the 1934 congressionally approved addition to the Navajo Reservation.

By the 1950s, the Hopi decided to take the boundary dispute to the federal courts. In 1958, Congress enacted legislation allowing the tribes to take the land fight into the courtroom. During federal hearings in Prescott, Arizona, the Hopi as plaintiffs pled that the 1882 reservation should be their exclusive use area. They argued that this area was only a small part of their original homeland, and they wanted at least the 1882 area for their own people.

The Navajo argued that the Hopi should be limited strictly to the District 6 grazing area, one-fifth of their Executive Order area and a very small sliver of what the Hopi claimed as their ancestral land. On August 2, 1961, the official court case, called *Healing v. Jones* (the names of the heads of the two tribal councils), was filed in United States District Court. One year later, on September 28, 1962, the court handed down a decision. Major points in the decision included:

1. Neither tribe obtained any vested rights in the 1882 Executive Order area.

2. Under a 1943 administrative action establishing the exclusive Hopi grazing district, the Hopi obtained exclusive rights to Grazing District 6.

3. Because of a clause in the 1882 Executive Order establishing the Hopi reservation stipulating "Hopis and other such Indians as the Secretary of the Interior sees fit to settle thereon," and as a result of Navajo movement onto the land with federal awareness and implicit federal permission, Navajo living on the 1882 area outside of District 6 could remain on the land.

4. The Hopi Tribe and the Navajo Tribe, subject to the trust title of the United States, have a joint, undivided and equal interest in the entire 1882 Executive Order Reservation, outside of Land Management District 6.

5. The federal court had no authority to partition the land, only Congress could approve such action.

Neither tribe was satisfied with the *Healing v. Jones* decision. Navajos maintained that they had legitimate claims to 1882 lands. Hopis were upset that they were unable to gain federally approved exclusive rights. So the tribes began pressuring Congress through their attorneys and lobbying firms.

Tensions between Navajo and Hopi reached a fever pitch during the years between 1962 and 1974 as a result of the court decision and the Hopi push for exclusive rights. In 1974, after extensive lobbying by both sides, after public relations campaigns and appeals for public support by both tribes, Congress enacted legislation calling for partition of the 1882 area and relocation of Indians living on the inappropriate side of the partition line. The law, called the 1974 Navajo and Hopi Land Settlement Act, was signed by President Gerald Ford on December 22, 1974. Each tribe received 900,000 acres of the 1.8 million acres of formerly shared land. Everyone on the inappropriate side of the partition line was to voluntarily move by July 6, 1986.

At the time the law was enacted, Congress was not really sure how many people were living in the affected area. A census indicated approximately 8,000 Navajo and 100 Hopi. Subsequent amendments to the relocation law would provide financial compensation for relocatees, replacement lands for the Navajo Tribe to ease their loss of land in the 1882 area, and replacement homes for all relocatee families.

The Hopi did not view the law as a victory. To the tribal council, they had helped their tribe regain only a small portion of ancestral lands that had been lost to the Navajo. To many Hopi traditionalists, the law meant absolutely nothing. They had never recognized the legitimacy of the federal government or the Hopi tribal council to interfere in their affairs with the Navajos anyway.

To the Navajo tribal council, the law was a defeat. Tribal Chairman Peter MacDonald and members of his staff and the Navajo tribal bureaucracy developed a public relations campaign alleging that relocation of Navajo from Hopi lands was tantamount to genocide. Non-Navajos and non-Hopis who support this point of view compared the law to everything from Nazi concentration camps to South African apartheid.

But it had taken the federal government almost a century to make the decision for partition and relocation. It was not a hastily conceived plan to undermine the development of the Navajo tribe. Nor was it the result of an energy conspiracy, as some would have the public believe, even today. Both Hopi and Navajo requested that the federal government make a decision about the boundary problem. After years of study, reports, and finally, court cases, the government made a decision.

Events leading up to the relocation law started in the 1860s, when American aggression drove the Navajo into the Hopi homeland. For years, the government tried to get the tribes to work out the problem themselves, but cultural differences, coupled with ignorance on the part of federal mediators about both Navajo and Hopi perspectives, made that impossible. Since both Navajo and Hopi continued to pound on doors in Washington, D.C., for assistance in the land squabble, Washington was finally forced to act. After a century of evaluation, federal bureaucrats felt that they had found the only viable solution.

The government established a Navajo and Hopi Indian Relocation Commission, headquartered in Flagstaff, Arizona, and mandated that completion of the awesome task of relocating thousands of Indians be completed by July 6, 1986. The stage was set for the next chapter in the struggle for land in the House of Dawn, the resistance to the land settlement act.

6

RELOCATION AND THE 1934 LAND FIGHT

Relocation came as a shock to traditional people. Even though they were familiar with the intertribal conflicts over land use, few were prepared to deal with the drastic changes intended to solve the dispute. Public Law 93-531 mandated the voluntary relocation of Navajo and Hopi people and established the Navajo and Hopi Indian Relocation Commission under the administrative guidance of three politically appointed commissioners to carry out the order and provide appropriate housing for relocatees. The law ordered that the Relocation Commission try to minimize the adverse impacts of relocation on the families and ordered replacement homes and cash incentives to encourage families to move as quickly as possible.

Thousands of Navajos signed up for relocation. The process of qualification for relocation homes and benefits is long and tedious, and many volunteers are still waiting to make their move. Some Navajos quickly obeyed the law and moved and then applied for benefits; some of them have yet to receive the replacement homes and benefits promised them under the law. Other Navajos have refused to sign up for relocation, vowing that they will never break the ties to their homeland.

Partition and relocation was not a hastily made decision, but surprised both Navajo and Hopi people living on the former Joint Use Area. Approximately 8,000 Navajos were affected by the relocation order. By contrast, only about 100 Hopis were affected, and for the most part, they quickly applied for relocation and moved. But interviews with both Hopi and Navajo relocatees have indicated that neither group was happy about moving. All the Hopis have complied with the law, and most Navajos have as well, but both have explained that they still have fond recollections of their former homes and are saddened by memories of the move.

Despite the fact that some families have done well since relocation, there have been aspects of the law and the move that have upset everyone. In the Navajo mind, the very word "relocation" conjures up a nightmare of memories from the Kit Carson days. "Relocation" was the word Americans used during the forced marches to Bosque Redondo, when the New Mexico Volunteers hunted down and captured Navajos, burned their homes, their orchards and cornfields, and slaughtered their livestock. To have relocation reimposed, regardless of the reasons, was a frightening prospect, especially to the older people. Confusion about why the law had been enacted, coupled with rumors about potential federal military round-ups and forced marches by the decreed July 6, 1986, deadline day if Navajos did not comply with the law, circulated throughout the former Joint Use Area. The Navajo Tribal Administration was disgruntled about losing in court and having their people subjected to the partition and relocation, and so they did little to cooperate with the relocation program or to dispel the rumors. Between 1974 and 1982, the Navajo Tribe spent millions of dollars in lobbying attempts to repeal or modify the law. Meanwhile, Navajos in the former JUA listened to rumors and became confused and depressed about what they heard. It was in 1982, after an election that brought new individuals into office, that the tribal administration made an aggressive effort to educate Navajos about relocation and to explain to people on the grass-roots level why the law had come to pass.

Further complicating the relocation scenario was the reintroduction of stock reduction to the JUA in 1973. According to BIA records, the agency was trying to restore lands badly overgrazed by both Navajo and Hopi sheep and goats. The reduction affected both Navajo and Hopi families, but it evoked bad memories of Collier's stock reduction program in the 1930s. Navajos felt as if the Hopi and the BIA were trying to starve them out. It seemed as if the collective nightmare of traditional Navajos had come true.

The stock-reduction years are remembered with bitterness by both tribes. When stock reduction measures were reintroduced, memories of the past added a horrifying element to the relocation scenario. Navajos and Hopis remembered that in 1937, land management and grazing districts had been established. Even though Collier had discussed the reduction plan with Navajo tribal leaders in the 1920s and received tribal council approval for the measure, Navajos still remember it as plan imposed upon them by the federal government. The most disturbing element to Navajos was the 10% reduction. In some instances, after buying the peoples' stock for cash, agents ordered the animals killed on the spot, before the horrified eyes of families who had raised them from birth. To see their animals bought and slaughtered for no apparent reason was horrifying to all Navajos. In their minds, it just didn't make sense, and what they perceived as senseless slaughter brought disharmony and sickness into their world.

Even today, the Collier era of stock reduction, BIA stock reduction in the disputed partitioned lands, and relocation are all interrelated in the Navajo psyche. Many times during research visits with Navajos in the disputed area, elderly women and men have broken into tears while recounting their stories of the origins of relocation, and many times the relocation story begins with the period of the Collier stock reduction programs. To these people, stock reduction was almost as bad as being forced to sell their own children to the government and then having the government kill them.

Upset about partition and relocation, facing stock reduction, and unable to improve or expand their own hogans to house their children or build special ones for ceremonies due to a construction freeze imposed on both Navajo and Hopi residents of the disputed land, their world seemed an oppressive place. Navajo chapters affected by the partition held meetings to discuss the situation and to try and figure out a way to change the law. "Why are the Hopis doing this to us," was a question raised at the time of partition and is one repeated today. "It seems like they are trying to destroy us," many Navajo nataani have said.

Most Navajos do not remember that Hopis were subject to stock reduction, too; most are so caught up in their own misery that they do not care that Hopi families had to move, too, and that Hopis have suffered the same sense of hopelessness, loss, and confusion as a result of relocation.

In contrast to the concerns of many traditional people, some Navajos saw the relocation law as an opportunity to get away from a difficult life. Since the 1950s and 1960s, younger Navajos had been moving off-reservation to work in the cash-based American economy and make money, while retaining weekend, ceremonial, and vacation ties to their parents' and grandparents' traditional use areas. Many younger Navajos saw relocation and relocation benefits as a way to become better integrated into American society—a way to get a better education, better employment, and a more contemporary lifestyle.

Housing and construction freezes imposed by the federal courts while awaiting a final determination in the 1882 dispute had made life in the JUA overcrowded and uncomfortable, and so the first rush of relocation applicants included many young Navajos who were eager to leave the JUA. Many of them had already had experiences living off-reservation, and they viewed relocation as a mixed blessing. Willing relocatees realized that by accepting relocation benefits, they would be forever closing the door to the peaceful traditional life of sheep-herding, medicinal plant gathering, farming, and a barter economy. They knew that they were leaving one way of life for another. It made them sad to think of leaving the traditional world, but the opportunity for housing with modern conveniences, electricity, hot and cold running water, and employment for those that chose off-reservation, border homesites was also appealing. Many young people were willing to take a chance and relocate, but they were worried about how relocation would affect their elders.

Even Navajos who eagerly signed up for relocation to other parts of the Navajo Reservation or to reservation border towns were concerned about the future of their parents, grandparents, and the traditional elders. While many relocatees were willing to accept benefits for themselves and their immediate families, they wanted their extended families and elders to be left in peace, living on their traditional homeland in their own Navajo way. But the law was clear—relocation of both Navajo and Hopi was to be completed by July 1986.

The "Life-Estate" Concept

Concerns for the elders and the adverse impacts relocation could have on the older traditional Navajos led Senator Barry Goldwater (R-Arizona) to seek alternatives to relocation for the old Navajo nataani. After consulting with Navajo and Hopi tribal leadership, Goldwater offered a solution for the Navajo elders. He suggested a life-estate concept, which would allow Navajos over a certain age to remain on the land, even if it was Hopi partition land, for the rest of their lives. Younger Navajos would have to relocate, but older people could remain.

The life-estate concept was opposed by the Navajo Tribe for many reasons. First, the tribe did not want to officially accept the partition of the land—they did not want to accept the Hopi side of the partition as Hopi land, as they officially and publicly maintained that it was Navajo land. Lobbying efforts to change or repeal the law were in progress, and the tribe felt that it would not be politically astute to accept the partition and the life-estate program. Second, the tribe opposed it on the grounds that families should not be split up and separated from each other. As a result, it was never adequately explained to the Navajo elders, and rumors circulated that the life-estate was really a cruel plan to isolate the elders and starve them out by preventing Navajo family members from giving their relatives the support needed for daily life.

Navajo family life revolves around the extended family, with each family member fulfilling certain roles. Children herd the sheep; mothers and aunties cook and take care of family business; men tend the livestock and haul the water; grandmothers and grandfathers look out after their animals during the lambing, calving, and shearing seasons; and everyone works to support the family. Because of the need for close family ties in Navajo agrarian life, few Navajos signed up for the life-estate plan, and all ultimately withdrew their requests after succumbing to pressure from the Navajo Tribe.

Explaining Relocation to the Navajo People

Navajo Tribal Chairman Peter MacDonald and other representatives of the Navajo Tribal Administration told traditional people that they would find a way to modify or repeal the law, so that Navajos would not have to move. They continued to make such promises, filling traditional Navajo hearts with hope, until MacDonald's 1982 electoral defeat by Peterson Zah, a man from Low Mountain Chapter in the affected area.

After reviewing the law and discussing the possibility of repeal with congressional leaders, Zah decided that repeal was not a viable option. As a result, Zah did not promise the Navajo people that he would repeal the law, but instead, began to look for ways to modify the adverse effects of relocation, and tried to offer the Hopi land exchanges in return for land on the Hopi side of the former Joint Use Area. Zah sent his staff people out to explain to Navajos on the grass-roots level why the law had happened and he worked closely with the federal Relocation Commission to find ways to minimize the effects of relocation on Navajo people. Zah understands relocation well, because members of his family have had to relocate three times as a result of redrawing grazing district boundaries and finally, due to the relocation law itself.

"I remember my grandmother and grandfather and other extended family discussing it [the land dispute]," Zah explained. "The way they couched the whole controversy was that somebody somewhere made a mistake and just put the two groups on top of each other on the land in a small given area and that it had to be resolved in some way and that it was unfortunate that my particular family and extended family had to take the brunt of what was happening just because somebody made a mistake years ago."

Zah sent out staff members to explain "the mistake" and the history of relocation to the people, while attempting to work out a comprehensive settlement plan that would include parts of the 1882 disputed area as well as the western Navajo lands affected by the 1934 land dispute. In the spring and summer of 1985, Miller Nez, a special assistant to Zah and a respected medicineman from the White Cone area on the edge of the disputed lands, travelled throughout chapters in the

Western Navajo Agency and chapters affected by the partition to explain why Navajos had to move. Nez made presentations at over twenty chapters and used the illustration of a giant tree to explain the situation to the people.

"Look at this tree," Nez explained to an audience packed in the stuffy heat of a summer afternoon at the Tolani Lake Chapter House. "The deep roots of this old tree go way back to 1882. Back then, even though many of our families were already living on this land, the president in Washington signed a law creating the Hopi Reservation. Look at the many branches of the tree. Some of them are legal cases that the Hopis filed against us. Others are laws that Congress enacted, like Public Law 93-531, which divided the land between Navajos and Hopis. Because of these branches and the relocation laws, some of us have to move."

Under the guidance of the Zah administration, people like Miller Nez explained relocation in a way traditional people could understand. But even with understanding, relocation is distasteful to the Navajo, and many families are still unwilling to move. Zah lost his 1986 re-election bid to current Navajo Tribal Chairman Peter MacDonald. MacDonald has continued Zah's work toward a comprehensive settlement plan for disputed lands in the 1934 and the old 1882 areas, and he seems to have given up any hope of repealing the relocation law.

Relocation of Navajos from the Hopi partitioned lands slowly proceeds, but not without some resistance, especially by Navajos whose families have been in the region for over a century.

Resistance to Relocation

The first shots of traditional Navajo resistance to a decision made by non-Indians two thousand miles and a different culture away were fired in 1979, by a Navajo grandmother from the Big Mountain area. Congress had enacted the relocation law, but left its implementation to the Relocation Commission and the BIA. As part of implementation, fencing of the partitioned areas was mandated to remind the tribes whose land was where. When a BIA fencing crew, composed primarily of Navajos, started fencing off the partition line around the traditional use area of Big Mountain nataani Katherine Smith, then seventy-nine years old, she got out her shotgun and fired warning shots over the crew's heads. She gave them a lecture about undermining fellow Navajos and sent them scuttling on their way. Since that day, a parade of journalists, politicians, and curiosity seekers have found their way to Big Mountain, and the parade continues today.

Residents of Big Mountain are not the only Navajos opposed to relocation, but they are the most organized of the relocatees, and their voices have been heard throughout the world. They opposed the relocation law prior to its enactment, and a determined handful of Big Mountain families have sworn that they will resist moving until the end of their lives. Relocatees from Coal Mine Mesa, Tolani Lake, and other affected chapters have made similar vows, but they have not received the attention of the Big Mountain Navajos.

In an interview two years after the shooting incident, Katherine Smith explained why she stopped the fencing crew. Her feelings reflect the sentiments of many Navajos from the JUA. "I went out to ask them what they were doing. And they said this land does not belong to the Navajos—it belongs to the Hopis. But that's a lie, a big, big lie," the elder explained. "It's our land and I fired over their heads to keep that fencing crew away . . . . This is our land, I know it."

Big Mountain residents have held meeting after meeting with representatives of the Relocation Commission, Congress, the BIA, the American Indian Movement, Navajo Tribal Chairmen Peter MacDonald and Peterson Zah, and Hopi Tribal Chairman Ivan Sidney in an attempt to explain what the land means to them and why some Navajos will never relocate.

According to reports of the Navajo Tribe, there are 828 families resisting relocation (Report of the Navajo-Hopi Land Dispute Task Force 1987). Resistance numbers vary, depending upon the agency or tribe involved. The Hopi Tribe maintains that there are no more than 50 resisting families; the Relocation Commission insists that there are approximately 300 families. It is difficult to assess which claims are most accurate.

Of about 1,000 Navajos living around the Big Mountain area, there is a core of between 15 to 35 families who have vowed to resist relocation. Many of these families receive assistance from what is now called the Survival Camp, originally known as the AIM camp in 1981, when Navajo AIM leader Larry Anderson and non-Navajo AIM members came to Big Mountain to show their support for Navajo elders resisting relocation and the accompanying fencing, stock impoundment, and stock reduction conducted by the BIA.

Not all Big Mountain Navajos have refused to comply with relocation, but all stand united in their concern about the future of their elders and the future of the traditional Navajo way of life. The most active, vocal, and articulate leaders of the resistance movement have been the Navajo women. Elders like Roberta Blackgoat and Mae Tso have taken time from their sheep herding, their weaving, and the daily routine of Big Mountain life to travel throughout the United States to explain their position to the American people. They have repeatedly appealed to the Navajo Tribal Council to assist them in their struggle. The women have been supported by family and clan members in their resistance and many of them have been arrested after run-ins with BIA fencing crews, stock impoundment crews, and BIA police.

On July 21, 1983, several Big Mountain women, accompanied by other Navajos opposed to relocation, travelled to the Navajo capital at Window Rock to present their views before the tribal council. Among the women who presented testimony to the council were Katherine Smith and her daughter Sally Tsosie,* Mae Tso,** and Grace Smith of Teesto. Their words before the council sum up how most Navajos resisting relocation feel. The women were concerned about livestock reduction and the relocation program. They were, and continue to be, concerned about the future of their children, and the survival of traditional Navajo culture.

"We at Big Mountain are a suffering group of people," Mae Tso told the council. "We are undergoing all sorts of pressure day and night. When you are under such pressure, men and women are dying off. We are suffering all kinds of losses—human losses . . . when you have a government do this to you, how can you honor it? . . . Actually, it is like undergoing a warfare. We can see how they come in on us with handcuffs, weapons, clubs. How can any uneducated female cope with this? We have our children being affected—they are young— but when they have to go through this you can see how it hurts them. I myself have been a herder and a weaver. This is all I can do to get by. When they took my livestock away, you could see that it meant [my own] being taken away [to jail]."

Mae expressed the feelings of hundreds of other Navajo people from the former Joint Use Area when she expressed concerns about people "dying off" from the pressure and confusion of relocation. In the Navajo belief system, illness and death come from being out of harmony with the world. The ultimate goal in Navajo life is to "walk in beauty," that is, to be in balance and harmony with the natural and supernatural world. It is difficult to achieve harmony in a world filled with fear, confusion, and paranoia. Any sickness, argument or acciden-

---

*Sally Tsosie had been involved in an earlier federal relocation program, which placed Indians in urban jobs. She is the mother of Clayton Lonetree, the United States Marine who became involved in a scandal while on embassy duty in Moscow. During a court-martial, Lonetree was convicted of thirteen counts of espionage and sentenced to thirty years imprisonment. Both prosecutors and defense attorneys have stated that the treatment of Native Americans and the relocation program influenced Lonetree's perceptions of the federal government.

**Previous to the Window Rock meeting, Mae Tso had an ugly run-in with BIA police, who were in the process of impounding her horses when she confronted them. Mae told them to stop, and in the resulting fracas, she was arrested and her wrist was sprained when police wrestled with her.

tal death is viewed with suspicion in the Big Mountain area (as in other traditional areas) and many people believe that these things are caused in part by the relocation.

Big Mountain elders, along with many Hopi Traditionalists, link strip-mining operations and mine dewatering with a lowering of local water tables and the drying up of springs that formerly flowed year round. Peabody Coal uses a water-based slurry line to transport coal from mining operations on Black Mesa over three hundred miles away to Bullhead City on the Colorado River. The water is dumped after it reaches its final destination. Elders view utilization of millions of gallons of water to move coal as bizarre; to people who live in this arid land, this is a shocking and shameful waste of water, their most precious resource.

Many elders view relocation as part of a greater conspiracy, a way for corporations and the federal government to move people off of the land to get at the minerals. They link the relocation law with high Navajo infant mortality rates and what they perceive as a rise in their own JUA death rate. They say that they have seen an increase in the number of suicides and the degree of public drunkenness and alcoholism since the advent of relocation.

Peabody Coal has denied any intention of moving mining operations into the Big Mountain area. They point out that 85% of their workers on Black Mesa are Navajo. Some Navajos have advanced to foremen and assistant supervisor positions, and have involvement in mine policy and decision making. In fact, many Navajos from the Big Mountain area are employed in Black Mesa coal operations, and both the Navajo and the Hopi tribes hold rights and accrue revenues from the operations. But the perception of relocation linked to energy resource exploitation lingers in the minds of Big Mountain Navajos, and the belief has been explained to non-Indians by Big Mountain people and their national support organizations. Whatever the reasons, stress is an important factor in the lives of former JUA residents, and to many traditional people, life has become a living nightmare.

Mae Tso and other Navajo women described the nightmare in their testimonies to the Navajo Tribal Council. "Having suffered lately in this fashion, I can see what it does to your mind," Mae Tso explained. "It is just terrifying . . . . We can see our children suffer, our homes are ruined . . . . [We have lived here longer than the] last one hundred years, for a long time we have had people there. I have nothing else but the living . . . . We don't ever want to move off. We want to stay on our land. Of course, everything goes with us. Perhaps they have their law. Same thing with us; we have our own religion, our sacred mountains. This is our law, the is the way we live."

The women were expressing sincere feelings and beliefs when they discussed stress and their ties to the land. Land is sacred to Big Mountain Navajos, and to other Navajos as well. It may be a difficult concept for non-Indians to understand, but it is very real. Thoughts of relocation do create trauma and stress among traditional Navajo, not only because they do not understand the relocation mandate, but because of religious and emotional ties to the land.

Relocation and Religion

Navajo residents of the partitioned JUA were among the most traditional Indians remaining in North America. The inroads of Americanization were making progress prior to the enactment of the relocation law, as the old herding and barter economy was being eroded by the shift to a cash economy. Many younger JUA Navajos were finding jobs in off-reservation towns and moving away from Navajoland to larger urban centers. However, relocation accelerated the gradual process and the resulting stress has made the elders worry about physical, cultural, and religious survival.

Big Mountain Navajos have a strong traditional relationship with their homeland. They have said that they believe they came into this world by crawling through the same reed from the lower world with the Hopi. Such a belief has not been expressed in conversations with Navajos from other parts of the reservation, and the long history of inter-marriage and kinship with certain Hopi villages demonstrates that genetically speaking, the two groups are uniquely related. Like other traditional Navajos throughout the Four Corners region, Big Mountain people continue the practice of planting a child's umbilical cord alongside a young tree, integrating the life of the child into the sacred ground and into the life of the tree itself.

Traditional Navajos are tied to the earth not only by the umbilical cord, but also by special religious shrines, trees from which wood is used for cradle boards, ceremonial bows and prayer sticks, and natural holy places. Springs are sites not only for water, but also for ritual purification. Some areas have special significance to particular families or clans, other sites are important holy places for the entire tribe.

Ceremonial plant-gathering sites and shrines important to Navajo and Hopi alike abound throughout the former JUA and especially around the Big Mountain region. Elements of traditional Navajo religion are linked with the use of special ceremonial herbs and plants. Some plants grow only in certain places, and it takes several generations for people to become familiar with specific plants' habitats. Big

Mountain and the Black Mesa region are full of such plants and such knowledge. Many Navajo nataani fear that once relocation is completed, all the knowledge and power of their way of life will be lost forever.

Navajos make offerings at special shrines, where their prayers are carried by the winds to the Holy People. Sometimes, an individual or family knows the appropriate prayers and offerings themselves; sometimes the services of medicine people are necessary in special prayers. Corn pollen and precious stones are frequent offerings. Prayers; blessings for crops, homes, families; and the location of family shrines and medicinal plant-gathering sites are passed down from generation to generation.

Traditional Navajos believe that there are natural rhythms to life, and that people are placed on a special space on earth. They are supposed to learn to understand that place, its terrain and its unique aspects. They feel that it is unnatural for any man to order another man where to live or how to live. This is one of many reasons why relocation is frustrating and disturbing to traditional people.

"Life is where the sheeps are," one old Navajo explained through an interpreter. "It will be up to me to tend them and through that I could get what I need and what I want. Then, they told me of a home, so I built a hogan . . . . Then I got a cornfield. But then I needed help so my folks suggested I get a wife and have children. That is part of life. All this made me think of the land, water, and grazing for livestock. I need all of that to survive. Then, besides that, there are offerings needed along the way. There are songs and prayers needed to help me along, so they taught me some songs and I learned some prayers. I learned of sacred places where I could go to and make my offerings and give my thanks . . . ." (Cahn and MacDonald 1982).

The old man explained that his parents had taught him that land is where all the family and ancestral memories are, and where his children and grandchildren will carry on. ". . . We know the land, we know the sacred places, we know where all the waters are and the land knows us. And so will my children. We will know it and the land knows us . . ." (Cahn and MacDonald 1982).

As JUA Navajos have signed up for relocation and left the area, they did it knowing that they were leaving family land and their past lives on that land. Many have found success in their new lives, but even those who have accepted relocation express concerns that their children will never know the serenity of traditional life. Many have said that they are happy to have had an opportunity to achieve success in the mainstream of the dominant society, but they are saddened by the erosion of the old ways.

Protecting the Elders

The overall concern for both Navajo relocatees and Navajos resisting relocation is the impact of relocation on the "elderlies," as they call older Navajos. Young people frequently comply, but they support the resistance of their parents or grandparents to the relocation program. One such supporter of resistance who has dedicated his life to the protection of the "elderlies" is Big Mountain Navajo Willie Lone Wolf Scott.

Scott, twenty-seven, is a full-time resident of the Big Mountain Survival Camp. During interviews in spring of 1986, he explained that he was a grandson of Katherine Smith and that he was worried about relocation and what would happen if people were forced to move against their wills. Scott was one of four young Indian men arrested by BIA police during a fracas with a BIA fencing crew on Big Mountain in March of 1986. The case was finally settled after hearings in Hopi Tribal Court, where prosecution was suspended after an agreement was worked out between the men and the Hopi Tribe.

"In this part of the country here, we follow direction from our elderlies," Scott explained. "All of us Navajos living at the camp here are home-based. I grew up around here and I still speak my traditional tongue and practice my traditional culture and my religion. I call myself a traditional. I am doing something here because I am a voice for my people. I am a voice for my elderlies."

Scott explained that many Navajo elders do not understand or read English, so he travels with them and translates for them. He said that he and other young Navajos were at the camp at the request of the nataani, to keep watch on the activities of the Hopi and the BIA and to help the elders herd sheep, chop wood, and get food and medical supplies.

Scott explained that he grew up hearing about the land dispute, but it was only in recent years that he had come to understand how the dispute developed and why relocation was ordered. "I was twelve years old when the law was made in 1974," Scott said. "I didn't really understand what was going on until the fencing started in 1977. I wondered why the law happened. I saw the fear and suffering it has caused to my relatives and I decided that I must do my part as a warrior and a protector for my people. I follow the instructions of my grandmother and Kee Shay and the other elders. That is why I am here, to help them."

Scott said that Navajos who want to move should go ahead and relocate, but no one should be forced to leave their home. When asked what he thought the best solution to the relocation problem was, he had a succinct answer that reflects the feelings of many others. "Repeal the law. That's the one thing that is behind all of this."

Concerns about Relocation Violence

For years prior to the slated July 6, 1986, relocation completion date, concerns about what would happen on the deadline day circulated throughout the former JUA and among assorted anti-relocation support groups. A number of non-Indian groups focused international attention on the Navajo struggle for repeal and the impact that relocation had on various Navajos.

Partially in an attempt to defuse the perceived potential for violence and partially out of a realization of the complexities of the Navajo-Hopi land struggle, AIM co-founder Russell Means travelled to the disputed area in March 1986 to study the situation. Means, a Lakota Sioux, was once married to a Hopi woman from First Mesa and has several children from that marriage. He is now married to a Navajo woman from Chinle, Arizona, and they have one child. He is thus familiar with both cultures and he has children who could be affected by the dispute.

After a tour of the Big Mountain area and a visit to the Hopi partition lands, Means made an appearance before the Hopi Tribal Council and admitted that the land dispute was an extremely complicated and sensitive issue—an issue in which AIM should never have taken a side. Means's statements came as a surprise to those people who viewed relocation as a genocidal conspiracy to destroy the Navajo tribe. In later interviews, the Indian leader expressed concerns for violence originating not with the Navajo or Hopi people themselves, but from those who had attached themselves to the relocation resistance.

Several months before deadline day, BIA Director Ross Swimmer had stated that no Navajos would be forced to move off of the partitioned lands until homes were ready for them, and he promised that no federal marshals would be called to the disputed area on the deadline day. Hopi Tribal Chairman Ivan Sidney also made public statements that no Navajos would be forced off of the land on deadline day, and that Navajos should come and talk to the Hopi tribal leadership about any problems or questions they had related to relocation. Despite the public promises, rumors and confusion prevailed in the region, and no one was sure exactly what would happen.

Events on July 6, 1986, demonstrated that concerns about federal troops removing Navajos from the former JUA and feared clashes between tribes were unrealistic. On the morning of July 6, the Hopi Tribe hosted a prayer breakfast on Second Mesa for several tribal leaders from the Four Corners region, including Zuni, Acoma, and other allied pueblos from the Rio Grande Valley. Together, the Hopi and their allies prayed for peace and the fruitful use of their reacquired homeland.

The next day, July 7, several hundred Navajo veterans joined hands with residents of the Big Mountain area and other land dispute Navajos to pray for peace and justice for Navajos affected by relocation. While over three hundred Navajos prayed for peace and justice, a large contingency of non-Navajos ripped down a section of the partition fence one mile south of Dinebito Trading Post. Other people in the fence protests were individuals who had travelled to Big Mountain to participate or assist in the Plains Sundance, which had wound up just prior to the deadline day.

The fence-cutting protest occurred in Hard Rock Chapter, and Percy Deal, the chapter president, was quoted in several news accounts condemning the action. He said that the damage to the fence could eventually hurt Navajo people because their livestock would wander through the fence and onto Hopi partition lands, where they would risk impoundment by the BIA.

On the whole, relocation deadline day was quiet in the former JUA. But in the weeks prior to and immediately after the deadline, there were some tense moments. In two separate incidents, Navajo police were attacked and disarmed by men in the disputed area. Some of the assailants were Navajo, others were not. The question of outsider provocation has been raised, but nothing has been clearly proven and things have been rather quiet in the region since the passing of the deadline.

In both disarming incidents, police were responding to calls for assistance by fellow Navajos when the confrontations occurred. The Navajo police had been briefed on the potential for violence in the region, and they did their best to avoid confrontation. Navajo police knew that any violent response on their part would fuel the fires of tension and propaganda in the former JUA.

The most celebrated of the provocations occurred after deadline day, on July 25, 1986, when Navajo police were travelling across Hopi partitioned land to a Squaw Dance in the Forest Lake Chapter on Navajo partitioned land. Accounts of the incident vary, but Navajo police have described their vehicle getting stuck in mud while en route to the ceremony, and finding themselves surrounded by approximately ten men, both Navajo and non-Navajo, brandishing rifles. Concerned about the explosive potential of the incident, the police allowed themselves to be disarmed. The threatening men then damaged the squad car radio to prevent police communication with fellow officers in Tuba City or Window Rock. The police later drove to Piñon and radioed for assistance.

The next day, Navajo police apprehended one of the armed men who had provoked the incident. He was a non-Navajo who gave his name as Freman Sanchez. According to news reports printed in the *Arizona Republic* and other papers, ten days later, an Anglo attorney turned up with the weapons in Flagstaff and gave them to the FBI.

It is clear that there was a potential for some violence in the region, particularly in incidents involving stock impoundment and fencing, but many concerns were exaggerated. Both Navajo and Hopi people have a great respect for human life, and it appears that neither group is anxious to ignite the flames of violence. Most non-Indians have left the region since the deadline has come and gone. Rumors of forcible eviction have diminished as more and more Navajo families sign up for relocation and quietly leave the area. Hard-core resisters remain on the land, but no one has yet tried to forcibly remove them.

Relocatee Numbers and Problems

Despite the highly publicized Navajo resistance to relocation, the project continues and has made quiet progress. According to Relocation Commission figures, some 1,416 families have yet to receive relocation certification and benefits. Commission officials have pointed out that approximately 300 of those families currently reside on the Hopi Partition Lands (HPL), and 1,116 Navajo families have already moved from the disputed lands and are waiting to receive their benefits and replacement homes from the government. The Navajo Tribe refers to families who have already moved from the former JUA, but who are still awaiting certification and benefits, as "refugees," saying that the government has not fulfilled its promises to them. Navajo tribal statistics put the number of uncertified "refugee" families at 1,200; the tribe is actively lobbying the federal government to deliver on promises made to these Navajos, who have complied with the law but still have not received their promised benefits. In a response to Navajo tribal allegations, the Relocation Commission released a report which pointed out that there was no deliberate intent to prevent families who had already relocated from receiving their rightful benefits. The report said that many families had moved despite advice to wait on the HPL until they received certification and benefits. "The majority of these families left the HPL to seek employment and for education in other places. As a consequence, most have established lives for themselves in these places," the report states (Evaluation of the Navajo-Hopi Task Force Statement 1987).

By July 1987, a total of 1,211 Indian families had relocated from the partitioned lands. All Hopis living on lands partitioned to the Navajo Tribe had moved, and thousands of Navajos had moved from lands partitioned to the Hopi Tribe.

Eligibility for relocation benefits is determined by federal guidelines interpreted by the Navajo and Hopi Indian Relocation Commission. A total of 36 Hopi families applied for relocation certification and benefits, 23 families were certified eligible, and 13 Hopi families were denied certification. Seven of those families are currently appealing the commission's refusal to certify them for relocation benefits. People can be denied benefits for a number of reasons: not residing full-time on the disputed lands is one of the main ones. Some 4,210 Navajo families have applied for relocation certification and benefits. Of these, 2,582 have been certified and 1,624 families were denied eligibility on the grounds that they were not full-time residents of the HPL. Currently, 568 Navajo families are appealing that denial.

Most relocatees, Navajo and Hopi alike, have accepted relocation and made the best of a difficult situation. Several hundred Navajos who accepted their replacement homes in off-reservation border towns have since sold their homes and returned to live with relatives on the reservation. Some have even sold their homes, accepted their $5,000 relocation compliance bonuses, and returned to live with relatives awaiting or resisting relocation on the disputed lands.

It would be untrue to say that all Navajos have succeeded in life away from their old homes. Many Navajo relocatees did not have the education or English-language skills necessary to blend into off-reservation society. In many cases, the $5,000 relocation bonuses were quickly spent, and relocatees could not find good jobs because they didn't have the skills necessary to find and keep employment. Many Navajo relocatees had never had to deal with utility bills, car payments, or property taxes. As a consequence, it wasn't long before some families got fed up and sold their homes to return to the reservation. Some sold their government-issued replacement homes for a profit and bought more modest homes; others became victims of a system with which they were not familiar.

In May 1985, the Relocation Commission released a report on the status of relocatee replacement homes. As of May 31, 1985, a total of 478 off-reservation replacement homes had been acquired for relocatee families. A review of court records indicated that 68% of relocatee families still owned their replacement homes (a total of 314 houses) and 30.87% (142 houses) had been sold. Of these, 1% (4 houses) had been relinquished to spouses via a Quit Claim Deed as a result of marriage dissolutions.

The older traditional people are among those having the most difficulty in adjusting to off-reservation life. In an interview with one, a Navajo elder, the sadness and confusion of life away from the traditional homeland was clearly illustrated.

The man was in his seventies when he signed up for relocation and moved into a tract house in the Sunset Crater area near Flagstaff, Arizona. He does not speak English, and prior to relocating, his life had revolved around his sheep, his cattle, and his cornfield. In an interview through a translator, he explained his dilemma.

"I once had forty sheeps and sixty cattles. My life was quiet and happy. Then, I signed up for the relocation and I came here. I didn't understand a lot of how things worked around here. Here, I have to pay for the water. Then there is the heat to keep the house warm and to cook. I didn't understand about the thermostat at first, and I used to open the windows when the house got too warm," he explained. "Then there is the land out here and the tax involved with it. It's expensive."

He was confused and disoriented after his move. He has tried to maintain a semblance of his old life by keeping a corn patch behind his new suburban home, but the life of comparative inactivity sapped his strength and has little meaning to him.

Many relocatees feel that they have become lost in a sea of bureaucracy. The Relocation Commission has contracted with a variety of social action groups, including Native Americans for Community Action in Flagstaff, Arizona, for assistance for relocatees mainstreaming into American society and finding suitable employment and counseling. Relocation Commission employees provided pre-move counseling, but there were limits as to how much time could be spent with each family. The Navajo Tribe took minimal steps to educate relocatees about the choices they faced or to provide information as to why they were being relocated and what would be expected of them. The tribe took the position that the law was unfair and they would do their utmost to change it, but also maintained that it was the responsibility of the Relocation Commission to move people and act as a guidance counselor for relocatees.

Many relocatees and Navajos resisting relocation have stated that they feel they have become a kind of political football for the Navajo Tribe. On the one hand, they point out, they either relocate to uncertain futures or sit out on the disputed land, worried about rumors, hearing promises of repeal, modification, or Constitutional challenges to the relocation law. On the other hand, their tribal leaders tell them that they are working on alternative plans to relocation and they should relax and let their leaders work out a solution.

While relocatees worry about their lives and their futures, the Navajo Tribe gains land and financial benefits from the relocation mandate. The tribe accepted the replacement lands guaranteed to it by the relocation law and its amendments. That land was given to the tribe to accommodate Navajo relocatee families. A large stretch of land in northeastern Arizona, contiguous to the Navajo Reservation and stretching along Interstate 40, was selected as replacement land and a few Navajo families have moved onto it. But one of the ranches selected by the tribe as replacement land is the billion-dollar coal rich Paragon Ranch in New Mexico, and plans are under development by the Navajo Tribe to mine the Paragon region. Life in a coal pit is unappealing, and not one Navajo family has yet relocated to the Paragon Ranch.

Relocatees have said that they feel lost in a war of words and paper. Some have even gone so far as to suggest that their way of life is being sacrificed by the tribal government so that the tribe as a whole may gain additional land and financial benefits. They point out that the Hopi Tribe accepted its relocatees onto its own reservation, while the Navajo Tribe has been unable to do the same for its own people. But relocation has many results, and stress in relocatee lives is only one.

ADDITIONAL RELOCATION CONCERNS

Aspects of relocation affect not only Navajo and Hopi relocatee lives, but daily life on the Navajo Reservation and the pocketbooks of American taxpayers as well. Navajo relocatees have expressed concerns about being forced to move off-reservation, because Navajo chapters on the main reservation have often told them they have no room to accommodate additional families.

On a reservation larger than the state of West Virginia, with a population of approximately 200,000 people, such concerns for space may be hard for non-Navajos to understand. But finding room for relocatees on Navajo land is a very real problem, and the problem has caused internal stress among the Navajo.

Within chapters, many families have established grazing rights, utilize traditional-use areas, and have been issued grazing permits for their family livestock. With the increase in Navajo population, many chapters are virtually bulging with people and livestock. Trying to balance a growing population with the traditional grazing areas and the old way of life has become a challenge. In order to move into a new chapter, relocatees must petition the chapter and receive approval of the move and a homesite by chapter officials and individual chapter members. Chapters are concerned about additional overcrowding and over-grazing, and many relocatee applicants have been refused. It is a sad situation, but it has not been done with deliberate malice. It is rather a fact of life. Thus, many relocatees are forced to move off-reservation onto the recently acquired replacement lands or into urban areas.

"It's a very complicated issue to begin with," Peterson Zah explained. "There are certain impacts that happen whenever anyone leaves one community for another. Having to move people against their wills really multiplies into so many other problems. For example, there are certain numbers of people who have moved to the New Lands [the 400,000 acres of replacement lands awarded to the Navajo Tribe] already. Let's say fifteen families . . . . All of those families have kids, children. Where are they to go to school? They are within Sanders School District. But Sanders School District never got itself ready to accept the children that come from those fifteen families, and so in the Fall of '88, let's say five or ten more families have relocated. We're talking twenty to twenty-five families relocated, and if each of those families has eight children, you have so many children that are un-housed for schooling, they don't have adequate school facilities . . . . So when a family moves, the problems multiply. There are multiple effects on families that someone may have thought, well, all you have to do is move them. But someone has to consider the children. Someone has to consider employment—where will they work? So they have enough land to graze sheep on—that is their natural lifestyle . . . . What about water? Out here in the desert, water is very, very important . . . . The same thing happens to a family that moves to a near-by chapter. All of a sudden, your chapter population is on the increase, and council delegates, chapter managers, and chapter officials are used to handling a certain number of constituents, then all of a sudden there is an increase. Then all of a sudden there is tension that develops between families, it causes a lot of problems and a lot of tension. It creates many, many kinds of problems. I've seen it at Lupton, I've seen it in so many other places . . . ."

Viewpoint of Hopi Relocatees

Much media attention has been focused on the plight of Navajo relocatees and Navajo resistance to relocation, but the situation and feelings of Hopi relocatees has received very little coverage. When Indians started relocating in 1977, Hopi families living on Navajo partitioned lands were among the first to move. There were fewer Hopi to relocate than Navajo, but many have experienced unhappiness and suffering as a result of their move, and most Hopi relocatees interviewed have said that they feel tensions have accelerated between the two tribes as a result of relocation.

"Most of the Hopi families who relocated didn't want to go," Sidney explained. "They are reluctant to talk to the press or anybody about their feelings and experiences. They feel it is time to put the past behind them and look to the future. Relocating was painful for them, but they put the good of the tribe ahead of themselves."

One family interviewed* relocated eight years ago, from their home in the Jeddito area to their relocation home, about fifteen miles south of Keams Canyon. Their home is accessible only by a dirt road. They have a ranch-style house, with a big barn and lots of livestock. They do not have line electricity, but solar collectors and a small generator. They have to haul water for themselves and for their animals, they have no indoor plumbing, and no running water. Life revolves around ranching, and the father works at odd jobs on the mesas to get cash.

"When we first moved out here, there was nothing but grass. Everything was nice and green," John, a young Hopi relocatee, explained. "They had planted alfalfa or something and everything was real green. It was like that for about a year and then everything went dry, including the waterhole for our cows."

John explained that the family did not want to leave Jeditto, because they had their fields there and they had Navajo friends. But when the law came to affect their lives, they complied and moved. "We were happier before. We didn't really want to move from there. But the thing was that we had to . . . . So when we moved, it was like starting all over again."

Family members explained that since the relocation law was enacted, Navajo family friends have stopped talking to them, and older members of the family have become depressed and confused. The family explained that they feel relocation would not solve anything.

"It's been going on for ten years and we don't see any conclusion. Some people are still waiting to be certified," John explained. "It's really none of our land anyhow. It's neither the Hopis nor the Navajos. It is whoever sits on that land, just that part. I always dreamed that one of these days I would go out and tell everybody, 'It's nobody's land. We shouldn't be fighting for this and we shouldn't be fighting for that.' We are set on this earth by Somebody to be tested out. It's not really

---

*To ensure their privacy and protection, names of family members have been changed.

nobody's land. But nowadays, we've got what is called government. That's the one that is telling us to fight over things."

Hopi relocatees have pointed out that they feel land distribution is the root of the problem. They said that they were tired of hearing and reading about the land dispute, and they were concerned about the effects of relocation on the people involved. They felt sorry for both Navajo and Hopi. When asked how the family felt about Navajos moving from lands partitioned to the Hopi, John explained, "I guess it will be hard for them to move, since it was hard for us to move. To me, the Navajos are okay. They are just people like us. But the Navajos seem to blame us for the whole thing . . . this partition and relocation won't solve anything . . . . Everybody's still going to be fighting."

Navajo-Hopi Mixed Marriages and Their Children

One area of suffering and relocation that has been largely overlooked is the impact the conflict has had on Navajos and Hopis who have married each other and have had children. Both tribes make loyalty demands on the children of mixed marriages, and both tribes are equally culpable for the stress and pain that those demands have inflicted on Navajo-Hopi children. The hostility engendered by the land conflict is perhaps most telling when directed against its most vulnerable targets.

In traditional Hopi and Navajo society, children were automatically affiliated with the mother's clan and tribe, but in the complicated world of the twentieth century, children are forced to make a choice of tribal loyalty. The tribes have established their own membership guidelines, but the emotional trauma of choosing tribal loyalty is difficult. Growing up in any society is never easy, but children caught up in the turmoil and hysteria of the land dispute are subjected to a uniquely painful type of suffering. While Navajo and Hopi relocatees have openly discussed their plight with reporters and tribal leaders, mixed-marriage children of the land dispute largely suffer in silence.

Some are quiet because they are proud and do not seek pity from the outside world. Others are quiet because their anguish, pain, and shame run so deeply that they cannot speak of it without breaking into tears. Being half-Navajo and half-Hopi forces them to live between two worlds, and as tensions accelerate between the tribes, some find themselves psychologically torn into pieces. Conflict between their relatives has seared their souls. Neither fully Navajo nor fully Hopi, they are pressured by elders of both tribes. In addition to the confusion and suffering of the land issue, these children are caught in the nightmare of not really being certain who they are or where they belong. Between two tribal worlds, they face the challenges of functioning in a cultural limbo.

Conservative estimates show approximately 2,000 mixed Navajo-Hopi couples. Each couple averages two children, and there are approximately 4,000 children of mixed Navajo and Hopi descent. Prior to the land partition and resultant relocation tensions, the children sometimes had a difficult time growing up. But in the past twenty years, many have become objects of derision and suspicion among relatives and tribal governments alike. All the children must answer fundamental identity questions—who are they, are they Navajo or are they Hopi?

Navajo-Hopi children have family and clan ties to both tribes. Enlightened tribesmen have acknowledged the plight of these people, and they say that they feel badly for children caught between two worlds.

"It is really sad to see what these children go through," Leonard Dallas, a former Upper Moencopi Village governor explained. "We have a lot of intermarriage between Moencopi and Tuba City and when the kids come of age, they must make a choice. They suffer a lot. Sometimes people tease them and sometimes they really don't seem to know who they are."

Interviews with mixed-marriage families have demonstrated that confusion and pain have become constant factors in daily life as a result of the land dispute. One couple, in which the wife was Navajo and the husband Hopi, has publicly protested relocation and was active in the Navajo-Hopi Unity Committee. The couple has four children and although they live in a Navajo chapter affected by partition, they have steadfastly refused to sign up for relocation benefits.

"Because I was born into the dispute, and know the kind of suffering children go through without a strong cultural and religious identity, I made a choice for my kids," the wife explained. "Navajos are a matrilineal people. So even before we had any children, my husband . . . and I decided that we would raise the children with Navajo as their first language and in the Navajo Way."

She went on to explain that 99.9% of Navajo and Hopi couples want to avoid any comment on or contact with the land dispute. "People don't want to talk about it because they feel that they have to take a position with one tribe or the other," she said. "All of us are forced to make a choice. Our own elders force us to make a stand. They force us to make a choice. In fact, we become the brunt of prejudice by our own families. Many times, we are made fun of by both tribes. My children are tormented by their own relatives. It isn't right and in recent years, it has become worse and worse . . . ."

The woman said that she has tried to instill pride in all of her children about being both Navajo and Hopi, but with all of the stress of the land dispute it is difficult. "Sometimes it is hard when you see the lack of respect with which Navajo and Hopi elders treat each other. They are always sniping and fighting with each other."

The woman said that the closer a family lives to the disputed land, the more likely that children will become a target. During the school year, the family leaves the former JUA, and moves to a reservation town over a hundred miles away.

"My children have been luckier in some respects than other Navajo and Hopi children, because they don't live in the middle of the disputed area [during the school year] . . . other children don't know that much about their background, so they don't bother them. But they are tormented by the older people."

She explained that when they go to her Hopi husband's village, Hopis make remarks like, "Here come the Navajos that are taking our land away." And when the family visits Navajo relatives, Navajos say "Oh, here come the Hopi people that are taking our land away."

The Navajo mother said that when snide comments and ugly family incidents occur, she has instructed her children to respond in a certain way. "When people say things like that to the children, I tell them to respond by saying, " 'Aren't you related to me . . . aren't you my uncle or my aunt? Why are you making me feel like I don't belong to this family?' And it stops right away."

Children of mixed marriages growing up on the Hopi mesas face the same dilemmas as mixed-marriage children growing up on Navajoland. They become targets of derision and suspicion, even after they grow up and have accepted a Hopi identity. One woman, whose mother is a Navajo and whose father is a Hopi, has aunts and uncles living on Big Mountain. Her little girl has been raised on the Hopi mesas, but she has sheep and goats in Big Mountain flocks.

"I am tired of hearing complaints against my relatives, and I am tired of always being caught in the middle," the woman announced. "I have aunts and cousins on Big Mountain and I don't think it is right for anybody to be forced to leave their homes, where they have always lived."

Children of mixed marriages have said that the whole thing is very confusing, and the love of children for their Navajo and Hopi parents and grandparents transcends tribal differences. They have pointed out that they don't understand how anyone can really own the land, and that they are tired of always living under the land dispute cloud.

"Why can't people just get together and be nice to one another," one child asked. "I am proud of both Navajo and Hopi, but people try and make it impossible to be proud. People try to pretend that people like me do not exist."

From early childhood days, Navajo-Hopi children are forced to realize that somehow, they are different. As they grow up, the years of teasing on the school playground begin to take a toll. Taunts and jeers frequently cause children to run home in tears. Words like, "Your father is a Navajo and Navajos are thieves. Stop taking our land," and "Your mother is a Hopi and you are killing our people," are not easily forgotten by vulnerable children who had no role in the making and resolution of the Navajo and Hopi land dispute.

Of course, playground battles happen everywhere and children of all cultures can be very cruel to each other. Children in Moencopi Village fight with each other over who is more traditional and who is more progressive. But the dilemma of the mixed Navajo-Hopi child is one of wondering about basic identity—wondering who they really are. If they knew, they could form circles of other mixed Navajo-Hopi children and fight back. It is a we/they conflict, but these children don't really know who is "we."

Many people of mixed descent have said that they hope the elders of both tribes can work out a settlement and force the two tribal councils to honor that settlement. They look forward to a traditional solution to the dispute. They worry about the survival of both Navajo and Hopi traditional cultures. "This land fight is tearing us all to pieces," one woman said. "Moving back and forth, fighting with each other, how can our cultures continue with so much outside interference?"

The Financial Aspects

The costs of relocation extend beyond relocatee stresses, the plight of mixed marriages and their children, and Navajo-to-Navajo and Navajo-to-Hopi tensions. Americans as a whole have been forced to shoulder a heavy tax burden by supporting relocation. At the time the law was enacted, a sum of $40 million was estimated to be the amount of tax dollars necessary to get the job done. That sum was exceeded within a year of establishing the Relocation Commission. By 1982, relocation costs had risen to $250 million, and projections for 1992, when relocation is projected to finally be completed, have doubled the costs again, to $500 million. Navajo tribal leaders have consistently pointed out that American taxpayers may be unwilling to support relocation costs, and in an attempt to stop relocation and its human and financial costs, they have developed a plan for the disputed 1882 and the 1934 areas.

The 1934 Dispute and the Navajo Comprehensive Solution

The groundwork for a second land struggle between the Navajo and Hopi tribes, and a possible relocation of tribesmen has already been laid. It is possible that even if every Indian relocates from the disputed 1882 area, federal courts or Congress may decree yet another partition and relocation from lands on the extreme western end of the Navajo Reservation—lands given to the Navajo Tribe by Congress in 1934.

The Navajo and Hopi tribes are currently preparing litigation over these lands, which consist of over 2 million acres in Arizona, from roughly just east of Tuba City, west toward the Grand Canyon, and southwest toward Cameron. When Congress made an extension of Navajo Reservation boundaries on June 14, 1934, the wording of the legal expansion stated that the lands were designated for the benefit of the Navajo "and such other Indians as may already be located thereon." The Hopi protested the expansion at that time, maintaining that all lands west of the 1868 Navajo Reservation to the Grand Canyon were part of Hopi aboriginal claims.

Expansion of the Navajo Reservation boundaries upset the Hopi, because they viewed the land as part of their ancestral homeland. Sipapu, the Hopi emergence point lies within the Grand Canyon area and many Hopi salt and trade trails crisscross the region, which also houses numerous Hopi religious and clan shrines. Further complicating the 1934 conflict are the claims of the San Juan Band of Southern Paiutes, who maintain that the area is part of their ancestral homeland as well. Federal courts have decreed that the Paiutes can be party to the 1934 case, and one factor that has delayed a final determination of the case has been whether or not the Paiutes regain federal recognition.

On December 30, 1974, the Hopi Tribe filed suit in United States District Court in Phoenix, claiming one-half interest in the 1934 reservation area. The Hopi claimed that there were very few Navajo living in the area and that by ancestral law and settlement rights, the land is Hopi. The Navajo say that their people have been living in the region for several decades and they maintain that the Hopi have no vested interest in the area and are attempting some type of land grab.

Hopi tribal representatives say that they are primarily interested in protecting land rights to 1.3 million acres around Tuba City and the Hopi village of Moencopi. Moencopi is approximately sixty miles west of Third Mesa, and was a satellite farming community of Oraibi. The village was left out of the 1882 Executive Order Hopi Reservation by federal oversight. Tuba City lies directly across the highway from Moencopi, and is essentially a boomtown. Tuba City was once called Hogan Village by Moencopi people, because until the uranium development boom of the 1950s, there were only government administrative offices, medical facilities, and a few sleepy hogans on the site. That changed as federal and tribal job opportunities, and employment in the uranium industry at Rare Metals on the edge of Tuba City (the site has since closed down) attracted more people to the area. Navajos left homes in other places on the reservation and came to Tuba City seeking employment. Some Hopi left their villages and moved into Moencopi to gain easier access to employment in Tuba City as well.

Today, Tuba City is acknowledged as the capital of the Navajo West. Approximately ten thousand people live in the community and it has become a medical, educational, business, and administrative center for the Navajo. Stresses between Navajo and Hopi have increased as the growth of Tuba City has accelerated. Moencopites have expressed concerns that they will become surrounded by Tuba City if an equitable settlement is not reached between the tribes over the 1934 case. Navajos in Tuba City are concerned about the quick growth of the region, the need to accommodate an ever-expanding population, and the need to assist the flood of Navajo relocatees applying for membership in the Tuba City chapter as a consequence of the relocation law. In a way, the 1934 dispute is a continuation of the 1882 case, with similar stresses, population problems, and ancestral settlement claims on all sides.

THE BENNETT FREEZE AREA

The Hopi are primarily concerned with gaining control of some 1.3 million acres of the 2-million-acre 1934 region. These 1.3 million acres are known as the Bennett Freeze Area, and lie primarily around Tuba City and Moencopi and points west. The region is named after Commissioner of Indian Affairs Robert L. Bennett, who in 1966 responded to Hopi requests for a freeze on land development west of the 1882 Hopi Reservation until the 1934 land ownership issue was settled.

According to correspondence between Bennett and then-BIA Navajo Area Director Graham Holmes, Bennett felt that the development freeze would be temporary. He apparently believed that some workable solution would be reached between the Navajo and Hopi tribes regarding land use and development in and around Tuba City. In August 1966, the Navajo asked Bennett to limit the construction freeze to certain areas around Moencopi. Bennett took no action. However, on Halloween 1967, Bennett mandated that the entire freeze be lifted so that public works projects could proceed (after his personal approval) without formal actions by either Navajo or Hopi. As a result of this thaw in the construction freeze, a school and a hospital were built in Tuba City.

The development and construction freeze was reinstated on July 8, 1980, when Congress enacted Public Law 96-305, which legislated restraints on development in the 1934 area. The law states that "any development of lands in litigation . . . shall be carried out only upon the written consent of each tribe except for limited areas around the village of Moencopi and around Tuba City . . . 'development' as used herein shall mean any new construction or improvement to the property and further includes public work projects, power and water lines, public agency improvements and associated rights-of-way."

What the law means in real terms is that neither Navajo nor Hopi living in the disputed area can add on to a house, build a new water line, repair living space, or make any construction or development move unless both Navajo and Hopi tribes have approved the planned changes in writing. Any construction, including roads, wells, irrigation projects, and even new bead sales stands along major highways in the 1934 area must be approved by both the tribes. According to law, this construction freeze will remain in effect until the courts or Congress decide who owns the land in the 1934 area. Some areas around Tuba City and Moencopi have been exempted by amendments to the mandate, but most people in the area are forced into cramped and uncomfortable living situations. Most of the people affected by the freeze are Navajo.

In April 1978, district court in Phoenix ruled that the Hopi Tribe was entitled to one-half interest in lands they had used and occupied in 1934. Hopi officials have said that they are not happy about the decision, particularly since they had based much of their case on ancestral claims dating back over a thousand years. The Hopi Tribe appealed the case, and it was taken to the United States Court of Appeals.

The appeals court held that the Hopi may have a 100% interest in the 1934 area. The court also said that lands jointly used by the two tribes in 1934 should be further studied, and final land ownership should be determined by the courts. The court pointed out that any lands jointly held could be partitioned when a final decision was reached. The Ninth Circuit Court then remanded the case back to Phoenix District Court.

The Ninth Circuit Court decision was appealed by both tribes and went on to the United States Supreme Court. But on December 1, 1980, the supreme court declined to review the case. This effectively upheld the Ninth Circuit Court decision and the 1934 land ball bounced back into the federal court in Phoenix.

One component of the case which affects the American public is that according to amendments in the 1974 relocation law, legal fees for both tribes in the 1934 conflict are subsidized by the secretary of the interior. Congress has not always appropriated all necessary money for the fees, and in recent months, Congress has placed the fee situation under review. But up to the present, the bulk of expense in the

1934-lands legal conflict has been absorbed by the taxpayer. According to tribal sources, hundreds of thousand of dollars have already been spent.

The Navajo Tribe has retained the Phoenix-based firm of Brown and Bain to look after their interests in the 1934 case. The Hopi Tribe started out the case with the Salt Lake City-based firm of John Paul Kennedy, but later gave the contract to the Denver-based firm of Arnold and Porter.

The courts have ruled that Paiute claims must be considered in the final determination of the case as well. The Paiutes have retained attorneys with the Boulder, Colorado-based, Native American Rights Fund to look after their legal interests. It is unclear whether or not the Paiutes want only a land settlement, a cash settlement, or a combination of both coupled with federal recognition as a tribal entity. Papers filed by their attorneys indicate that the group wants some land, and they have stressed areas in the Willow Springs, Paiute Canyon, and Navajo Mountain regions being of special interest.

Attorneys involved in the case have pointed out that the Paiute entry into the case has further delayed a decision, and no one is certain how their claims will affect the final determination. Attorneys for the Navajo Tribe have requested that a hearing date be set for the summer of 1989, when Navajo and Hopi land claims can be reviewed and the case finally determined by the judge. Navajo attorneys have stated that they don't want the Paiute claims to be included in that hearing, because dealing with the Paiutes would add extra hours and financial costs to case discovery. Hopi attorneys have yet to make an official comment on the Paiute involvement in the case, but Chairman Sidney has said that Hopis do not want to ignore Paiute claims in the case, since they feel that the Paiutes have been victims of federal aggression as a result of federal action undermining federal recognition of the Paiutes as a tribe. Therefore, the tribe has made no move to oppose federal recognition or Paiute intervention in the 1934 case.*

The history of the 1934 case is long and complicated, but the land has become increasingly important to Navajo and Hopi since the July 6, 1986, deadline for completion of relocation has passed. Sidney has stressed that his tribe wants to get the case back into court as quickly as possible so there will be a final resolution. The Navajo Tribe has pointed out that they would like to see a combined settlement of the 1882 area and the 1934 area, and it is actively lobbying Congress to consider a determination that will link the two areas together in a

---

*A hearing date has been set for September 6, 1989, and Paiutes are to be included.

comprehensive solution. Navajo tribal officials have said that they would prefer a legislative solution to a judicial settlement. The Navajo say they want to see the case settled out of court, but the Hopi Tribe has repeatedly stated that they feel their interests will be better served through federal court decisions.

The idea of a comprehensive settlement for 1882 and 1934 disputed lands was developed by the Zah administration and was continued with the MacDonald administration. In May 1987, details of the plan were made public in a report issued by the Navajo Tribe's Navajo-Hopi Land Dispute Task Force. According to the report, the two tribes should sit down and renegotiate both 1882 and 1934 claims, reaching a compromise that would prevent any further relocations. The Navajo Tribe has offered money and land exchanges to the Hopi Tribe as part of the settlement, but the Hopi refuse to negotiate on the 1882 area. They maintain that the 1882 case has been settled in court and they will not reopen that case.

The Navajo Tribe stated in its report that they are concerned about the physical and psychological well-being of Navajos in the 1882 area and the 1934 area, and they said they are especially worried about the 1966 development and construction freeze imposed on residents of the 1934 area. According to the report, the impacts of the construction freeze have been devastating. "The result has been to impose . . . hardships on approximately 10,000 people living in that area by retarding economic development, housing construction, and infrastructure development where they are most needed . . . . Many Navajo people have been prohibited from . . . making improvements . . . that would allow Navajos to live in a home fit for human beings. Additionally, roads remain dangerous and unpaved as a result of the freeze" (Report of the Navajo-Hopi Land Dispute Task Force 1987).

The report recommends several solutions to problems in the disputed areas. The report and the comprehensive solution to the report were officially endorsed by the Navajo Tribal Council in its 1987 summer session. Solutions sanctioned by the Navajo Tribe are:

1. No one should be forced to move against their will.
2. Navajos anxious to return to land partitioned to the Hopi shall be allowed to do so.
3. No one should continue to abuse Navajos awaiting relocation as a "political football." Those wanting to relocate should be assisted by the federal government and those wanting to return to their old HPL homes should be permitted to do so.
4. The federal Navajo and Hopi Indian Relocation Commission should deliver homes and relocation benefits to some 1,200

Navajo families who have signed up for relocation but have not received their benefits, even though they have physically moved from the JUA. Other Navajos willing to relocate should be quickly awarded their replacement homes, bonuses, and financial compensation.

5. The relocation commission should provide better counselling for Navajo relocatees.

6. Both the 1882 dispute and the 1934 dispute should be resolved without any financial impact on the Navajo Tribe, and all land claims lawsuits filed by the Hopi Tribe against the Navajo Tribe should be dismissed.

7. Developmental freezes in both areas should be lifted and the federal government should provide financial and economic assistance to all Navajos in the areas.

8. Approximately 350,000 to 400,000 acres of land partitioned to the Hopi Tribe should be transferred to the Navajo Tribe, thus minimizing the number of Navajo relocatees, and the Hopi Tribe should receive compensation in the form of land, money, or both, not from the Navajo Tribe but from the federal government. Any land given to the Hopi should be free of Navajo occupants.

The report further stressed that the best thing for Navajo relocatees would be repeal of the relocation law. It admitted that congressional support for the repeal recommendation was unrealistic, but it offered some hope for congressional support of the comprehensive solution, stating that "the strong stance taken by Chairman MacDonald on this option has created a more positive atmosphere in Washington."

The idea of allowing Navajos to return to the HPL and linking the 1934 case with the 1882 case in any kind of comprehensive solution has not been well received by the Hopi Tribe. "This land is not for sale. We will not give an inch of the reacquired land back to the Navajos . . . . I would certainly like to see that those [Navajo] people living on what was Hopi's land in 1934 would be relocated," Sidney explained. "Because it has yet to be shown to me that anyone has taken active control of the Navajo people . . . . The Navajos are telling Congress and the outside world 'we want to sit down with the Hopis. We want to sit down with the 1934 case and negotiate,' but they really don't want to negotiate at all. They just want everything and it seems like Congress and the courts give them everything they want."

Sidney was adamant that none of the HPL will be ceded to the Navajo. "I have been approached by the Navajos and their comprehensive settlement attitudes. The whole idea is nothing new . . . . We may not show up at any meetings to discuss it. Because we are not the ones subjecting the Navajos to the fate of relocation that they say is hurting them so much . . . . I feel that it is their own people who have recklessly allowed them to settle in the areas where they [are], knowing full and well about the traditional boundaries of their own elders . . . ."

Sidney further pointed out that while the comprehensive settlement offers Hopis financial compensation for land, it says nothing about the Navajo Tribe returning the replacement acreage it acquired as a result of amendments to the 1974 relocation law. "They're wanting to keep everything," Sidney complained.

But Zah, the originator of the comprehensive settlement solution, has stressed that both tribes must be willing to compromise, and both must be willing to make land sacrifices.

"I think a comprehensive solution, perhaps with Congress as an arbitrator, would be the best solution," Zah said. "Because in the 1934 case, to the lawyers on both sides, it is in their best interests to litigate these cases in court . . . . And I support a comprehensive solution and a negotiated settlement because it is better if we work it out ourselves without allowing these lawyers to make money off the Navajo and off the Hopi . . . . All in all in the Navajo-Hopi situation, I think that the two tribes just simply have to resolve this issue. They may not be happy with what happens, but that is something that we as responsible citizens in America have to accept . . . . If for some reason, one of the tribes doesn't want to negotiate, then the other [tribe] ought to go to Congress and the Congress ought to impose some sort of comprehensive solution on the tribes—again. The 1974 law was an imposition by Congress, and I don't like the idea, but if everything else fails, that may be the only option we have . . . ."

Tensions in the 1934 Area

Mindful of the misery and confusion many Navajos in the 1882 area have experienced, many Navajos residing in the 1934 area are worried. Families in the Tuba City and Gap-Bodaway regions have started to organize against any possible relocation, and regular community meetings to discuss the situation and develop plans to protect their homes have been held, since the beginning of 1988.

Tensions are running high in the 1934 region. Each side accuses the other of wrongdoing and illegal construction. Hopis say there were no Navajos living in the area prior to World War II. Navajos counter that their families have been in the region since before the 1860s.

An incident occurred in the summer of 1985 that illustrates the type of pressure fueling tensions in the 1934 dispute. A Navajo hogan was destroyed by a Hopi demolition crew near the Coal Mine Mesa Chapter that summer. The hogan was located on Bennett Freeze land. The Hopis maintain that they thought the hogan was abandoned, and they believed that it was on the HPL; they say that they did not realize they had crossed from the Hopi Reservation to the Bennett Freeze area when they reclaimed the site.

Despite official Hopi statements that the demolition was an accident, a family member said he believes that the incident was deliberate, because that hogan had been built by his grandfather, whose land claims are a key factor in the 1934 dispute. "I think the Hopis singled out his homestead because it had been there since before 1930 and it supports Navajo claims for the land," he explained.

Many Navajos are worried that they will have to move if the Hopis prevail in court. Hopis, especially people in the Moencopi area, are worried that they will not have room for farming or village expansion if Navajo claims prevail. If the Paiutes receive official recognition, they may actively pursue their traditional land claims in the region, and that may further complicate a difficult situation. Confusion prevails in the region. Continued tensions and additional hard feelings between tribesmen are the only certainties, until a solution equitable to all is somehow hammered out.

7

TOWARD THE FUTURE

In the House of Dawn, the key to unlocking the door to the future is in the understanding of the past. Events in the past three centuries have laid the foundations for tomorrow. The struggle for land between Hopi and Navajo will continue. How far the struggle is allowed to escalate and how much land each tribe will occupy will be determined by the newest arrivals, the Anglo-Americans, who are themselves in the midst of a migration to the region.

The Southwest is unique among the regions that make up the United States, because it is the area that has maintained the widest diversity of languages and cultures, and its indigenous populations culturally intact. Southwestern tribes have been fortunate, because until recently, their isolation in a remote region of mountains, deserts, and little water made their lands uninviting to non-Indians. As long as tribes maintain a land base, religion, language, and culture survive. But when the land base is eroded or taken away, everything else begins to die. Land creates the essential fabric of Indian society, central to both physical and spiritual survival.

Today, Southwestern tribes are under more stress than ever before. They do not face extermination by foreign enemies or forced marches to remote lands, but they face crushing economic problems, growing populations, and threats to religious and linguistic survival as a result of the growing inroads of the dominant society. Navajo and Hopi, as well as other groups, face serious challenges and must make difficult decisions if they are to retain a recognizable traditional identity. Despite the struggle for land between Navajo and Hopi, the tribes may have more in common than they realize. Each group will have to make its own decisions.

Challenges and Strengths

Of all the tribes in the Southwest, it has been the Navajo who have made the most spectacular gains in terms of population growth and territorial expansion and this growth will continue. While other tribes have also increased in population, they have not had access to the vast mineral wealth or growing economic development of the Navajo, nor have they been able to regain lands lost to the Americans, or in some cases to the Navajo Tribe itself. The Navajo have evolved their own unique form of Manifest Destiny, and they have served as a role model and an inspiration to other tribes since they assumed aggressive control of their own minerals and other resources.

Navajo Tribal Chairman Peter MacDonald was one of the founders of the Council of Energy Resource Tribes, a type of Indian OPEC. The Navajo Tribe has fought for and gained the power of taxation on their reservation and has a surplus of almost $300 million in the tribal treasury as a result of taxation and tribal development (AP 1988). The tribe has developed an effective court and judicial system and daily works to strengthen its sovereignty and self-sufficiency. Navajo success has influenced other tribes to follow their example. These tribes may soon tax their own resources and perhaps expand their own reservation boundaries through land investments.

In the coming years, the Navajo Nation will have to struggle with many difficult issues. Over half the tribal population is under eighteen years old (Education Assessment 1987), and chronic unemployment and under-employment are constant problems; despite tribal attempts to develop a successful private sector, progress has been slow. Navajo population has broken the 200,000 mark, and there is a space problem on the reservation. As the under-eighteen age group matures and has children, there will be more and more Navajos. Where are all of those people going to find places to live, employment, and education to make them competitive in both the Navajo and outside worlds?

Under amendments to the Relocation Law, the Navajo Tribe was guaranteed 400,000 acres of replacement lands. The amendment act, Public Law 96-305, was to assist Navajos in land needs and replace lands the Navajo had lost to the Hopi as a result of partition and ensure that Navajo relocatees had a place to go. The tribe has acquired almost all of the promised replacement lands and thousands of additional acres since 1985. Utilizing the replacement lands and buying additional lands may be part of a solution for the growing population problem. But additional Navajo expansion into New Mexico and Arizona has not been received favorably among many Anglo residents of the region, or the neighboring smaller tribes.

Under the tenets of the law, the Navajo Tribe was to receive 250,000 acres of land under the jurisdiction of the Bureau of Land Management (BLM) within the states of Arizona and New Mexico and contiguous to the Navajo Reservation. An additional 150,000 acres of private land was to be given to the Navajo Tribe as part of their reservation. The lands selected were to be within 18 miles of current reservation boundaries, and no land adjacent to Grand Canyon National Park was to be made available for tribal selection.* The tribal land selection was limited to 35,000 acres in New Mexico, so the bulk of replacement land lies in Arizona.

On June 16 and 17, 1983, the tribe selected 371,400 acres of Arizona land for relocatees and their replacement houses. The lands came to be called the New Lands and comprised acreage from five ranches: Fitzgerald, Wallace, Roberts, Kelsey, and parts of the Spurlock Ranch. The land selected in New Mexico was on the Paragon Ranch. The Paragon Ranch consists of some 35,000 acres of coal-rich land northwest of Chaco Canyon in the San Juan River country of northwestern New Mexico; it encompasses BLM land, some private lands, and some state land and it is located in a region of New Mexico called the Checkerboard Area.

The Checkerboard Area is made up of BLM lands, private lands, and state lands interspersed with Navajo Reservation land, and is inhabited by both Navajo and Anglo ranchers. The region is a jurisdictional nightmare. Federal, Navajo, and New Mexico State law enforcement agencies must work closely with each other to determine where one jurisdiction ends and another begins.

At the time of tribal selection of Paragon, much of the land was used for cattle. The Public Service Company of New Mexico had developed plans for construction of a coal-fired electricity-generating plant on the land, and were planning ways to extract coal from it. Disputes between the energy company and the tribe have slowed down the acquisition process, although the tribe still plans to proceed with mining and power-generating plans. As of January 7, 1987, only a portion of Paragon land, some 10,178 acres, had been made officially available for transfer into trust for the tribe because of resistance by the state of New Mexico and other land claimants.

The Navajo Tribe has worked closely with the federal Relocation Commission and the federal government to wrest subsurface rights

---

*This decision was made after extensive lobbying by American ranchers, environmentalists, and the Sierra Club, who opposed Navajo ownership of public lands lying north and west of the Colorado River in Arizona. The Navajo Tribe had selected House Rock Valley near the Grand Canyon as replacement land prior to the 1980 law. Environmentalists complained that Navajo sheep would disturb the area's delicate ecological balance.

from the Public Service Company of New Mexico. As the situation currently stands, the tribe has officially selected 33,714 acres of Paragon Ranch land. The remaining 1,286 acres are being held in abeyance, pending identification of settlement areas for relocatees who want to live near a generating station. Technically, the full acreage has not yet been taken into trust for the tribe.

There has been heavy resistance to additional Navajo land acquisition in both Arizona and New Mexico. Ranchers in Arizona have voiced concerns that their state will become "checkerboarded" like northwestern New Mexico. They have said that they are afraid that the carrying capacities of their own ranches will be damaged if large numbers of relocatees move near their borders, and are also worried about the impact of Navajo sheep on range management.

The city of Winslow, Arizona, and many non-Indians publicly stated that they were concerned that the selected lands would go into trust and there would be a loss of tax base. Ranchers and other concerned citizens held numerous meetings from 1982 to 1986, and were vocal about their opposition to the land selections. They contacted their congressional delegations and met with representatives of the Navajo Tribe to air these concerns.

By 1986, when replacement homes had been built on the New Lands and relocatees began moving in, much of the controversy had died down. Approximately 20 relocatee families have moved onto the New Lands, and the local cities and school districts now face challenges revolving around the accommodation of education and employment needs for the new residents.

Navajo Land Purchases

Since 1986, a new controversy had arisen, eclipsing the old replacement lands problem. Under the leadership of Chairman Peterson Zah, the Navajo Tribe began buying land and grazing rights in and around Winslow and Flagstaff. When Peter MacDonald took the helm of the Navajo ship of state in 1987, he continued this policy. After approval by the Navajo Tribal Council, in a move that has stirred more controversy, MacDonald signed a contract to buy the 491,432 acre Boquillas Ranch for $33 million. Boquillas Ranch, the largest ranch in Arizona, lies near the Grand Canyon, approximately 150 miles west of Flagstaff and adjacent to the Hualapai and Havasupai reservations.

When the tribe bought 92,500 acres of land in and around Winslow in July 1986, the city fathers panicked. The Navajo Tribal Council paid $9.48 million for the land, which is in a checkerboard pattern, with some pieces touching the southern Navajo Reservation border and some 64 acres lying within the Winslow city limits. Winslow city officials publicly stated that they were unhappy about the purchase, and they demanded to know how the Navajo Tribe planned to use the land.

Further controversy was stirred by tribal acquisition of land and grazing rights near the San Francisco Peaks, north of Flagstaff. On August 6, 1986, thousands of Navajos gathered at the base of the peaks, which are sacred to all tribes in Arizona.

The San Francisco Peaks are called *Dok'oo'sliid* in Navajo and are known as the place "Where the Thunder Sleeps." They are one of the four sacred mountains marking the traditional boundaries of the Navajo world. To the Hopi, the peaks are the home of the kachinas and a number of other spirits. Hopi shrines dot the peaks, and the region is very sacred. Navajo believe that a number of Holy People frequent these mountains. The mountain complex is Arizona's tallest, and the highest peak towers almost thirteen thousand feet above sea level. The peaks are a virtual cornucopia of medicinal and ceremonial herbs and plants.

Navajos joined hands in celebrating their tribe's purchase of rights to 174,000 acres of land near the peaks. The land, held by the Espil family since 1904, was relinquished for $6.5 million. The tribe holds seasonal grazing rights to United States Forest Service acreage on the land, and outright title to 900 acres of the Espil Ranch.

"I just want to welcome you to the new Navajoland," Zah announced after accepting title before the assembled Navajo multitudes. "I am very happy that we have acquired the grazing rights to one of the holy places of the Navajo people."

Navajo reaction to Zah's land acquisition was positive. But there has been some tribal opposition to MacDonald's purchase plans because the Boquillas Ranch, locally known as "Big Bo," is not adjacent to the Navajo Reservation, and many Navajos have complained that they believe there were irregularities in the purchase contract. They have expressed concerns that the tribe paid too much for the ranch. The ranch purchase has become the subject of investigation by several federal agencies and the Dineh Rights Organization, a Navajo group that advocates the adoption of a tribal constitution and a limitation on executive powers of Navajo tribal government. Zah has expressed concern that the purchase was hasty and expensive.

"When I was the chairman, I had the opportunity to buy that land . . . . It was always advertised for $25 million," Zah said. "We didn't take up the idea of purchasing that land because it was away from the reservation and . . . I knew that some of the tribal people living around that area were opposed to the selling of the land. Also, I didn't have the resources. I couldn't come up with the money to buy that land. I had other priorities . . . ."

The Hualapai and Havasupai have complained about the Big Bo purchase, as have Anglo ranchers in the region. The Pai tribal leaders have said that they should have been consulted by the Navajo Tribe before buying the ranch, as it is part of their ancestral homeland.

Chairman MacDonald has defended the purchase, saying that it will benefit the Navajo people in the long run. "It is the . . . tribe's intention to utilize the land for the benefit of the Navajo people," MacDonald explained in a press statement. "There is no question in our minds that the tribe's development plans will serve only to increase the value of the Big Boquillas." MacDonald said that the Boquillas land has mineral development potential, and he plans to take steps to ensure that more revenues pour into Navajo tribal coffers as a result of the ranch purchase.

Despite opposition to Navajo land investment, the tribe continues to buy more. The Navajo Tribe receives millions of dollars annually from royalties and tax revenues and as the tribe's population grows, more land will be needed. Land with development and mineral potential can provide jobs. From the Navajo point of view, land buying and wise investment is a viable solution. The Hopi Tribe is also looking into additional land investment, and is currently considering the development of a tourism and recreation area near Winslow, Arizona. Some people have even suggested that the Navajo Nation (and the Hopi Tribe) should separate from Arizona and New Mexico and become the first all-Indian state.

Hawley Atkinson, a long-time member of the federal Navajo and Hopi Indian Relocation Commission, and one of the three commissioners guiding relocation policies said he believes that the Navajo tribal leaders have a long-term land acquisition plan that will help Navajo people.

"Both Peterson Zah and Peter MacDonald are men of great vision and great leaders for their tribe," Atkinson explained. "Their resistance to relocation, their badgering Congress for more and more money, and the taxation and severance taxes for energy development on the reservation have combined to create a surplus of money in the tribal treasury. With this money, they are buying land and ensuring the further survival and expansion of their people . . . . When I first joined this commission, I didn't have a grasp of what the Navajo strategy was. I thought they were just fighting the relocation. But now, I see the determination and the tenacity forming up into a much larger and greater plan. It is a brilliant plan . . . ."

Why shouldn't Navajos utilize their natural resources and profits accrued from development of their land to gain more land and better employment for their people? They are a pragmatic people, with a unique ability to adapt and survive under adverse conditions. They have always pushed against boundaries, and their worldview centers around the belief in an expanding universe. Federal dollars, energy dollars, and dollars gained by tribal taxation of reservation businesses are contributing to expansion of the land base to sustain the Navajo world and ensure Navajo survival. The Navajo are working on solutions to their problems. But many other Indians are concerned about their own problems and what impact Navajo land gains may have on their own cultural survival.

Predictably, the Hopi are concerned about the increase in Navajo lands, fearing that Navajo gains will be made at Hopi expense. The Hopi were traditional allies not only of Rio Grande pueblos but also of the Havasupai and Hualapai; the tribes used to trade and intermarry with each other. Since the Navajo purchase of the Big Boquillas Ranch, Pai leaders have met with Hopi leaders to discuss how to cope with Navajo expansion.

"You know, we have our own plans about how to try and attract the tourist dollar to our reservation," Edgar Walema, head of the 1,200-member Hualapai Tribe explained during a meeting with Hopi and Havasupai leaders. "Now the Navajos have bought the Boquillas Ranch, part of our ancestral homeland. If we had money, maybe we could have bought some of that land. But now, we don't know what to think and we don't know how it will affect us."

Common Threats

The Hopi and their allies face many of the same problems that the Navajo face in terms of growing populations, providing education and employment for their people, and the need to develop viable private sectors on their own lands. Tribal populations are on the rise throughout the Four Corners region, and each tribe faces similar problems and challenges.

Stresses between Navajo and Hopi are a central focus of public interest because of the relocation law. But conflicts between other tribes have developed as well. Stresses have been observed between the Navajo and the Zuni and Utes, again because of growing populations and limited land bases. In recent years, the Zuni, whose reservation was once confined to New Mexico (south of Gallup), have received federal recognition and expanded reservation boundaries more in line with their traditional homeland, and some Zuni Reservation land now extends into Arizona. This brings the Zuni again into conflict with the most populous tribe, the Navajo. On the Ute Mountain and Southern Ute reservations in southwestern Colorado, concerns have been expressed about Navajo families grazing their cattle and building temporary residences on Ute land.

What many tribes have yet to realize is that all face a common threat—the undermining of their cultures by the dominant American culture. It is true that Navajo population will continue to grow at a geometric rate, and they will continue to be the biggest and most powerful tribe in the United States. But they will not absorb their Pueblo neighbors, or their Ute neighbors, or their Pai neighbors as long as the tribes retain a land base. Tribes will continue to compete for land and resources, but their competition with each other will not be as fierce as the competition between traditional cultures and the dominant Anglo-American society.

Unless all the tribes can develop sound economic bases and provide bilingual education and strong cultural and traditional religious backgrounds to their children so they can operate successfully in both Indian and non-Indian worlds, more and more Indians will leave the reservation for life in mainstream America. Unless sound infrastructures and solid economic bases are developed on the reservations, educated Indians and Indians desperate for work will be forced to leave their traditional homelands. Tribes need to develop their job markets. They need to attract industries and investors to their lands. They need to have small businesses, restaurant, and tourist trades. The tribes need to develop a way to keep their educated young people at home. Otherwise, the indigenous people of the Southwest will be absorbed into the dominant European culture and forgotten, like so many other tribes before them.

Navajo and Hopi, Navajo and Paiute, and other tribes in conflict with the Navajo over land usage and rights need to develop solutions to their problems. It is unlikely that the tribes will unify and stand together to face the gathering cultural and economic storm, but somehow, the land fights must be solved in an equitable manner. If Navajo and Hopi can solve their long-standing dispute, it is likely that other tribes would follow suit and benefit from the solution as well. Despite the frustration of the land dispute, not all is grim. There have been cases of intertribal cooperation, and there are some glimmerings of hope.

Signs of Hope

In spite of centuries of tension and cultural misunderstanding between Navajo and Hopi, in the past two decades, they have periodically cooperated on projects important to both. Sometimes, the cooperation has produced success, and sometimes the joining together has served only to further document tribal resistance to American incursions. The moments of cooperation have shown that in some cases, the tribes are able to put aside traditional differences and work together. Working together for mutual benefit and survival is one step that may hold future promise.

One important example of intertribal cooperation happened in the late 1970s, when American commercial interests announced that they wanted to expand an existing ski resort on the San Francisco Peaks, north of Flagstaff, Arizona. In November 1979, Navajo, Hopi, Apache, and Zuni people travelled to Flagstaff to protest the proposed Arizona Snow Bowl expansion. Pueblo priests, Navajo nataani and medicinemen as well as academicians, American religious leaders, environmentalists, and civil rights attorneys stood united in their opposition to the resort expansion.

The local office of the Coconino National Forest initially approved the Arizona Snow Bowl's request to build new ski lodges, cut down hundreds of trees, and develop an extensive series of additional ski runs. In the minds of the traditional religious leaders, the proposed activities were sacrilegious. Just prior to the Coconino National Forest's approval, a law had been passed by Congress, the American Indian Religious Freedom Act (Public Law 95-341), which had directed federal agencies to re-evaluate their policies and procedures, "as they impact upon the exercise of traditional Indian religious practices." The law said Indian religious rights should be respected and not violated. The San Francisco Peaks case was the first major test case under the American Indian Religious Freedom Act.

After reviewing the concerns of indigenous people, in February 1980, the Regional Office of the United States Forester, based in Albuquerque, New Mexico, overturned the initial decision of the Coconino National Forest supervisor. In his decision, Forester M. J. Hassell pointed out that "the expansion could violate the rights of American Indians to practice their religion on the San Francisco Peaks" (DNA 1981). The Arizona Snow Bowl developers were upset at the regional decision, and appealed it to the chief United States forester in Washington, D.C. The chief forester agreed that development could proceed.

Following the instructions of Navajo and Hopi religious leaders, DNA Peoples' Legal Services, (a grantee of the federal Legal Services Corporation that provided services to Indian people living on and around the Navajo Reservation) and attorneys for the traditional Hopi and the Hopi Tribal Council filed suit in federal District Court in Washington, D.C., on March 30, 1981. The lower federal courts upheld the decision of the forest service to allow expansion. Ultimately, the case was referred to the United States Supreme Court, which refused to review it, effectively allowing the expansion to proceed. Indians viewed the loss as a defeat of the American Indian Religious Freedom Act, and many religious leaders have stated that they do not feel the act made any guarantees protecting religious freedom and expression.

The expansion of the Arizona Snow Bowl was a blow to native Americans, but it did illustrate something positive. Navajos and Hopis, along with other Four Corners tribes, could stand unified against a common threat.

Moving away from esoteric areas and into solid physical realities, Navajo and Hopi have been able to cooperate in the cleanup of an area contaminated by radioactive tailings, heavy metals, and industrial toxins at a site near Tuba City and Moencopi. In the 1940s and 1950s, the Western Navajo Agency (much of which is affected by the 1934 Navajo and Hopi dispute), was the focus of uranium mining and milling. Rare Metals, a site approximately eight miles northeast of Tuba City and Moencopi, was the location of a massive uranium mill. When the bottom fell out of the nuclear market in the 1960s, the mill was abandoned, but stagnant tailings ponds and tons of waste, tailings, and industrial by-products were left behind.

The Rare Metals site was ignored for almost twenty years. But in the 1980s, Navajos and concerned Moencopi residents started to study site contamination and the possible effects wind-blown tailings could have on living things. Eventually, the local groups were able to get their tribes involved in pursuing a cleanup of the site, and today Navajo and Hopi team leaders are burying the tailings and monitoring air and water for signs of contamination.

"The uranium covering that was initiated for Rare Metals in 1985 is a really good example of cooperation," Zah explained. "It was something that had to be done because uranium itself is dangerous to human beings and [contaminants] are not going to say 'let's not sit on these guys because they are Hopis.' [Contaminants] will sit on any human being and they will deteriorate their lives . . . I am glad that both of our tribes are working together to change that . . . ."

In other areas, the two tribes have been able to cooperate in permitting power lines to cross over the disputed 1934 lands to provide electricity to housing projects. Before congressional funding ran out for a road across the former JUA, which would have connected the Hopi mesas and Big Mountain region with Kayenta, both Navajo and Hopi tribes worked together on highway construction. The road was called the Turquoise Trail, and has yet to be completed. Failure of the project was not due to a lack of cooperation between the tribes, but a lack of federal dollars to complete it.

To many people, these small steps in tribal cooperation may seem insignificant, but they are hopeful signs when one considers the preceding centuries of stress and antagonism.

The traditional Hopi leaders and many traditional Navajos have said the time has come for political leaders to step aside and allow religious leaders to sit down together and negotiate a solution through traditional problem solving. Hopi kikmongwis and Navajo medicinemen and nataani have said that they are certain they could work out a solution. But someone has to take the initiative and make the first move. Until a solution is reached, both tribes will ignore traditional leaders and look to Congress and the federal courts for solutions.

Until some solution is reached, the struggle for land and resources will continue in the House of Dawn. Up to now, Navajo and Hopi people have appeared unwilling to work out their problems in the traditional way. While Indian people debate among themselves, their leaders struggle with an alien system to defend tribal rights and territories. The future of the people who live in the region is being shaped right now. There are no guarantees as to what shape that future will take.

While Navajo and Hopi fight over land boundaries and cultural continuity, more and more Anglos move into the Southwest. The Americans are buying land. American children are interacting with Indian children. Television is entering every hogan, trailer, and stone house. Christian missionaries continue seeking converts among the native populations. Traditional barter and trade economies continue to be undermined by the dominant cash-and-wage economy. State and federal governments continue to lobby, cajole, and coerce the tribes for favors and access to tribal water and resources.

But through it all, one thing becomes clear—Navajo and Hopi have no choice but to continue the struggle over land rights. This last of the Indian wars will be fought to its finish by lawyers rather than warriors, using words instead of arrows. It is a war that must be fought because land is the primary value—not profit. The prize will be as it always has been: land, sacred land, so that their people can follow the dictates of their ancestors and be at peace with their Gods.

AFTERWORD

Most Americans do not know why relocation is so upsetting to the Navajo and Hopi. Having been reared in a society where money is the key factor to material survival, they do not understand that to these people, land is more important than money because it allows them to preserve their cultural integrity. It enables them to resist assimilation into an alien culture. To Americans who have become conditioned to the consumer society of mass production, money is the stuff of dreams because with it, things and places are interchangeable and can become something else upon demand. But to native people, place *itself* is everything. It is the source of sustenance, and as such, becomes more dear with the passage of time. For the Western world, sustenance is something that comes in cans produced in a distant place and delivered by ships or trains or trucks rather than wrought from the earth by their own hands. Because of this, place has become relatively unimportant to most Americans; only currency holds a primary value.

The average American would welcome an opportunity for a new home at no cost to themselves and a $5,000 bonus for moving. But traditional Navajo and Hopi have different perspectives on the casual exchange of place for material and money.

The First Amendment Lawsuit

Because of this concern for place and cultural survival, in January 1988, a group of traditional Navajos living on the partitioned former JUA filed a lawsuit challenging the Navajo-Hopi Relocation Act on constitutional grounds. The group claims that the relocation law violates their religious freedom and their right to equal protection under the law. The suit was filed by the Big Mountain Legal Office under a section of its operation named "In Defense of Sacred Lands." A number of other law

137

firms are also involved in the case. Most of the Navajo families involved are from the Big Mountain region.

The lawsuit claims that Navajo religious rights are violated by the relocation law because their religious practices are intricately linked to their traditional homeland. Navajo Tribal Chairman Peter MacDonald and the Navajo Tribal Council have verbally supported the lawsuit, and Navajo Tribal Attorney General Michael Upshaw has said that the tribe will file an *amicus curiae* brief supporting Navajo religious claims.

"The Relocation Act has caused untold hardship for these individuals and tens of thousands of other Navajo people," MacDonald said. "These traditional Navajos are courageously asserting their individual liberties, and the Navajo Nation fully supports their right to do so."

The case was originally filed in United States District Court in Washington, D.C., but has been remanded to United States District Court in Phoenix. No Hopi are party to the case; only Navajo religious rights are to be placed under consideration. Many Navajo are hopeful that their position will be regarded favorably by the courts, and they will not have to relocate from lands partitioned to the Hopi. But relocation proceeds.

How Relocatees Feel about Repeal

A survey of Navajo relocatees released in August 1987 revealed that despite the official opposition of their tribal council to relocation and the 1974 Navajo and Hopi Land Settlement Act, many relocatees interviewed did not support repeal of the law. The survey was conducted by Relocation Commission staff in March and April 1987. Commission researchers interviewed 1,007 Navajo relocatee families about living conditions in their new homes and asked them how they felt about repeal of the law. According to survey information, over 60% of the relocatees interviewed currently live on the Navajo Reservation; 52% of those interviewed were over the age of thirty, and 22% were over forty.

"We wanted to know people's reaction to the possibility of repealing the law," David Shaw-Serdar, a commission statistics analyst explained. "So we added a question that said, 'for yourself and your immediate family, which would you prefer? A—Repeal the law and not get benefits and be able to move back as if the law had never passed, no or yes. Or, B—Keep the law the way it is and get benefits, no or yes,' plus, they could make comments."

Over 220 of the 1,007 families interviewed responded to the question. Of these families, 67% did not want the law repealed and supported receiving relocation benefits. Only 26% supported repeal of the law, revocation of benefits, and a return to life in the former JUA. The survey indicated that 6% responded yes to both—they wanted the law repealed and they also wanted to receive relocation benefits.

Critics of the survey have pointed out that they believe the sampling was too small to adequately reveal how relocatees really feel. Whether or not the survey reflects the feelings of all relocatees, however, the comments revealed both pragmatism and resignation. They showed that Navajo do not feel good about the law—they feel that it was wrong—but also that they feel it is too late for repeal of the law, and repeal of the law would also be unfair. One relocatee wrote, "but the law was passed. It is not up to us anymore, so why not get something out of it? It's better than getting left with nothing" (Relocation Commission Survey 1987).

A dominant theme in relocatee comments was concern about the future of their extended families. As has been stated in previous chapters, Navajo life revolves around the extended family. It is only natural that people would continue to be concerned about the survival of the extended family and clan system.

Hoping for the Best

The Navajo Tribe has continued to lobby Congress for a comprehensive settlement of both the 1934 and the 1882 areas. The Hopi Tribe remains adamant that they will accept no comprehensive settlement; they feel that they have lost enough land to the Navajo and they will not reopen the 1882 land issue. Meanwhile, the 1934 land case, involving Navajo, Hopi, and Paiute claims looms on the horizon.

In March 1988, United States District Court in Phoenix considered several motions by Navajo and Hopi tribal attorneys regarding the 1934 case. In pleadings before Judge Earl Carroll, Navajo tribal attorneys asked that the judge set a hearing date for the issue, preferably in summer 1989.* Navajo tribal attorneys said they wanted only Navajo and Hopi claims to be heard at the 1989 hearing, because to include the Paiutes would delay their case discovery. Hopi tribal attorneys said their clients have not opposed the Paiute petition for federal acknowledgement as an Indian tribe and they do not mind if the claims of Hopi, Paiute, and Navajo are heard together. The BIA has granted preliminary recognition to the San Juan Paiutes, but Judge Carroll will determine in what specific way they will be party to land claims in the

---

*A hearing date has been set for September 6, 1989. The hearing will include Navajos, Hopis, and Paiutes.

1934 area, if they receive any land at all, and how much.

According to attorneys for the tribes, it appears that Judge Carroll is leaning toward hearing the claims of all three tribes together in 1989, but until the final order from the judge is handed down, nothing is certain. Meanwhile, many Navajos in the 1934 area have fears and concerns about another relocation. Small groups from throughout the region have banded together under the leadership of a man called William Long Reed, and these groups have developed land protection strategies; they are beginning to mobilize to teach the outside world about their concerns in the 1934 case. The Hopi Tribe has retained a number of public relations and lobbying firms to fight for their interests through the media and in Washington, D.C. While it is unlikely that Judge Carroll will order another relocation, it is not impossible. All tribes involved are hoping for the best, but individually, are preparing for the worst.

BIOGRAPHIES

Catherine Feber-Elston

Navajo Tribal Chairman Peter MacDonald

Peter MacDonald was born at Teec Nos Pos, Arizona, in the heart of the Four Corners region on December 16, 1928. MacDonald was born into a traditional Navajo family, and grew up with Diné as his first language. As a child, MacDonald spent his time herding sheep and learning how to live in the Navajo Way. He is now one of the most articulate and charismatic of modern Indian leaders.

The Second World War ripped into the fabric of Navajo life and tore MacDonald away from his homeland. He enlisted in the United States Marine Corps in 1944, and served as a Navajo Code Talker in the South Pacific. He attained the rank of corporal and completed his enlistment in 1946. He returned to Dinétah and started thinking about ways to improve the lives of Navajo people.

MacDonald left the reservation and studied at Bacone Junior College, where he received an Associate of Arts degree in 1951. He received a Bachelor of Science degree in electrical engineering from the University of Oklahoma in 1957, and conducted graduate studies in his chosen field at the University of California at Los Angeles from 1958-62.

Before entering the political arena, MacDonald was involved in several classified technological projects. He was a project engineer and a member of the technical staff at Hughes Aircraft in El Segundo, California, from 1957-63, and the director of the company's Office of Management, Methods and Procedures from 1963-65.

MacDonald returned to Dinétah in 1965 to work with the Office of Navajo Economic Opportunity. It was at this time that MacDonald entered the complicated world of Navajo politics. In 1970, he was elected tribal chairman, serving three terms until his 1982 electoral defeat by Low Mountain leader Peterson Zah.

MacDonald worked with the engineering firm Cataract, Inc., founded by Indian millionaire Mel Pervais, while considering whether or not to return to public life after the 1982 defeat. He made his decision to seek another term in 1986, and his electoral bid was successful. MacDonald is now in an unprecedented fourth term as chairman of the Navajo Tribal Council.

MacDonald has long been in the limelight as a champion of Indian rights and Indian sovereignty. Perhaps his greatest contribution to the Indian people has been his opening of avenues for Indian self-sufficiency. MacDonald founded the Council of Energy Resource Tribes (a type of Indian OPEC) and is co-founder of the American Indian National Bank. Through his vision for the Navajo people, he took them from the nineteenth century into the twentieth, through economic and energy development. His efforts have helped to make the Navajo Tribe the most influential and powerful Indian tribe in America.

MacDonald laid the legal groundwork to ensure that Navajos have the right to tax businesses and energy development on their land. His efforts have helped not only the Navajo people in their struggle for self-sufficiency, but all American Indian tribes.

MacDonald, a Republican, was a member of President Reagan's Energy Policy Task Force. He was a member of the Board of Directors of Great Western Bank, CP National, Valley Life, and the Patagonia Corporation.

MacDonald was an outspoken opponent of Public law 93-531 and vehemently opposed to the relocation of Navajos from the disputed lands. During his first block of tenure as chairman, after his reelection in 1986, he studied ways to minimize the adverse impacts of relocation, and is now pushing for a comprehensive solution to the 1934 and 1882 dispute land cases.

Catherine Feher-Elston

Hopi Tribal Chairman Ivan Sidney

Ivan Sidney was only 34 years old when elected chairman of the Hopi Tribe in 1981. He was the youngest Hopi ever elected to that office. Now 41, Sidney has entered his second term.

Sidney was born at Polacca on August 19, 1947. He graduated from Phoenix Indian High School and studied police administration at Phoenix College. He worked as an officer with the Hopi Bureau of Indian Affairs Police after completing his college work. In 1969, Sidney went to work with the Arizona Department of Public Safety (Highway Patrol) for four years. He became Hopi BIA Police Chief in the 1970s, and served as chief for nine years.

Sidney entered the political arena in 1981, when he ran for tribal chairman. As an initiate into a Hopi religious society, Sidney has stressed that Hopi tradition, religion, and culture cannot be ignored in the running of the tribal government. In his seven years of office, Sidney has attempted to walk the tightrope between Hopi tradition and the contemporary world of American politics and economic development.

Perhaps Sidney's most significant contribution to the Hopi people has been his success in defeating Navajo legislative assaults against the relocation law. The Navajo Tribe has attempted to modify or repeal the relocation law since its inception, but Hopi lobbying and education of Congress have prevented any repeal of the law. Hopis maintain that the 1974 relocation law returned only half of their land to them. Sidney and the Hopi tribe are preparing litigation in the 1934 case, in an attempt to wrest away lands given to the Navajos. Hopis maintain that the western boundaries of the 1934 Navajo Reservation violated their territorial integrity, and say they need access to land that was traditionally theirs long before the Navajo Reservation was expanded.

Sidney, a Republican, is currently lobbying the White House and the Republican Party to establish an Indian Liaison Office to act as an information conduit to the president. Sidney has pointed out that Blacks and Hispanics have such offices, and that Indians need direct access to the president as well.

Sidney views the establishment of the Hopi High School on the reservation in 1986 as a major accomplishment since it will keep the children at home and, thus, help keep traditional Hopi culture, language, and traditions alive. Hopi children had previously been sent away from the mesas for high school education.

Sidney has encouraged appropriate technology in Hopi economic development. He negotiated the establishment of a hat factory with a South Korean firm in order to provide Hopi employment. The factory is located at the Hopi industrial park.

Sidney envisions a future of unity, peace, and prosperity for his people. He has worked hard to protect the lands Hopis received as a result of the partition of the 1882 disputed area and is focusing current efforts on the 1934 dispute. He has said that the Hopis will not accept a comprehensive settlement linking the 1882 and the 1934 boundary disputes.

BIBLIOGRAPHY

Published Sources

Abel, A., ed. *The Official Correspondence of James S. Calhoun.* Washington, D.C.: Government Printing Office, 1914.

Bancroft, H.H. *History of Arizona and New Mexico, 1530-1888.* San Francisco: The History Company, 1889.

Bartlett, Katherine. "The Navajo Wars." *Museum Notes* 6 (1934). Flagstaff: Museum of Northern Arizona.

———. "Spanish Contacts with the Hopi." *Museum Notes* 6 (1934). Flagstaff: Museum of Northern Arizona.

Benavides, Fray Alonso de. *Memorial of 1630 and Revised Memorial of 1634.* trans. by F.W. Hodge, G. Hammond, and A. Rey. Albuquerque: University of New Mexico Press, 1945.

Big Mountain Navajos. *Endangered Diné.* Photographs by John Running. Flagstaff, Arizona: Big Mountain People, 1981.

Bolton, H.D. *Coronado on the Turquoise Trail, Knight of Pueblo and Plains.* Albuquerque: University of New Mexico Press, 1949.

Clemmer, Richard O. *Continuities of Hopi Culture Change.* Ramona, California: Acoma Books, 1978.

Espinosa, J. Manuel. *First Expedition of Vargas into New Mexico, 1692.* Albuquerque: University of New Mexico Press, 1940.

Farmer, M.F. "Navajo Archaeology of Upper Blanco and Largo Canyons of Northern New Mexico." *American Antiquity* 8 (1943):65-79.

Friday Locke, Raymond. *The Book of the Navajo.* Los Angeles: Mankind Publishing Company, 1976.

Grant, Blanche, ed. *Kit Carson's Own Story.* Taos, New Mexico: n.p., 1926.

Hammond, G.P., and A. Rey. *Expedition into New Mexico Made by Antonio de Espejo, 1582-1583, as Revealed in the Journal of Diego de Luxan, a Member of the Party*. Los Angeles: The Quivera Society, 1929.

————. *Narratives of the Coronado Expedition, 1540-1542*. Albuquerque: University of New Mexico Press, 1940.

————. *Don Juan de Onate, Colonizer of New Mexico, 1595-1628*. Albuquerque: University of New Mexico Press, 1936.

Hill, W.W. *Navajo Warfare*. Yale University Publications in Anthropology, no. 5. New Haven, Conn.: Yale University Press, 1936.

Indian Law Resource Center. *Report to the Hopi Kikmongwis and Other Traditional Hopi Leaders on Docket 196 and the Continuing Threat to Hopi Land and Sovereignty*. Washington, D.C.: Indian Law Resource Center, 1979.

James, Harry C. *Pages from Hopi History*. Tucson: The University of Arizona Press, 1974.

Kammer, Jerry. *The Second Long Walk*. Albuquerque: University of New Mexico Press, 1980.

Kappler, Charles J., ed. *Indian Affairs, Laws and Treaties*. 3 vols. Washington, D.C.: Government Printing Office, 1904, 1915.

McNitt, Frank. *Navajo Wars: Military Campaigns, Slave Raids and Reprisals*. Albuquerque: University of New Mexico Press, 1972.

Nequatewa, Edmund. *Truth of a Hopi*. Flagstaff, Arizona: Northland Press in cooperation with the Museum of Northern Arizona, 1967.

Qua'Toqti Newspaper. Interview with Duke Pahona. July 14, 1977.

Twitchell, E. *The Spanish Archives of New Mexico, II*. Albuquerque: Torch Press, 1914.

Whiteley, Peter. *Deliberate Acts*. Tucson: University of Arizona Press, 1988.

PUBLICATIONS OF THE HOPI TRIBE

The Hopi Perspective: 1979. New Oraibi, 1979.
Hopi Tunat'ya: Hopi Comprehensive Development Plan, A Summary. Kykotsmovi, 1987.
We Care. New Oraibi, 1979.

PUBLICATIONS OF THE NAVAJO TRIBE

Navajo-Hopi Backgrounder. Window Rock, 1980.
Report of the Navajo-Hopi Land Dispute Task Force. Window Rock, 1987.

Unpublished Sources

Associated Press. July 17, 1987, newswire.

Cahn, Edgar, and Peter MacDonald. Unpublished, untitled manuscript underwritten by the Navajo Tribe, 1981–82. Flagstaff, Arizona: Southwest Information.

Commission for Accelerating Navajo Development Opportunities (CANDO). Phone conversation with author, March 1988.

Feher, Catherine Frances. "Perceptions of Land Ownership in the Navajo-Hopi Land Dispute: An Ethnohistoric Study." Research paper. Flagstaff, Arizona: Southwest Information.

Feher, Catherine Frances, and William E. Wilson. "A Study of Mortality and Natality by Tribe and Chapter in the Former Navajo-Hopi Joint Use Area of Northern Arizona, U.S.A." Research project and funding proposal. Flagstaff, Arizona: Southwest Information.

Navajo Tribal Development Office. *Navajo Tribal Education Assessment,* 1987. Window Rock, Arizona.

Stephens, C.H. "The Origin and History of the Hopi-Navajo Boundary Dispute in Northern Arizona. Master's thesis, Brigham Young University, 1964.

Wood, J.J., and K. Stemmler. "Land and Religion at Big Mountain." Report. Bound by Navajo Times Press, Window Rock, Arizona. 1981.

Wood, John, Walter Vannette, and Michael Andrews. "A Sociocultural Assessment of the Livestock Reduction Program in the Navajo-Hopi Joint Use Area." Report for the Flagstaff office of the Bureau of Indian Affairs, 1979.

Interviews with Author

These interviews were conducted from 1981 through 1988. Specific dates and places are not given because, in most cases, the author developed friendships and working relationships with these people and met with them many times over the last seven years.

HOPI

Bahnimptewa, Stanley (Kikmongwi, Oraibi)
Banyacaya, Thomas (Kymotsmovi)
Dallas, Leonard (Upper Moencopi Village)
Dallas, Patrick (Director, Office of Hopi Lands)
Dan, Heber (Kikmongwi, Moencopi)
Hamilton, Clarence (Former Hopi Tribal Chairman)

Johnson, Caleb, Rev. (Spokesman for Oraibi kikmongwi, born in Moen-
    copi)
Leslie, Ebin (Kikmongwi, First Mesa)
Lomakema, Milland (Director, Hopi Crafts Guild, Second Mesa)
Mahle, Ethel (Walpi, First Mesa)
Monougue, David "Grandfather" (Hotevilla)
Sekaquaptewa, Abbott (Former Hopi Tribal Chairman)
Shingoitewa, LeRoy (Upper Moencopi)
Sidney, Ivan (Hopi Tribal Chairman)
Talaswaima, Terrence (Honvantewa) (Curator, Hopi Museum/Hopi
    Cultural Center)
Other Hopi and Tewa people who wish to remain anonymous.

NAVAJO

Arviso, Katherine Dahozy (Ft. Defiance)
Billy, Irving (Former Supervisor, Western Navajo Agency, Tuba City)
Blackgoat, Roberta (Nataani, Big Mountain)
Boone, Sam, Sr. (Coppermine, herbalist, supporter Native American
    [Peyote] Church)
Cody, Nephi (Medicineman)
Daizy, Colbert (Navajo-Hopi Task Force)
Deal, Percy (Big Mountain)
Homes, Annie (Big Mountain)
Joe, Mary Lucy (Navajo-Hopi Task Force)
Keams, Geraldine (Navajo actress from White Cone)
MacDonald, Peter (Navajo Tribal Chairman)
MacDonald, Wanda (First Lady, Navajo Nation)
Nez, Miller (Medicineman, White Cone)
Ration, Norman (DNA Legal Services, Navajo-Laguna)
Scott, Peggy (Navajo-Hopi Land Commission)
Shay, Kee (Nataani, Big Mountain)
Smith, Katherine (Nataani, Big Mountain)
Thompson, Johnny (Navajo Tribal Vice Chairman)
Tsosie, Sally (Big Mountain)
Walters, Nancy (Big Mountain)
Watchman, Lydia (Nataani, Big Mountain/Cactus Valley)
Whitesinger, Pauline (Nataani, Big Mountain)
Zah, Peterson (Former Navajo Tribal Chairman, FJUA resident)
Other Navajo people who wish to remain anonymous

PAIUTES

James, Evelyn (Spokeswoman, San Juan Band of Paiutes)

OTHER INTERVIEWEES

Atkinson, Hawley (Navajo and Hopi Indian Relocation Commissioner)

Beaver, Bill (Trader, Sacred Mountain Trading Post)

Berger, Leon (Former Executive Director, Navajo and Hopi Indian Relocation Commission; Former Executive Director, Navajo-Hopi Task Force)

Crystal, Susan (Attorney, Navajo and Hopi Indian Relocation Commission)

Goodrich, Steven (Former Executive Director, Navajo and Hopi Indian Relocation Commission)

Gurwitz, Lewis (Founder, Big Mountain Legal Defense/Offense Committee)

Havatone, Wendall J. (Hualapai Tribal Vice-Chairman)

Hoffman, Charles (Professor of Anthropology, Northern Arizona University

Inouye, Daniel (U.S. Senate, Chairman, U.S. Senate Committee on Indian Affairs)

Kealiinohomoku, Joann (Founder, Cross-Cultural Dance Resource Center; Professor Emeritus, Northern Arizona University, Department of Anthropology

Lewis, Roger (Former Navajo and Hopi Indian Relocation Commissioner)

Lujan, Manuel (U.S. House of Representatives, New Mexico)

Massetto, Sandra (Navajo and Hopi Indian Relocation Comissioner)

Means, Russell (Lakota, co-founder, AIM)

Phillips, Lee (Big Mountain Legal Defense/Offense Committee, attorney)

Shaw-Serdar, David (Research Analyst, Navajo and Hopi Indian Relocation Commission)

Stuhff, Michael (Attorney)

Walema, Edgar B. (Hualapai Tribal Chairman)

Watkins, Ralph (Navajo and Hopi Indian Relocation Commissioner)

Waxman, Alan (Physician, Medical Consultant, Navajo Nation Family Planning)

Government Documents

Dorrington, L. A. Letter to the Commissioner of Indian Affairs, 7 January 1925. Washington, D.C., Department of Interior.

Eastman, Galen. Letter to E. A. Hayt, 21 January 1880. Washington, D.C., Department of Interior.

————. Letter to Commissioner of Indian Affairs, 20 March 1880. Washington, D.C., Department of Interior.

Hayt, E. A. Letter to William Mateer, 14 August 1879. Washington, D.C., Department of Interior.

Howard, C. H. Letter to H. M. Teller, 14 July 1882. Washington, D.C., Office of the Secretary of the Interior, Indian Division.

Merritt, E. S. Letter to Commissioner E. A. Hayt, 23 February 1880. Washington, D.C., Department of Interior.

Miller, Edgar K. Letter to Commissioner of Indian Affairs, 20 March 1930. Keams Canyon, Arizona, Hopi Agency Files.

————. Letters to the Commissioner of Indian Affairs, 1925, 1927. Keams Canyon, Arizona: Hopi Agency Files.

————. Memo about the Flagstaff Conference, 1930. Keams Canyon, Arizona: Hopi Agency Files.

Sullivan, J. H. Letter to Commissioner of Indian Affairs, 31 January 1881. Washington, D.C., Department of Interior, Bureau of Indian Affairs, Letters Received.

Tipps, Betsy L. *Cultural Resource Investigations near Big Mountain, Arizona: Inventory and Ethnohistory Along the Turquoise Trail Road Project.* Phoenix, Arizona: Bureau of Indian Affairs, Phoenix Area Office, 1987.

U.S. Bureau of the Census. *1980 Census.* Washington, D.C., 1980.

U.S. Congress. House. Executive Document 263, 49th Cong., 1st Sess., 1868.

U.S. Congress. Senate. *Report of H. J. Hagerman—Navajo Reservation.* 72nd Congress, 1st Session, 1932.

U.S. Congress. Senate. Subcommittee of the Committee on Indian Affairs. *Hearings: Survey of the Conditions of the Indians in the United States,* 71st Cong., 3rd Sess., 1932.

U.S. Department of Commerce. *Federal and State Indian Reservations and Indian Trust Areas.* Washington, D.C.: Government Printing Office, 1976.

U.S. Department of Interior. Office of Indian Affairs. *Reports of the Commissioner of Indian Affairs,* 1852-99, and especially 1874, 1876, 1878, 1881, 1902, 1972. Washington, D.C.: Government Printing Office.

U.S. Navajo and Hopi Indian Relocation Commission. *Evaluation of the Navajo-Hopi Task Force Statement:* Washington, D.C.: Government Printing Office, 1987.

————. *Report and Plan.* Washington, D.C.: Government Printing Office, 1981.

APPENDIX A

CHRONOLOGY OF EVENTS
IN THE 1882 EXECUTIVE ORDER AREA

(*Source:* Bureau of Indian Affairs, Phoenix, Arizona Office)

600-1300   Hopi settled in Arizona and New Mexico area.

1500   Evidence Navajo settled in northwestern New Mexico area.

1863   A government agency for the Hopis established at Keams Canyon.

1868   The U.S. enters into a treaty with the Navajo under which the Navajos are granted an extensive reservation to the east of what is to become the Executive Order reservation of Dec. 16, 1882 (1882 area).

1863-1880   Executive Order issued adding to the Navajo reservation which totals eight million acres by 1880.

1882   President Chester Arthur issues an Executive Order setting aside
(12/16)   a reservation of approximately 2.5 million acres for the Hopis (Moquis)—"and such other Indians as the Secretary of the Interior may see fit to settle thereon."

This order does not include the Hopi village of Moencopi to the west.

Approximately 300 Navajo are living within this area at the time of the Executive Order.

1890   U.S. troops are sent to Keams Canyon because of growing Hopi-Navajo disputes and an internal Hopi dispute in the village of Oraibi over a new school.

1931   Secretary of the Interior and Commissioner of Indian Affairs, in a
(2/7)   letter to a special commission that had been asked to make a recommendation on the Navajo-Hopi problem, effects an *implicit* legal settlement of all Navajos *then* residing on the portion of the 1882 area which lies outside the exclusive Hopi section.

1934   By Congressional action, the Navajo reservation boundaries in Arizona are established. This act set aside land for the benefit of Navajo and "such other Indians as are already settled thereon."

            This includes the Hopi village of Moencopi and certain Paiute Indians whose occupancy dates back to antiquity.

1937   Commissioner of Indian Affairs signs and promulgates a map de-
(12/28)   fining land-management districts established within the Navajo and Hopi reservations, setting down the carrying capacity for livestock in each of the districts. The Commissioner notes in transmitting this action to the field—"It is understood, also, and it should be clearly explained to the Navajo and Hopi councils, that the delineation of District 6 is not a delineation of a boundary for the Hopi Tribe, but is exclusively a delineation of a land-management unit."

1943   The Office of Indian Affairs approves new boundaries and carrying
(4/24)   capacity for land management District 6. A statement of administrative policy concerning the use of this area also is issued. Total land area in District 6 is 631,000 acres.

1958   Congress enacts a jurisdictional statute authorizing a three-judge U.S. District Court to adjudicate the conflicting claims of the tribes to the 1882 area lands and to determine the relative rights and interests of the tribes to the land.

1961   *Healing v. Jones* case filed in U.S. District Court.
(8/2)

1962   The court hands down a decision in the case of *Healing v. Jones*.
(9/28)   The court decides:

            (1) Neither tribe obtained any vested rights in the land under the 1882 Executive Order. The rights are vested in the tribes by the

1958 jurisdictional act and thereupon became protected by the 5th Amendment to the U.S. Constitution.

(2) By a 1943 administrative action establishing a grazing district for the exclusive use of the Hopi surrounding the Hopi villages, the Hopi obtained exclusive right subject to the trust title of the U.S. to that area, known as land management District 6.

(3) Because of administrative action taken between 1937 and 1943, the Secretary implicitly settled the Navajo Tribe within the 1882 reservation under the authority of the Executive Order.

(4) The Hopi Tribe and the Navajo Tribe, subject to the trust title of the U.S., have a joint, undivided, and equal interest in the entire 1882 Executive Order reservation outside of land management District 6.

(5) The jurisdiction act of 1958 did not confer authority on the court to partition joint interest between the two tribes.

1963 (6/3)	The Supreme Court affirms the judgment in the case of *Healing v. Jones.*
1970 (March)	The Hopi Tribe petitions the District Court to issue a writ of assistance enforcing the Hopi rights to the Joint Use Area.
(August)	The District Court dismisses the Hopi petition on grounds that it has no jurisdiction over the question of tribal control of the disputed area.
1971 (12/3)	The Court of Appeals for the 9th Circuit reverses the District Court decision, holding that the District Court has authority to issue a writ of assistance and remands the matter for further proceeding.
1972 (5/22)	The U.S. Supreme Court denies a Navajo petition for a writ of certiorari. (Review of lower court decision.)
(10/14)	The District Court issues an order directing the Navajo Tribe to:

(1) Afford Hopi Tribe its proper joint-use of the disputed area.

(2) Reduce its livestock in the Joint Use Area to one-half of the carrying capacity.

(3) Administer the area jointly with the Hopi Tribe.

1972   The Navajo Tribe appeals from the court's order and then, at the court's request, submits an alternative plan to implement the order.

1973   The court rejects the Navajo plan and adopts a U.S. plan for achiev-
(4/23)   ing true joint use of disputed area.

(July)   Hopi petition the court to cite the Navajos for contempt of court as a result of non-compliance with the court order on four specific items:

            (1) Removal of livestock.

            (2) Division of rental.

            (3) Exchange of documents.

            (4) New construction.

(12/1)   The government petitions the court for one additional year to comply with the Oct. 14, 1972, order. Navajos join in this petition with a request of a two-year extension.

            The court denies the request for additional time.

1974   The court finds Chairman MacDonald and the Navajo Tribe guilty
(5/29)   of contempt in failing to reduce livestock and in failing to control new construction within the Joint Use Area.

(12/22)   President Gerald Ford signs the Navajo-Hopi Land Settlement Act (P.L. 93-531), ending a two-year legislative struggle to settle the dispute.

1976   JUA office in Flagstaff, AZ, starts livestock reduction program.
(4/15)

1977   Federal District Court issues order and injunction against Hopi and
(3/11)   Navajo tribes. Secretary of the Interior is given exclusive responsibility and jurisdiction on all matters relating to livestock reduction, fencing, monumenting, surveying and grazing control.

1978   A Federal District Court order is issued basically comprised of four
(11/30)   parts:

            (1) Total permits issued to Navajo awaiting relocation shall not exceed one-half of the total carrying capacity.

(2) No permit for grazing may be issued to any Navajo who was not grazing livestock at the time of the decree of partition.

(3) If any Navajo permit holder discontinues grazing for any reason, the permit shall be cancelled and no new permit shall be issued. Also, the number of animals being grazed by the permit holder shall be reduced by the number covered by the cancelled permit.

(4) The Secretary is expected to diligently pursue full enforcement of the regulations prohibiting overgrazing and trespassing by livestock of the permit holders. The Secretary will, under his law enforcement authority, see to it that persons and property of members of both tribes are protected lawfully within the respective grazing areas.

1979 (4/18)	Entry of the final judgment of partition by the federal court.
(11/1)	JUA office in Flagstaff issues permits to eligible Navajo relocatees.
1980 (7/8)	Navajo and Hopi Indian Relocation Amendments Act (P.L. 96-305) becomes law. Emphasizes three points:

(1) Abolishes the administrative office of the BIA in Flagstaff, AZ.

(2) Transfers administrative office program responsibilities to Phoenix and Navajo area offices.

(3) Authorizes tribal jurisdiction of partitioned areas to become effective April 18, 1981.

(10/9)	Secretarial Order No. 3057 signed. Transfers administrative jurisdiction over land partitioned to the Navajo and Hopi tribes to the BIA Navajo and Phoenix area offices.
1981 (3/13)	Hopi Tribe files in federal District Court challenging Secretarial Order No. 3057.
(4/22)	Impoundment of livestock in HPL begins. Four horses and three cows impounded first day.
(5/4)	Navajo demonstration at Hopi Agency at Keams Canyon, AZ. Protesters march from Jeddito Chapter House to the BIA agency. No serious incidents.

(5/5)   Navajo demonstrators protest in Flagstaff. Seek to meet with Washington BIA official Ted Krenzkie but do not.

(5/11)   Acting commissioner of Indian Affairs Kenneth Payton informs Acting Phoenix Area Director Curtis Geiogamah of the decision to suspend impoundment of livestock.

Navajo demonstration at Keams Canyon, AZ. Marchers from Jeddito Chapter House number 800 to 1,200, more than three times as many as May 4, 1981. No serious incidents.

(5/18)   Navajo demonstrators, numbering about 300, march on Phoenix Area Office. No serious incidents.

(8/12)   Acting Deputy Assistant Secretary Kenneth Payton writes Chairman MacDonald informing him that impoundment will resume.

Payton said Hopi Chairman Sekaquaptewa had stressed the requirement that livestock be reduced to carrying capacity by Jan. 8, 1982.

He also said the Phoenix Area Office would accept and process grazing applications made by the Navajo Tribe on behalf of individuals unable or unwilling to file their own application.

(10/15)   Phoenix Area Office announces teams will hand deliver valid grazing permits to Navajos living in the Hopi Partitioned Area.

Phoenix Area Director William Finale signs the general notice of intent to impound.

Permits to Navajos will be issued for a one-year period from Nov. 1, 1981, to Oct. 31, 1982.

(Oct., following)   Because of the holidays and legislative action, it is decided to delay impoundment action until after the first of the year.

1982 (1/21)   U.S. District Court Judge Earl H. Carroll issues an order concluding—"All conservation practices undertaken by the Secretary of Interior, including grazing control and range restoration activities, shall be coordinated and executed by the Secretary with the concurrence of the tribe."

The order also said the Secretary continues to be responsible for relocatees living in the area.

1982
(3/29)

Judge Carroll holds Chairman MacDonald and Navajo tribal officials in contempt of court for failing to comply with the 1977 order to remove existing Navajo-owned structures in Hopi Partitioned Area.

Carroll orders a $500-per-day fine starting April 15, 1982, if structures remain.

(4/30)

Judge Carroll issues his judgment in the case of *Hopi Tribe v. Secretary of the Interior*. Major issues include:

(1) The Secretary is responsible to administer and execute conservation practices including grazing control and range restoration on Hopi Partitioned Lands.

(2) The Secretary must seek concurrence from the tribe owning the land (applied both to Navajo and Hopi partitioned areas) before executing conservation practices on the land.

(3) The Secretary shall have the right to take such action as he deems necessary to protect rights and property of life tenants and persons awaiting relocation, but must issue a written order, with appropriate findings of fact justifying the action before taking such action where he is unable to obtain concurrence.

(4) Life tenants and persons awaiting relocation have grazing rights which are property.

(5) Each tribe has jurisdiction and authority over its partitioned lands and all persons located thereon.

(6) The Secretary is enjoined from: (a) failing to actively administer conservation practices; (b) failing to coordinate with and obtain concurrence of Hopi Tribe before executing practices; (c) from administering grazing and range restoration in matters in accordance with 25 CFR 12 and 153 without first obtaining concurrence.

(7) Secretary is ordered to promulgate rules and regulations consistent with P.L. 93-305 within 60 days (June 29, 1982).

(6/30)

Phoenix Area Office sends letter to the Hopi Tribe with proposed regulations for concurrence.

| 1982 (8/3) | Judge Carroll orders the Navajo Tribe to pay a $19,000 fine for violating court order of March 29, 1982, to remove residential structures in Hopi Partitioned Area. |

He also rules the Navajo Tribe may have to pay an additional $500 for each day the structures remain standing, and directs Navajo leaders to post a $75,000 bond with the court to cover possible future charges.

(8/18) Phoenix Area Office officials meet with Hopi Tribe; tribal leaders inform Phoenix Area Director they do not concur with proposed regulations.

(8/19) Tribal attorney for Hopi notifies Field Solicitor that the tribe does not concur with the proposed regulations because of lack of consultation in the development of regulations.

(8/27) The Phoenix Area Director is formally notified that there is non-concurrence by the Hopi Tribe on the proposed regulations; a hearing is scheduled for Sept. 14, 1982.

(8/31-9/1) At a hearing before Judge Carroll, the court implies that if the Secretary does not affirmatively act in accordance with the April 30, 1982, judgment within 10 days, he may be considered for contempt of court.

(9/10) Interim regulations are published in the Federal Register and made effective.

(9/13) Phoenix Area Director James H. Stevens issues a general impoundment notice for Hopi Partitioned Area; notices are posted and circulated to area newspapers.

(9/14) At an administrative hearing held in the Phoenix Area Office, the Hopi Tribe formally presents a brief on the proposed regulations and reaffirms non-concurrence and objects to implementation.

Steps are taken to reissue permits on Hopi Partitioned Lands; individual notices of intent to impound are sent by Phoenix Area Office.

(11/30) Assistant Secretary of the Interior for Indian Affairs Kenneth Smith finds grazing regulations are necessary to protect the rights and property of Navajos awaiting relocation and issues an order amending the interim grazing regulations (25 CFR 168) and adopting them over Hopi Tribe non-concurrence.

1983
(January)

Peterson Zah inaugurated as Navajo Tribal Chairman. Announces new policy of working toward settlement of Navajo-Hopi problems in partitioned areas; will sit down with Hopi Tribal Chairman Ivan Sidney to discuss mutual concerns.

(2/2)

Navajo individuals file suit against the Secretary of Interior *(Zee v. Watt)* seeking declaratory and injunctive relief, contending the HPL grazing program is not in conformance with P.L. 93-531.

(3/10)

The United States files a motion to dismiss *Zee v. Watt* on grounds individuals may not bring such action.

(4/15)

Case of *Hopi v. Watt* argued in 9th Circuit Court on appeal from the decision of District Court in Arizona. Case pending.

(5/25)

All valid Navajo HPL grazing permits now in effect; approximately 200 permits covering 3500 SUYL (Sheep Units Year Long).

(5/27)

Hopi Tribe notified of the Navajo grazing demand on the HPL for the 1983 grazing season and informed it could allocate the balance of the stocking rate, or some 6300 SUYL, to Hopi livestock owners.

(6/8)

District Court hearing in Flagstaff, AZ, on all matters involving Hopi Partitioned Lands. Purpose is to determine whether outstanding issues can be settled by agreements between the parties or will require court action.

(6/22)

First amended complaint for injunctive and declaratory relief in *Zee v. Watt* filed in District Court by DNA.

(6/27)

Joint report to the court concerning negotiations by the Navajo and Hopi tribes on "new construction" and grazing issues as requested in June 8, 1983, hearing. Filed by the Justice Department in concert with Navajo and Hopi tribes.

Affidavit of Assistant Area Director Pat Ragsdale of the Phoenix Area Office. Discusses Secretarial responsibility under the Settlement Act and the Phoenix Area's policy and program to carry out this responsibility.

(7/28)

Phoenix Area Director Stevens notifies Hopi Tribe it has 30 days to issue permits to Hopi livestock owners or any Hopi animals grazing on HPL will be in trespass.

1983
(8/2)

Supplemental memorandum of the United States in support of its motion to dismiss *Sidney v. Navajo Tribe*. Filed by the Justice Department.

(8/10)

Notices sent to individual Navajos requesting applications for the upcoming 1984 grazing permit period.

(8/26)

Letter from Navajo Tribe to Judge Carroll discussing lack of progress of negotiations between the two tribes on "new construction" and grazing issues as set forth in June 8, 1983, hearing.

(8/31)

Hopi Tribe requests a stay in the impoundment of Hopi livestock on HPL. Tribal council has been actively pursuing a permitting procedure but has failed to reach a final agreement.

(9/12)

General trespass notices posted throughout HPL and published in local newspapers.

(9/14)

Report from Justice Department to Judge Carroll affirming the lack of progress in negotiations between the two tribes on "new construction" and grazing issues.

(9/20)

Interior Secretary Watt rescinds Phoenix Area Director's order of July 28, 1983, to impound Hopi livestock on HPL.

(10/12)

Home visits to eligible Navajo permittees begin. Purpose of visit is to secure signature or approval letters and permits.

(10/31)

Preliminary draft report from Dames and Moore, biological analysis of rangeland in the Hopi Partitioned Area.

(11/10)

Individual Navajos begin to file appeals of Phoenix Area Director's decision on their 1984 permit eligibility.

(12/31)

Total livestock impounded on HPL in 1983: 80 horses, 52 cows, and 10 calves. Of impounded livestock, 15 horses and five cows were sold at public auction. Six horses were illegally removed from the impoundment corral and 15 cows were forcibly removed from a livestock trailer as they were being transported to the impoundment corral. The balance of impounded livestock was redeemed by owners or Navajo Tribe.

For the 1983 grazing season there are 210 Navajo permittees grazing livestock on the HPL with a grazing demand of 3500 SUYL. This is 1435 SUYLs less than in 1982.

1984	Memorandum from Assistant Secretary saying the Department can-
(2/8)	not compel the Hopi Tribe to implement tribal range conservation

1984
(2/8)

Memorandum from Assistant Secretary saying the Department cannot compel the Hopi Tribe to implement tribal range conservation measures on the HPL. However, the Department has the power and duty to enforce conservation measures if necessary to protect the rights and property of Navajo relocatees.

The memorandum directed the Phoenix Area Director to take such measures as necessary to remove trespass Navajo livestock from the HPL and authorized the impoundment of Hopi livestock if its presence adversely affects the rights and property of Navajo relocatees or life tenants.

(2/14)

Hopi Tribe is awarded a P.L. 93-638 contract in the amount of $1.3 million for range restoration and conservation in range units 551-556.

(3/10)

Soil Conservation Service completes the range site and condition class delineation on the HPL and provides draft copies of site maps and write-ups.

(3/15)

Final report from Dames and Moore, biological analysis of rangeland on the Hopi Partitioned Land, is received.

(4/9)

Begin work on calculating stocking rate for HPL and District 6.

(5/11)

Hearing in District Court on *Hopi v. Clark*. During the hearing Judge Carroll is informed of the vegetative study recently completed on HPL, the apparent improvement in vegetative condition, and the grazing control efforts of the Bureau.

Judge Carroll questions why the Bureau is not enforcing trespass regulations and not collecting trespass fees.

(5/21)

Meeting with Office of Natural Resources of Hopi Tribe to deliver a copy of the biological analysis of rangeland on the HPL and conduct a seminar on the technology and methods used by the Bureau in conducting a vegetative inventory.

(5/25)

Completed stocking rate determination for HPL and District 6.

(June)

In a meeting in Albuquerque, NM, Assistant Secretary Smith agrees to hold monthly meetings to keep all parties informed of the activities occurring in Navajo and Hopi partitioned areas. Navajo and Phoenix area directors will schedule and coordinate these meetings with the two tribes.

1984 (6/22)	Coordination meeting is held at Navajo Community College with Hopi and Navajo tribes, Phoenix and Navajo area office officials. Purpose of meeting is to discuss mutual items of interest on partitioned areas. Deputy Assistant Secretary John Fritz attends.
	Navajo Tribe agrees to provide assistance in removing trespass livestock by hiring range riders.
(6/25)	Hopi Partitioned Lands Office moves from Flagstaff, AZ, to Phoenix Area Office.
(7/9)	Plaintiff's interrogations and request for production on the Owelty issue (both partitioned areas should be of equal value) filed by Hopi Tribe in *Sidney v. Watt*.
(8/10)	Notice sent to individual Navajo requesting application for upcoming 1985 grazing permit period.
(8/20)	The Hopi Tribe and Justice Department file stipulation to maintain "status quo" on fence closures on the partition line.
(9/6)	Hopi Tribe passes resolution H-117-84 to move Hopi Partitioned Lands Office to Keams Canyon, AZ, on Hopi reservation.
(9/30)	Soil Conservation Service files final report and maps for soil survey and range site condition class investigation on both District 6 and HPL with Phoenix Area Office.
(10/2)	Coordination meeting held at the Navajo-Hopi Relocation Commission offices in Flagstaff, AZ, with Hopi and Navajo tribes and Phoenix and Navajo area office personnel.
(10/9)	Navajo Tribe ordered by District Court to pay Hopi Tribe $403,000 in contempt charges for illegal construction of houses on HPL by individual Navajos.
(10/26)	Coordination meeting held in Gallup, NM, with Hopi and Navajo tribes, Phoenix and Navajo area offices.
(12/3)	Federal defendants supplemental responses and objections to plaintiff's interrogations and request for production of documents on the Owelty issue filed in District Court by Justice Department.
(12/31)	Total livestock impounded on HPL during 1984: 23 horses, one mule, 10 cows and four calves. Of the impounded animals, one

mule and two yearling cows are sold at public auction. The remainder of the animals either are returned or redeemed by owners or Navajo Tribe.

For the 1984 grazing season there are 179 Navajo permittees grazing livestock on HPL with a grazing demand of 2972 SUYL. This is 658 SUYL less than in 1983.

1985 (1/18)	Response to inquiry by Deputy Assistant Secretary Fritz regarding letter from Cactus Valley-Red Willow Springs sovereignty.

(1/25)   Navajo first set of interrogatories and request for production of documents. *Sidney v. Zah.*

(1/28)   Arizona Governor Bruce Babbitt declares an emergency in northern portions of the Navajo and Hopi reservations due to heavy snow and mud. National Guard is called out to provide assistance to the two tribes in delivering food, water and medical supplies to individuals, including several Navajo relocatees in the northern portion of the HPL.

(1/29)   Notice sent to Navajo Tribe informing its officials of individual Navajo permittees who failed to pay the Hopi permit fee.

(1/31)   Hopi Agency Superintendent is provided a copy of the appraisal, "Report Grazing Rate Analysis Hopi Partitioned Lands 1982-1985," by Burke, Hansen, Homan and Klafter. Minimum acceptable grazing rental rate $4.50/AUM on District 6 and $6.00/AUM on Hopi Partitioned Lands.

(2/8)   "Federal Defendants Response to Plaintiffs Motion for Partial Summary Judgment" and a "Motion to File a Brief in Excess of the Range Limitation." *Hopi Tribe v. Navajo Tribe.*

(2/12)   Former Interior Secretary William Clark, serving as the personal envoy of President Reagan, meets with tribal chairmen Sidney and Zah at Keams Canyon. Clark delivers letter from Reagan saying the land dispute "cannot be allowed to persist." Clark and aide Richard Morris will attempt to secure an agreement between the two tribes in coming months.

(2/15)   Final determination of the grazing rental value for Navajo livestock on the HPL from September, 1978, through December 31, 1984 (BIA-NH-1), is mailed both to the Hopi and Navajo tribes.

1985
(2/25)

Navajo Tribe pays the Hopi fee for individuals listed in the Jan. 29, 1985, notice.

(3/13)

Phoenix Area Director, Assistant Area Director and Hopi Agency officials meet with the Joint Conference Committee to discuss livestock permitting on District 6 and explain the Bureau's position concerning Ordinance 40.

(3/25)

Letter from Hopi attorney to Hopi Tribe expressing legal position on grazing control both on District 6 and the HPL. No change from past position.

(3/27)

Complaint is filed by Hopi Tribe. *Hopi Tribe v. Navajo Tribe and Hodel.* Action to collect rental payments due the Hopi Tribe from the Navajo Tribe pursuant to the Settlement Act. The Secretary and the United States are joined to compel them to perform statutory, trust and fiduciary duties imposed by Congress in connection with the determination of the amount of such rental payments with their collection.

(3/29)

Judge Carroll dismissed *Zee v. Watt* case. Individual Navajo relocatees have no standing in this matter as the grazing rights on the HPL rest with the Navajo tribe.

Hopi Superintendent grants 60-day extension to the Hopi tribe to allow time for implementing a permit program on District 6 and the HPL. The 60-day extension expires on May 15, 1985.

(4/29)

Notice of appeal filed by Hopi Tribe in BIA-NH-1, the grazing rental determination on HPL, 1978-1984.

(5/1)

Notice of appeal filed by Hopi Tribe in BIA-NH-1, grazing rental determination on HPL for the period 1978-1984.

(5/31)

Navajo motion to dismiss Hopi appeal BIA-NH-1.

(6/24)

In accordance with P.L. 96-305 and subsequent court decisions, 11 range units turned over to Hopi Tribe for its exclusive management and control.

(7/2)

Plaintiff's motion for partial summary judgment-damage case filed by Hopi Tribe in *Sidney v. Navajo Tribe*. Plaintiffs reserve the right to determine at a future date: (1) the amount of damage to the lands in question; (2) the amount of liability of the Navajo Tribe; and (3) the amount of liability of the United States.

Plaintiffs memorandum in support of motion for partial summary judgment, *Hopi Tribe v. Navajo Tribe.*

1985
(8/1)

Acting Area Director Walter Mills writes letter to Chairman Sidney informing the Hopi Tribe of 1985 Navajo grazing demand and the stocking rate available for Hopi use on the HPL by range unit.

(8/13)

U.S. District Court order in *Hopi Tribe v. Navajo Tribe* ordering parties to comply with Local Rule 42(c) in its entirety no later than December 5, 1985. Rule 42 calls for a statement of facts and a statement of law.

(8/29)

Letter to Bureau of Indian Affairs from Chairman Sidney requesting (1) names and addresses of all occupants known to BIA who "are legally occupying" the HPL; (2) funding sources for dwellings that have been illegally constructed or improved on the HPL; and (3) if the BIA has developed a comprehensive plan for the removal of illegal occupants from the HPL on July 7, 1986.

(10/3)

Reply of Hopi Tribe to Navajo motion to dismiss BIA-NH-1.

(10/10)

Hopi Resolution H-117-85 urging Sandra Massetto to voluntarily resign from Navajo-Hopi Relocation Commission. Sen. Dennis De-Concini, D-Ariz. responds by calling for Chairman Sidney to step down instead.

(10/18)

Acting Area Director Walter Mills response to Chairman Sidney's August 29, 1985, letter.

(10/21)

Mediator Richard Morris reports to former Interior Secretary William Clark that problems dealing with the land dispute "cannot be resolved by voluntary agreement between the Hopi and Navajo." Morris adds: "Lacking agreement between the tribes or changes in existing law, it is clear the relocation of Navajo from Hopi land must go forward."

(12/22)

P.L. 99-190 (continuing resolution) passed by Congress. Provides for the Assistant Secretary of Indian Affairs to participate in the relocation of Navajos awaiting relocation to the New Lands. During the congressional hearings on relocation there was considerable discussion about the number of Navajo families residing on the HPL and the apparent lack of data.

1986
(1/3)

Secretary Swimmer establishes a New Lands Task Force to assist in planning and moving Navajo families to the New Lands.

1986   Navajo Tribe files an appeal with Interior Board of Indian Appeals
(1/8)   IBIA regarding Acting Deputy Assistant Secretary-Indian Affairs determination of the rental to be paid by the Navajo Tribe to the
Hopi Tribe for homesite and farmland on the HPL for the period
1978-1984.

(1/13)   Assistant Secretary for Indian Affairs Ross Swimmer dismisses Hopi
appeal concerning BIA-NH-1.

(1/26)   BIA and Relocation Commission engages in field review to determine number of Navajo families remaining in HPL. This exercise
is an attempt to dispute Navajo claims of 10,000 individuals still
living on the HPL and to answer congressional questions.

(1/27)   Board of Indian Appeals receives filing from the Hopi Tribe sug-
gesting the board may lack jurisdiction in the *Navajo Nation v.
Deputy Assistant Secretary Indian Affairs*, Docket No. IBIA 86-
24-A.

(1/29)   First meeting of New Lands Task Force.

(2/4)   IBIA rules against Hopi Tribe on its jurisdiction filing in Docket
No. IBIA 86-24-A.

(2/25)   Draft Memorandum of Understanding between Secretary Swimmer
and Navajo-Hopi Relocation Commission which allows for BIA
counseling with Navajos awaiting relocation and greater involvement in the New Lands planning and development.

(March) Field tribes to the New Lands undertaken with interested Navajo
families. This is in accordance with P.L. 99-190.

(3/7)   Order clarifying procedures from IBIA concerning submission of
briefs and administrative record regarding Docket No. IBIA 86-
24-A.

(4/10)   Letter to Assistant Secretary from Chairman Peterson Zah regarding BIA personnel conducting surveys, constructing fencing, tearing up roads and forage in the vicinity of the relocatee homes, and
vehicle speeding on the HPL. Chairman Zah requests all these activities halt immediately and expresses strong objection to such
treatment of Navajo individuals by those under the Secretary's control.

1986 (4/11)	Group of Navajo residents in the Mosquito Springs area in Range Unit 257 protest the Hopi Tribe's range conservation and restoration activities which are being conducted under a P.L. 93-638 contract.
	During this same period of time, seven miles of internal management fences in Range Units 255, 256, and 257 and a newly completed metal stock tank and float system in Range Unit 256 are destroyed by persons unknown.
	All activity on the 638 contract is temporarily halted in the Coal Mine Mesa resource area due to protests while the situation is evaluated.
(April)	A large group of Navajo and other individuals surround several Navajo BIA law enforcement officers in the Manysheep Valley area of the HPL after the officers' vehicle became stuck in Dennibito Wash. The individuals demanded all firearms and told the officers to leave the area and not come back. After leaving the area, the officers returned to the Pinon police substation where they were detained by several hostile individuals at gun point for several hours.
(4/23)	Letter from Chairman Sidney to Assistant Secretary Swimmer regarding the Area Director's correspondence of January 31, 1986, concerning the Hopi range water maintenance program 93-638 contract proposal. In his letter, Sidney accuses the Area Director of instituting a policy to hold the mandates of P.L. 93-638 and P.L. 93-531, as amended, hostage to discretionary administrative policies and requested a formal hearing.
(5/1)	MOU between Navajo Area Office and Relocation Commission outlines responsibilities and general arrangements for a Social Service demographic survey of Navajo heads of household residing on HPL.
	U.S. Geological Service agrees to undertake a water feasibility study of New Lands. Purpose of the agreement is to determine availability of a water source for domestic and livestock use.
(5/7)	Notice of dockets from IBIA concerning Docket No. IBIA 86-24-A.
(5/10)	Roads into Parker Draw and Little Silversmith range units on the New Lands completed.

1986
(5/16)   Construction of pilot home on New Lands begins.

(6/10)   Order granting extension of time to the Navajo appeal in Docket
                No. IBIA 86-24-A.

(6/17)   A house under construction by the Relocation Commission for the
                Goldtooth family adjacent to the HPL west of Whitecone is de-
                stroyed by fire and the family threatened by several Navajo indi-
                viduals. In addition, a camp trailer belonging to a Hopi livestock
                owner, Ferral Secakuku, located in Range Unit 559, also is de-
                stroyed by fire.

(6/20)   Letter from Navajo Attorney General Claudeen Arthur expressing
                Navajo concern over the violence in Teesto against Navajo families
                and specifically the burning of the Goldtooth house and the threats
                and intimidation against the Goldtooth and Scott families. Also, she
                complained of contact being made by Hopi tribal officials toward
                individual Navajos in the Redlake area concerning livestock tres-
                pass. In both cases, she said, "it is the federal government's re-
                sponsibility to protect the rights and property of the Navajo fami-
                lies awaiting relocation."

(6/23)   Assistant Secretary Swimmer says the July 6, 1986, deadline for
                Navajo relocation is no longer valid. There will be no forcible re-
                moval of Navajo families from the HPL because of the so-called
                July 6 deadline.

(6/24)   Grazing regulation for the New Lands, 25 CFR 700, are published.
                All grazing permits issued pursuant to the regulations 25 CFR 168
                will not expire on July 6, 1986, but will continue to be processed
                and administered in conformance with the regulation until final
                relocation is completed.

                Letter from Chairman Zah to Assistant Secretary Swimmer request-
                ing that regulation under 25 CFR 168 be amended to provide
                management and protection of Navajo grazing rights on the HPL
                after July 6, or make agreement to provide such management pro-
                tection.

(6/25)   Extension of the expiration date beyond July 6, 1986, for grazing
                permits issued to Navajos living on lands partitioned to the Hopi
                Tribe in accord with 25 CFR 168 is published in the Federal Regis-
                ter.

(6/29)   Road construction for first range cluster site on New Lands begins.

1986
(July)

An alleged obstruction of religious freedom complaint is filed by the Big Mountain Offense and Defense Committee with Assistant Secretary Swimmer on behalf of several Navajo individuals.

(7/6)

Date of so-called termination of voluntary relocation passes without incident.

(7/17)

A group of local Navajo individuals surround two Hopi Agency law enforcement personnel and a Hopi tribal ranger in the Teesto area near Finger Paint and demand the officers' sidearms. Officers are told to leave the area and to inform the Hopi Tribe to stop fencing and water development in the area.

Two miles of internal boundary fence in Range Units 558, 559 and 562 are destroyed during the same period of time.

(7/28)

U.S.G.S. begins test well drilling program on the New Lands.

(8/1)

Notice of withdrawal of counsel by Hopi Tribe.

(8/8)

Complaint filed with Assistant Secretary Swimmer on behalf of Mae Wilson Tso and others by Lee Phillips of the Big Mountain Offense/Defense Committee. The complaint alleges that the Secretary, Assistant Secretary, and employees of the BIA have violated their statutory duties and the rights of the plaintiffs.

(8/25)

Motion for request for extension time from Hopi Tribe, Docket No. IBAI 86-24-A.

(9/11)

Order granting extension of time to Hopi Tribe in Docket No. IBIA 86-24-A.

(9/15)

Following an investigation by the Solicitor's office, BIA and the National Park Service on Mr. Phillips' August 8, 1986, allegations, Assistant Secretary Swimmer responds, dismissing the complaint.

(9/30)

Fair rental value determination of lands partitioned to the Hopi Tribe for the period from January 1, 1985, to December 31, 1985, is mailed to the Hopi and Navajo tribes for their deposition. Determination includes livestock grazing, homesite and farmland rental.

(10/6)

Report on permit eligibility for the New Lands is submitted to Assistant Secretary Swimmer.

1986   Motion for request for extension of time from both Hopi and
(10/17)   Navajo tribes, Docket IBIA 86-24-A.

(10/22)   Order granting extension of time to both Hopi and Navajo tribes,
            Docket No. IBIA 86-24-A.

            Investigation report submitted to Secretary Swimmer in response
            to alleged harassment of Navajo individuals awaiting relocation in
            the Big Mountain area. This investigation is in response to a con-
            gressional inquiry dated September 15, 1986.

(11/1)   Livestock permits for 1987 issued on HPL to 123 families for 2,310
            SUYL.

(11/7)   Hopi Resolution H-178-86 authorizing the CEO and the grazing
            committee to negotiate with the Secretary of the Interior to imple-
            ment 25 CFR 166, 25 CFR 168, or some other neutral permitting
            system that will adequately protect the lives and property of Hopis
            that are grazing cattle within the Bennett Freeze Order area as
            specified by P.L. 93-531, as amended.

(12/8)   *Benally v. Hodel*, et. al., Civil No. 86-0912, USDC, filed by Navajo-
            Hopi Legal Services Program. Case against the Department of Inte-
            rior and the Navajo-Hopi Relocation Commission seeks a declara-
            tion regarding the lawfulness of the relocation program conducted
            by the defendants. Plaintiffs seek to permanently enjoin the defen-
            dants from continuing the relocation of Navajos and the expen-
            diture of funds directly or indirectly used until such time as the
            statutory constitutional requirements are met.

(12/9)   Hopi motion to dismiss Navajo appeal in BIA-NH-1.

(12/18)   Letter from Chairman Sidney to Assistant Secretary Swimmer re-
            questing immediate attention to the increase of Navajo livestock
            trespassing on to the HPL, which Sidney attributes to political
            rhetoric by Navajo Chairman-elect Peter MacDonald.

1987   Letter from Chairman Sidney to Assistant Secretary Swimmer re-
(2/2)   garding future trust status of the Hopi reservation. The Hopi Tribe
            contends the federal trust responsibility will remain status quo,
            and will not be affected by the turning over of the HPL to jurisdic-
            tion of the Hopi Tribe.

(2/24)   Assistant Secretary Swimmer dismisses Navajo appeal on BIA-NH-1.

1987   Navajo motion for substitution of counsel.
(3/13)

(4/30)   Letter from Assistant Secretary Swimmer to Chairman Sidney explaining the Bureau's trust role on the Hopi reservation. Swimmer said although the trust responsibility arises from various treaties, statutes, executive orders and regulations, these do not define the scope of the responsibility. Questions involving specific trust responsibilities, other than range management, on Hopi lands will have to be addressed on a case-by-case basis. Thus, while the United States has a trust relationship with the Hopi Tribe, the Settlement Act, as proven by the Hopi Tribe in its litigation, alters that relationship. The trust responsibility cannot remain "status quo" as suggested in Sidney's February 2, 1987, letter.

(5/15)   Order of Decision IBIA Docket No. IBIA 86-24-A. The board approves the methodology used and conclusions reached by the defendants, but remands it back to the Phoenix Area Director to make factual corrections in data and finalize the rental determination.

(6/5)   Letter from Phoenix Acting Area Director Walter Mills to Chairman Sidney expressing the conclusion that Assistant Secretary Swimmer's letter of April 30, 1987, regarding the trust applies to District 6 as well as the HPL.

(7/7)   The first seven Navajo relocatees from the HPL move to the Little Silversmith Range Unit on the New Lands. This move was accomplished 18 months after Congress authorized Assistant Secretary Swimmer to assist the Navajo-Hopi Relocation Commission in relocating families from the HPL to the New Lands.

(7/17)   Livestock belonging to permittees who moved to Little Silversmith on July 7 is transported from the HPL to the New Lands.

(July)   "Distribution of radionuclide and trace elements in groundwater, grasses and surfical sediments associated with the alluvial aquifer along the Puerco River, northeastern Arizona." A reconnaissance sampling program: U.S. Geological Survey Open File Report. Both the grass and sediment samples showed low concentration of radionuclides.

(8/5)   Notice of deposition upon oral examination and request to produce documents. *Ivan Sidney v. Peter MacDonald.*

1987
(10/1)

Preliminary proposal to study the occurrence and movement of radionuclides and trace elements in the Puerco River and lower Little Colorado River basin. Prepared and submitted by U.S.G.S. Proposes an additional six-year study to: (1) Determine types, concentration, spatial variability, and recent origin of radionuclides and other trace elements in surface water, fluvial sediments, and groundwater in and near the Puerco and lower Little Colorado rivers. (2) Quantify transport rate of selected radionuclides and other trace elements in surface water from Gallup, N.M., to the Colorado River near Grand Canyon, Ariz. (3) Estimate the amount and extent of contaminant movement between surface and groundwater.

(10/6)

"Preliminary assessment of water quality in the alluvial aquifer of the Puerco River basin, northeastern Arizona." U.S. Geological Survey Water Resources Investigation Project. Samples from 14 wells and one spring were analyzed to determine if a contaminant plume of radionuclides or trace elements are present. Statistical analysis of the water quality data suggests that no contaminant plume can be defined on the basis of samples from existing wells. Contamination in the alluvial aquifer apparently does not change in the downstream direction along the Puerco River. The geochemistry of the radionuclides indicates that most radionuclides from the uranium decay series are immobile or only slighly mobile, whereas uranium will not precipitate out of the solution but may be removed by sorption in the alluvial aquifer.

(11/7)

Second group of nine Navajo relocatee families from the HPL move to the Parker Draw Range Unit on the New Lands.

(11/10)

Livestock belonging to the permittees who moved to Parker Draw on November 7, 1987, are transported from the HPL.

(12/31)

To date a total of 19 Navajo families have moved to the New Lands.

1989
(9/6)

Hearing date for 1934 Disputed Lands Case for Hopis, Navajos, and San Juan Paiutes.

APPENDIX B

The following is excerpted from one of the most recent lawsuits filed on behalf of Navajo plaintiffs and is included for its presentation of the historical background as well as its statement of Navajo philosophical/religious tenets and the type of grounds upon which the legal system continues to consider civil relocation suits. (See Afterword)

Religious Freedom Suit Filed 1988
(*Source:* United States District Court Records)
Civil Action Number 88-0181
In the United States District Court for the District of Columbia
Jenny Manybeads, et al., Plaintiffs
v.
United States of America, et al., Defendants

COMPLAINT
(For Declaratory Judgment and Injunctive Relief)

Introduction

• This is an action for a declaratory judgment and injunctive relief challenging certain actions of the United States of America, through the Department of Interior, the Bureau of Indian Affairs and the Navajo-Hopi Indian Relocation Commission, in planning, approving and carrying out the compulsory relocation of Navajo or (Dineh, their name in Navajo language) people from their ancestral homelands located in northern Arizona. The challenged actions are being carried out by the federal government as a result of pursuant to P.L. No. 93-531 (the Navajo Hopi Indian Land Settlement Act of 1974) as amended by P.L. 96-305 (1980) ("the Relocation Act").

• The challenged governmental actions of forcibly removing plaintiffs from their ancestral homelands will sever the spiritual relationship which exists between plaintiffs and their ancestral homelands, thus irreparably interfering with the free exercise of plaintiffs' religion, in violation of the Free Exercise Clause of the First Amendment of the United States Constitution. The Dineh people have, since the beginning of their history, considered this spiritual relationship between themselves and the land to be sacred, and the source and definition of their religious belief and practice, as well as the source of spiritual balance and supernatural powers. Further, plaintiffs' religion mandates that plaintiffs maintain this spiritual relationship by assuming responsibility for caretaking the land on which they reside, and this religious teaching defines plaintiffs' ultimate purpose in life. The relocation activities of the federal government will unlawfully destroy this spiritual relationship, depriving these Indian people of their ability to maintain and continue their traditional religious beliefs and practices.

• The forced relocation policy of the Relocation Act violates the due process clause's guarantee of equal protection under the law. The Relocation Act was passed ostensibly to resolve a dispute between the Hopi and Navajo Tribes to title to certain reservation lands occupied by plaintiffs, and the Act mandated forcible relocation of the Navajos to achieve a resolution. This dispute was caused by boundaries. In every case, however, in which there has been an Indian claim to land occupied by white settlers, Congress and the courts have never required the white settlers to relocate, but have instead paid monetary or other compensation to the Indian claimants. Here, however, when the alleged settlers (Navajos) are Indian, the government, in violation of equal protection principles, has required the settlers to relocate, rather than providing for compensation to be paid to the Indian Claimant (the Hopi).

• The Congressionally mandated program of forced relocation of Navajo Indians, which prevents their free exercise of religion, violates the American Indian Religions Freedom Act, 42 U.S.C. § 1996 ("AIRFA"), which expressly establishes as this nation's official policy, the duty of the United States to protect and preserve for all Native Americans their inherent right of freedom to believe and exercise their traditional religions.

• The federal government's role in the planning, development and implementation of the relocation program also violates the federal trust relationship and duties which result and are owed to the Plaintiffs. The "trust relationship" between the Federal government and Indian people arises out of a unique set of historical circumstances which has given this relationship a distinct judicial status recognized by the Federal government since the founding of this nation. This trust relationship imposes upon the Defendants the duties and responsibilities of a fiduciary and/or guardian in all of its dealings with Native Americans including Plaintiffs. The United States and all

Defendants named herein are required in the performance of the fiduciary obligations arising from this trust, to exercise the highest degree of diligence, care, skill and loyalty to protect and preserve Plaintiffs' rights, including their right to preserve and exercise their religion. The forced relocation of Plaintiffs from their ancestral lands which deny Plaintiffs their right to the free exercise of their religion thus constitutes the most serious type of violation of this trust relationship.

• The proposed removal and relocation of Plaintiffs against their will would deprive Plaintiffs of their right to freedom of religion, a right which is secured to them by international human rights law as established and recognized in treaties and in the customary law of nations and by the United Nations Charter. Moreover, the forced relocation of Plaintiffs will subject them as a group to both physical and spiritual suffering which violates their human rights under international law. Finally, the relocation policy violates plaintiffs' rights as a non-self-governing people as recognized by international law and Article 73 of the United Nations Charter.

JURISDICTION AND VENUE

• This action arises under and alleges violations of the First Amendment of the United States Constitution; the American Indian Religious Freedom Act, 42 U.S.C. § 1996; the federal trust responsibility owed to American Indian people; the equal protection guarantee of the due process clause of the Fifth Amendment of the United States Constitution; the international prohibition against genocide under customary international law and the Treaty on Genocide; the right to freedom of religion under customary international law and the United Nations Charter; and plaintiffs' rights as a non-self-governing people pursuant to Article 73 of the United Nations Charter.

• Jurisdiction is based upon 28 U.S.C. § 1346, this being an action against the United States as a defendant; and upon 28 U.S.C. § 1331, this being an action arising under the Constitution, laws and treaties of the United States.

• Venue lies in the District of Columbia pursuant to 28 U.S.C. § 1391 (e) (1), as defendants United States of America, the Department of the Interior and the Bureau of Indian Affairs reside in this District.

• The questions of law and fact relating to plaintiffs are common to all members of the class predominate over all questions affecting only individual members to such extent that a class action is the only available method for the fair and efficient adjudication of this controversy. Defendants have acted on grounds generally applicable to the class, thereby making appropriate injunctive relief and corresponding declaratory relief with respect to the class as a whole.

General Allegations

PLAINTIFFS' RELIGION

- According to plaintiffs' religious teachings, plaintiffs and their families have lived continuously on the land on which they currently reside since the creation of this world and the Emergence of the Navajo (Dineh) onto this world. Historians confirm that ancestors of plaintiffs have lived in the area for more than one thousand (1000) years, with evidence of such occupancy dating to approximately 900 A.D. to 1130 A.D.

- Navajo society is divided into hereditary clans, which are each composed of hereditary family groups. Each clan, and each family within each clan, has traditionally occupied and used an area of land which is recognized by other members of the Tribe as each clan's and family's "traditional use area" of "ancestral homelands." Each family has lived on, occupied and used its traditional use area for numerous generations. Children, when they reach majority, build a dwelling on their mother's traditional use area and continue to live on their family's ancestral homelands.

- For each plaintiff, his or her family has lived on, occupied and used its family's ancestral homelands for numerous generations.

- The Navajo religion, like other tribal or traditional Native American religions, is "site-specific," in that a practitioner of the religion communicates with the spiritual world only at certain specific geographic locations, which are openings to the spiritual world. These sacred spaces, such as specific springs, buttes, canyons, trees, rock formations, burial places or sites of sacred medicine plants, to the traditional Navajo practitioner, each mark the spot of some special manifestation of the divine order and is a necessary "passageway" to communicate with the heavenly world.

- In the traditional Navajo religion, the practitioner prays to the spiritual beings of an area who then act as emissaries by communicating the prayers to the Holy People or Deities. These prayers can only be communicated to spiritual beings which are known to the individual practitioner and at the specific sites where the spiritual beings are found. Contrary to the western religions, there is not one single "god" in the traditional Navajo religion.

- There are no churches or houses of worship at which a traditional Navajo prays, as according to the Navajo religion it is only at a specific geographical opening to the spirit world that prayers can be heard by the spiritual beings (called "the Holy People"). The location of these specific geographic sites is determined by specific events which happen or happened at each site.

- Moreover, in the traditional Navajo religion, there is a pervasive relationship between religion and life. Many thoughts and actions in everyday life are intimately related to religious belief and practice, and require prayers and offerings to the Holy People, which can only be offered at these specific known sacred sites.

- The teachings of the traditional Navajo religion regarding the location of specific sites for communication with the Holy People and regarding religious practices have been passed down from generation to generation by Navajo medicine men and other spiritual leaders.

- In the traditional Navajo religion, there are many spiritual beings, and each can be communicated with only at different and separate geographic locations. Contrary to the western religions, there is not one single "god" in the traditional Navajo religion.

- A principal teaching of the traditional Navajo religion is that the Creator placed the Dineh upon their ancestral lands at specific geographic locations to be caretakers of the land, and gave the Dineh the responsibility to maintain balance in the universe by making offerings and prayers to the Holy People at specific sacred sites throughout the land. The Navajo religion teaches that if the Dineh are unable to fulfill this responsibility, there will be spiritual unbalance in the universe, life will no longer be in harmony and this world will end.

- A principal teaching of the traditional Navajo religion is that the Creator instructed the Dineh that they must live within the boundaries of the four sacred mountains and the two sacred rivers. The mountains are (Sisnagajini) Blanca Peak in the East, Mt. Taylor (Sootdzit) in the South, the San Francisco Peaks (Dook'o'stlid) in the West, and the La Plata Mountain (Dibentsaa) in the North. The two sacred rivers are the San Juan, which is located in the North, and the Little Colorado, which is to the South.

- The traditional Navajo religion also teaches that each Navajo clan was placed by the Creator in a specific area within the sacred mountains, and was instructed to live in that area and be caretakers of that area, and that the fulfillment of this responsibility is essential to the continued well-being of the entire world.

- Plaintiffs' traditional religion teaches that if Plaintiffs are moved from the land which they have been instructed by the Creator to caretake, they will die and this world will end.

- Plaintiffs' religion teaches that Plaintiffs are only to make prayers and offerings to the Holy People at geographic locations which they know are sacred passageways to the spiritual world at which they know they can communicate with the spiritual beings.

- In the traditional Navajo religion, there are sacred geographical sites that are sacred to all Dineh people; locations that are sacred to all members of each clan; locations sacred for each family; and locations sacred for each individual. These locations are sacred because of events that occurred there that held special significance for the tribe as a whole, for a clan, for a family, or for an individual, respectively.

- The daily practice of the Navajo religion by an individual entails regular offerings, prayers, and communication to the Holy People and the individual's spiritual guardians, who can be communicated with only at known sacred sites where the individual has become introduced to and is known by the Holy People there. For each Plaintiff, these sacred sites are specific geographic locations surrounding the home and the land on which each lives. These prayers seek protection from evil and sickness and for guidance on the spiritual path of the individual.

- Continually, throughout each day, as a traditional Navajo practitioner performs his or her daily acts, such as preparing food, weaving, herding sheep, hauling water, planting or harvesting, he or she offers prayers and offerings to the spiritual beings which they know protect the family and the individual and surround them on their family's and clan's homelands.

- In addition, each Navajo practitioner of the traditional Navajo religion numerous times throughout the year goes to other specific special and sacred locations on their family's or clan's traditional use area to pray and make offerings to the spiritual beings, either for protection or to cure some spiritual imbalance. Because of the many generations of each Plaintiff's family and clan that have lived on the same homelands, the individuals of each family and clan are known and protected by the spiritual beings in their area.

- The traditional Navajo religion also teaches that certain geographic locations are places of evil spiritual beings, and that these geographic locations must be avoided, because if an individual was at one of those evil spots, it would create spiritual imbalance in the individual, and that were he to make prayers at these evil locations it would cause serious spiritual and physical harm to the individual.

- Plaintiffs are thus inextricably connected to their homeland by their religion. They are known by the spiritual beings on their homeland, because of the many generations of their families and clans that have lived there in harmony with spiritual people there. Plaintiffs are instructed by their Creator never to leave their sacred homeland. Their religion teaches them that their purpose in life is to take care of their homeland. If they were relocated from their homelands, they would be unable to fulfill their spiritual obligations to the Creator to caretake the land, and would have no purpose in life.

- If Plaintiffs were relocated, they would be unable to perform their religious practices. On the new lands to which they would be relocated, plaintiffs would not "know" the spiritual beings of that area nor would they "know" the location of the special or sacred sites where the spiritual beings could be found. This lack of knowledge would sever the spiritual relationship and pathway of communication between Plaintiffs and their Holy People and deprive them of the spiritual beings' protection. In addition, Plaintiffs would not know whether the supernatural forces at any particular location were good or evil when attempting to make prayers and offerings. In this situation Plaintiffs would be cut off from their spiritual beings, the Holy People and their religion.

- If plaintiffs were relocated, they would be unable to perform their religious practices. On the new lands to which they were relocated, plaintiffs would not know where the sacred sites are, and thus would be unable to communicate with the Holy People. The spiritual beings on the new lands would not know plaintiffs, and would not protect them. Plaintiffs would not know whether good or evil spiritual beings were at any location where they might make prayers and offerings.

- Plaintiffs' religious belief is that they are connected to their Mother Earth through the spiritual beings on their ancestral homelands, and if they are forced to relocate, the spiritual tie that gives their life meaning will be destroyed and they will not survive.

Historical Background

- In 1848, the land now inhabited by plaintiffs was included in the area of land which was transferred to the United States from Mexico by the Treaty of Guadaloupe Hidalgo. The Treaty expressly recognizes and confirms the right of the Indian peoples to practice their religion and affords them the protection to continue to do so.

- In or about 1863, the United States government, through the United States Army led by Colonel Kit Carson, began a search and destroy campaign designed to capture or kill the entire Dineh nation. Thousands of Dineh were killed, and approximately 8500 Dineh men, women and children were captured, and were forced to march, in the infamous "Long Walk", over 400 miles in the dead of winter to Fort Sumner in eastern New Mexico, where they were imprisoned. The Dineh who were not killed or captured, including relatives of plaintiffs herein, escaped and hid themselves in the remote canyons of the area including the lands now occupied by plaintiffs, until the army left. The 8500 Dineh subject to this catastrophic relocation policy were imprisoned for five years, until the Treaty of 1868 was signed between the United States and the Dineh. During their five years of captivity, over 2,000 of the Dineh died. Upon their release, the Dineh people who survived the imprisonment returned to their ancestral homelands within the four sacred mountains, including the area now in dispute, where they resettled their families.

- The Treaty of 1868 created the original Dineh reservation, which later was extended by statute and by executive order, so that it encompassed the land now occupied by plaintiffs herein.

- In 1882, President Chester Arthur signed an executive order establishing a reservation "for the use and occupancy of Moqui (Hopi), and such other Indians as the Secretary of the Interior may see fit to settle thereon." The 1882 Executive Order area consisted of 2.4 million acres, located west of the Dineh treaty land, and included land occupied and used by Dineh and some villages occupied by the Hopi. Its arbitrary shape and location bore little relationship to the actual qualities or use of the land. Both Navajo and Hopi lived within the borders of the 1882 area, and extensive archeological studies at the time revealed hundreds of old Navajo sites.

- For years, the Navajo and Hopis lived as neighbors. Prior to the 1920s, there was no conflict between the Hopis and Navajos regarding this land. The Hopis, who are a "Pueblo" or communally based tribe, lived in several villages in the 1882 executive order area and farmed the surrounding land. The Navajos lived in extended family units away from the villages on land not used or occupied by the Hopis, each family living and raising sheep on an area of land which had been used and occupied by that family for many generations (called a family's "customary use area" or "traditional use area"). This division of the land continues until the present. There are no Hopi villages located on the land subject to relocation.

- There was little conflict between the traditional Navajos and the traditional Hopis in the 1882 executive order area, and their relationship has been characterized by a great deal of cooperation and goodwill. While there were the normal neighbor to neighbor problems concerning land, water and resource use which were exacerbated by the fact that both the Navajo and Hopi were required to live only on reservation lands much smaller than their aboriginal lands, due to encroachment on their ancestral lands by white settlers, but these conflicts were not of a substantial magnitude. The relationship between the traditional Hopi and Navajo was and continues to be one of friendship, trading and intermarriage with the agrarian Hopi lifestyle complementing the lifestyle of the pastoral Navajo.

- From the 1880's up through the 1950's the Federal government acting through the BIA, both allowed and encouraged continued Navajo settlement of the 1882 area. Throughout this period, the government took no action to prevent or ameliorate the land use problems which were developing between the Hopi and Navajo people and in fact greatly exacerbated the problems through its acts and omissions.

- Despite this historic neighbor relationship between the peoples themselves, as the value of the land in question continued to increase dramatically throughout the 1940's and 1950's, the pressure to resolve the question of title and to develop the land also increased.

- After administrative attempts to resolve the competing claims of the Hopi and Dineh tribes, in the 1882 executive order area, in 1958 Congress passed P. L. No. 85-547. This Act authorized the Navajo and Hopi Tribal Councils to participate in a lawsuit in federal district court to determine the rights and interests in the 1882 executive order area. The 1958 Act also "vested" title to the land in both tribes.

- In 1962, the District Court, in *Healing* v. *Jones*, 210 F.Supp. 125 (D. Ariz. 1962), *aff'd*, 373 U.S. 758 (1963), held that, except for the one-sixth of the reservation Hopis had customarily used exclusively, "the Hopi and Navajo Indian Tribes have joint, undivided, and equal interests as to the surface and sub-surface including all resources pertaining thereto, subject to the trust title of the United States." The JUA was an area exclusively occupied by Navajos; the District Court found, however, that the Hopis had been granted an equal interest in this area by the 1882 executive order establishing the Hopi reservation, even though Hopis had never occupied the land. The area of exclusive Hopi use was called District 6; the remainder of the 1882 area became known as the "Joint Use Area" (JUA). The court left open the question of how, if at all, the joint interest might be divided between the two tribes.

- After this determination, the Hopi Tribal Council, substantially aided by energy development interests, lobbied intensely for passage of legislation which would force the Navajo people off of half the JUA land.

- In 1974, Congress passed P. L. No. 93-531, the Navajo-Hopi Land Settlement Act ("the Relocation Act"). The Act gave the District Court jurisdiction to partition the JUA and directed a 50-50 division. It also created the Navajo-Hopi Indian Relocation Commission ("NHIRC"), an independent agency of the executive branch, to relocate Navajo and Hopi residents who, after partition and fencing, were on the "wrong side of the line."

- Congress relied on several untruths in its decision to pass the Relocation Act: that only a small number of persons would be relocated; that the Navajos would in any event have to leave the land because of overgrazing; that the Hopis, in their District 6 (exclusive use area) were overrun by Navajo livestock, while in actuality the Hopis had refused fencing; that there was a great deal of unused land in the HPL, while in actuality the land was filled to capacity; and that the Navajos were very rich, while in actuality the Navajos in the JUA were very poor.

- The partition of the JUA benefits only a small number of Hopis, *i.e.*, those that are affluent cattle ranchers. Few, if any, Hopis have moved from their villages in District 6 to the H.P.L. The occupancy of the Navajos in the HPL represents no threat to the Hopi culture, but is a hindrance only to a minority of Hopis who want to develop the land for personal gain.

- Unlike the pro-development, pro-relocation forces within the Hopi Tribe, both traditional Hopi and Navajo people share a deep spiritual tie to their ancestral home and medicine lands which constitute the integral and indispensable part of their respective religions. Both the traditional Hopi and Navajo believe they were placed by their Creator upon the lands they occupy and that they share a responsibility as caretakers of those lands and of the earth.

- In 1977, the United States District Court for the District of Arizona, pursuant to the authority granted it by the Relocation Act, approved a partition line dividing the JUA into two equal geographical areas, one of which would belong to the Hopi tribe ("Hopi Partition Land") and one which would belong to the Navajo tribe ("Navajo Partition Land"). That order was affirmed by the Ninth Circuit on September 11, 1980. Neither decision considered the First Amendment religious free exercise implications of forced relocation.

- Approximately 10-15,000 Dineh people were then living on the Hopi Partition Land, and were thus, pursuant to the terms of the Relocation Act, required to relocate to other lands.

- Approximately 100 Hopis were then living on the Navajo Partition Land, and were thus, pursuant to the terms of the Relocation Act, required to relocate to other lands.

- Plaintiffs all reside on the Hopi Partition Land, where their ancestral homelands are located, and are all subject to relocation pursuant to the Relocation Act.

- The number of Dineh currently residing on Hopi Partition Land, and subject to relocation under the Relocation Act, is estimated to be from 1,500 to 3,500 individuals, including the named plaintiffs herein.

- The vast majority of the inhabitants of the Hopi Partition Land are Navajo, and few Hopi had ever attempted to settle there because of the distance from the Hopi mesa-villages. Moreover, even at present, few if any Hopis have moved onto land vacated by the relocating Navajo. The main use of the vacated land proposed by the Hopi Tribal Council is for cattle grazing, recreation, agriculture and energy resource development all of which will benefit only a minority of Hopis and the outside development interests. None of the competing interests involve constitutional rights or concerns nor constitute a compelling government interest.

- The traditional Hopis support plaintiffs, and oppose partition of the JUA and relocation of plaintiffs. The traditional Hopi religion also teaches that there is a strong spiritual connection between the Hopis and the land, and they believe that the traditional Navajos on the JUA share with them in caretaking the land for the Creator.

- Defendants, through the BIA and the NHIRC, have implemented a relocation program, pursuant to which thousands of Navajos have been coercively relocated from their ancestral homelands, and which threatens plaintiffs with coercive or forcible relocation. The relocation process has caused significant social, economic, psychological and cultural injuries to plaintiffs and other relocatees, resulting from, *inter alia*, loss of access to or involvement with traditional religious and cultural activities, the severance of the spiritual relationship between the relocatees and their ancestral lands, inadequate and defective housing, inability to adjust to an urban lifestyle and economy, and victimization by organized financial and real estate schemes which defrauded relocatees of their homes and other benefits.

- Pursuant to the Relocation Act, and as part of defendants' relocation program, defendant BIA has reduced Navajo livestock on the H.P.L. by 85%, and prohibited new construction. Defendant BIA has enforced this livestock reduction and construction freeze by seizing livestock from residents of the HPL, including plaintiffs, and by prohibiting new construction and by causing recently constructed buildings to be destroyed. This construction freeze and livestock impoundment have combined to create intolerable living conditions and deprive plaintiffs of the food, shelter and economic resources necessary to sustain themselves and their families on their ancestral homelands. These conditions have coerced many Navajos, and currently threaten plaintiffs, to relocate from the H.P.L., even though such relocation violates their religious beliefs and denies these Navajos the ability to practice their religion.

- Defendants have constructed and are constructing fences, water diversion and other relocation-related construction projects on the HPL, which have interfered and threaten to interfere with plaintiffs' practice of their religion by desecrating sacred sites and blocking access to sacred sites. In addition, the construction freeze interferes with plaintiffs' ability to practice their religion as they are unable to construct shelters necessary for the practice of their religion on their ancestral land.

- Plaintiffs face not simply forcible relocation by Defendants, but coercive relocation due to the effects of Defendants' enforcement of the livestock impoundment and construction freeze. Defendants' actions are in essence a "surrender or starve" program designed to coercively force plaintiffs to relocate from their ancestral homelands, or face starvation, serious overcrowding, and separation from their children and families.

- The challenged relocation policy of defendants benefits Hopi property rights, at the expense of Navajo human and constitutional rights.

- The actions and threatened actions of defendants have inflicted and will inflict on plaintiffs irreparable injury for which there is no adequate remedy at law.

Claims for Relief:

(1) Violation of Right to Free Exercise of Religion (First Amendment to the Constitution)

(2) Violation of the American Indian Religious Freedom Act

(3) Violation of Equal Protection

(4) Violation of Federal Trust Responsibility

(5) Violation of Right to Freedom of Religion Under Customary International Law and the United Nations Charter

(6) Violation of International Prohibition Against Genocide

(7) Violation of Plaintiffs' Rights Under Article 73 of the United Nations Charter as a Non-Self-Governing People

Complaint ends with "Request for Relief"

Suit filed on behalf of plaintiffs by attorneys connected with The National Emergency Civil Liberties Committee, the Center for Constitutional Rights, and the National Lawyers Guild, as well as individual attorneys.

APPENDIX C

See also Congressional Record *for the 93rd and 96th Congresses for precise terms of the following relevant laws:*

Public Law 93-531, 93rd Congress, H.R. 10337
December 22, 1974

An Act to provide for final settlement of the conflicting rights and interest of the Hopi and Navajo Tribes to and in lands lying within the joint use area of the reservation established by the Executive order of December 16, 1882, and lands lying within the reservation created by the Act of June 14, 1934, and for other purposes.

Covers: Mediator, Interagency committee, Negotiating team, Negotiating session, Full agreement, Partial agreement, Report to District Court, District Court review and recommendations, Hearing, Settlement guidelines, Restoration of land, Joint ownership of minerals, Paiute Indian allotment, Establishment of Navajo and Hopi Indian Relocation Commission, Rules and regulations, Report to Congress, Voluntary relocations, Assistance payments, Replacement housing, Fair market value, Additional payment, Disposal of dwellings, Payment of fair rental value, Land exchange, Appropriations, and Repeal, among other issues.

Public Law 96-305, 96th Congress, 94 Stat. 929
July 8, 1980

An Act relating to the relocation of the Navajo Indians and the Hopi Indians, and for other purposes.

Covers: Navajo and Hopi Indian relocation amendments; Tribal lands in issue; Determination of rights; Defense; Partitioned lands; Tribal jurisdiction; Effective date; Land transfer to the Navajo Tribe; Navajo and Hopi Indian Relocation Commission, selection authority; Report to congressional committees; Public notice; Negotiation authority; Assistance to Commission by Federal agencies; Replacement housing; Surveying, monumenting, fencing; Livestock reduction program; Relocation benefits; Appropriations authorization; Use of funds; Litigation or court action; Life estate leases, application; Priority ranking; Awarding of leases; Residents; Tenant death; and Voluntary estate relinquishment, among other issues.